SOMERVILLE & ROSS
A CRITICAL APPRECIATION

Hilary Robinson

SOMERVILLE & ROSS

A Critical Appreciation

Gill and Macmillan
St. Martin's Press, New York

First published 1980 by
Gill and Macmillan Ltd
15/17 Eden Quay
Dublin
with associated companies in
London, New York, Delhi, Hong Kong,
Johannesburg, Lagos, Melbourne,
Singapore, Tokyo
and in the United States of America by
St. Martin's Press, Inc.
175 Fifth Avenue
New York, N.Y. 10010

0 7171 0934 8 (Gill and Macmillan edition)

0-312-74426-9 (St. Martin's Press edition)

Grateful acknowledgment is made to the following for the use of extracts from the works of Somerville & Ross: Sir Patrick Coghill and Chatto and Windus Ltd of London, *The Real Charlotte*; John Farquharson Ltd of London, *The Enthusiast*, *Mount Music* and *An Irish R.M. and his Experiences*; and William Heinemann Ltd of London, *The Big House at Inver*.

Photoset by
Photobook (Bristol) Ltd,
28/30 Midland Road, St. Philips, Bristol, and
Printed and bound in Great Britain by
Redwood Burn Ltd, Trowbridge and Esher.

To my parents, William and Marjorie Berrow

Contents

Acknowledgments	ix
Manuscript Sources	xi
Introduction	1
Chapter I	5
Biography and Background	
Chapter II	38
The Collaboration and the Use of Dialect	
Chapter III	57
An Irish Cousin	
Naboth's Vineyard	
Through Connemara in a Governess Cart	
In the Vine Country	
Beggars on Horseback	
In the State of Denmark	
Chapter IV	85
The Real Charlotte	
Chapter V	118
The Silver Fox	
The Irish R.M. and his Experiences	
Dan Russel the Fox	
Chapter VI	147
Mount Music	
An Enthusiast	
Chapter VII	177
The Big House of Inver	
French Leave	
Sarah's Youth	
Select Bibliography	205
Notes	211
Index	215

Acknowledgments

I am grateful for the permission granted by Sir Patrick Coghill to quote from published and unpublished writings of Edith Somerville and Violet Martin, and to Mr Gordon Wheeler, of the Special Collection in the library of the Queen's University of Belfast, for his patience and kind co-operation. Dr John Cronin of the same University has been a source of encouragement with his own love and knowledge of the work of Somerville & Ross. I am indebted to Mr O'Sullivan of the Manuscript Room, Trinity College, Dublin; and to Dr Roger McHugh who supervised my doctorate thesis on Somerville & Ross when he was Professor of Anglo-Irish Literature at University College, Dublin. I should also like to say thank you to my friend Bea Jackson for her bright enthusiasm, and to my husband, Ian Robinson, for his comments on *The Real Charlotte*. I am of course entirely responsible for the opinions expressed in this book.

HILARY ROBINSON
21 March 1979

Manuscript Sources

Manuscripts from the National Library of Ireland, the New York Public Library, and the libraries of Trinity College, Dublin and the Queen's University of Belfast have been consulted. The ones most used are those in the Queen's University of Belfast; as well as the Common-place books the following have been most frequently used:

The Diaries of Edith Somerville 1873–1948.

The Diaries of Violet Martin 1875–1915.

Edith Somerville's Letters to Colonel John Somerville, 1033 A.LSS, 1 March 1889–18 December 1948.

Edith Somerville's Letters to Dame Ethel Smyth, 300 A.LSS, 3 January 1921–3 February 1930.

Dame Ethel Smyth's Letters to Edith Somerville, 470 A.LSS and 13 postcards, 15 July 1918–22 July 1943. First editions of the published work have been used except for *An Irish Cousin* and the *Irish R.M.* stories.

Introduction

Edith Œnone Somerville (1858-1949) of Drishane, Castletownshend, County Cork, and Violet Martin (1862-1915) of
Ross, Oughterard, County Galway, were second cousins, and
great-granddaughters of Charles Kendal Bushe, Lord Chief
Justice of Ireland at the time of the Union. They were proud of
this ancestor and proud of their respective families. An obsession
with genealogy and family history was as much a characteristic
of the Anglo-Irish as it was of the Gaelic nation.

Edith Somerville and her brother, Admiral Boyle Somerville,
wrote and published privately the records of their family. The
first Somerville who came to Ireland, in 1690, came to escape
religious persecution in Scotland. Eight generations of the
family had lived in Drishane; in *Wheeltracks* Edith Somerville
wrote of the 'aboriginal Somervilles and Townshends' of
Castletownshend, compared with the later arrivals, the 'colonist
Bushes and Coghills'.

The Martin family were amongst the first planters; they came
to Ireland with Strongbow, in the reign of Henry II. In the
Cromwellian wars the Royalist family moved out of Galway
town and took possession of much of Connemara. There were
four family seats. Ballinahinch was the biggest stronghold; it
extended over nearly 200,000 acres. Elizabeth, Countess of
Fingall, told in her memoirs, *Seventy Years Young*, how the Martin
of Ballinahinch, in the days of George IV, boasted to the king
that his avenue was forty miles long (she added that rumour had
it that every mile of the avenue was lined with beggars). Ross
became the seat of the senior branch of the family in 1590. The
House there which Violet Martin knew was built by her great-
grandfather in 1777.

From the days of the Norman ancestors to the late eighteenth century the Martin family was Roman Catholic. Violet Martin's great-grandfather married a Protestant and became one himself. It is likely that he turned back to his Church before he died, but the children were Protestants. The eldest son, Violet Martin's grandfather, married a Catholic. In Violet's childhood, daily Mass was said at Ross; and the foster-mothers took the children to their priest for secret baptism. But Protestantism quickly took hold of them, so that Violet Martin praises her family's Anglican clemency, 'the Protestant instinct, and a tolerance for the sister religion, born of sympathy and personal respect'. In her short family history she does not mention the aunt who lived at Ross for sixteen years, nor the aunt's dramatic reunion with one of her sons:

> As for Aunt Moore she was certainly a Roman Catholic, she married young and had a large family, what became of them it is hard to say, Edward Moore was left under the care of a priest in Malta I think. One day a young man came to Ross and stood on the drive, Aunt Moore came out. Edward Moore advanced and said, 'Do you know me mother? I am your son.' 'Stuff and nonsense you are no son of mine.' And she rejected him with scorn. Grandpapa heard the contention, 'Well,' he said, 'whoever you are, come in and have your luncheon.'[1]

Violet Martin did try to find out about her grandmother's family, but she was told, 'as it was unfashionable in those days to be R.C. her family was never much spoken about'. She discovered that her grandmother, Mary Blackney, was a daughter of an Ellen Walsh, a family known as 'Walsh of the Mountain', a Celtic family located 'somewhere on the borders of Waterford and Carlow'.[2]

Violet Martin's pseudonym shows her desire to be in the tradition of her family's noble heritage. 'Martin Ross' is close to the head of the family's title, 'Martin of Ross'. Edith Somerville's pseudonym, Geilles Herring, was an ancestor's name, chosen in desperation when Mrs Somerville refused to allow her daughter's own name to appear. It was confused with 'Grilled Herring' and used only once, for the first edition of *An*

Irish Cousin. The 'E.Œ.' is merely a mark of the formality in names on which Dr Somerville always insisted. Christian names were for use by close family and friends; initials were for the public. In this book 'Violet Martin' and 'Edith Somerville' are used to refer to the people, and 'Somerville & Ross' to refer to their literary partnership.

Somerville & Ross were traditional novelists: they were concerned with the way people behave in society. They wrote about what they knew intimately: the Anglo-Irish and, sometimes, the way their finely layered society was beset by political pressures. They focused on individual members of Anglo-Irish society with a subtlety of characterisation which illuminates not only the social and religious conflicts of the time but the more general human condition. They threw into relief the troubles of an entire class and showed godlessness and greed in the most ordinary people. They were less concerned with the Gaelic and Catholic Irish, about whom they knew less; but when they did write about them it is often with a sense of pathos and their comedy never degenerates into the buffoonery of Lover and Lever. They have been misjudged. Their feminine laughter was sharper and more critical than anything which gave rise to the Stage Irishman, but it was usually reserved for those of their own religion. There was no malice in their attitude to the Irish people.

Their ability to capture the dialect of the people is remarkable. The Irish turn of phrase, the striking image, the singular inflexion, never degenerate into stock stage brogue or Kiltartanese. They had no desire to change or improve the people, and they enjoyed them as fellow creatures. They were not blinded by the sentimentality which spoiled the work of many nineteenth-century writers, nor by the patriotism which coloured the vision of many of their contemporaries. This extract from a letter from Violet Martin to Edith Somerville in 1885 is a fair example of their kind of observation—its detachment, its superiority and its sympathy:

> Poor Thady died on Thursday night, a very gallant quiet end, conscious and calm. Anne Kinnearey did not mean to say anything remarkable when she told me that he died 'as

quiet, now, as quiet as a little fish', but those were her words. I
went up there on Thursday to see old Anne, and coming into
a house black with silent people was suddenly confronted
with Thady's body laid out in the kitchen. It was very awful
. . . Andy Connor, three parts drunk, advanced and
delivered a loud horrible harangue on Thady and the Martin
family—the people sat like owls, listening—and we retired
into a room where were whiskey bottles galore, and the cream
of the company—men from Galway, respectably drunk and
magnificent in speech. At all events the pale tranced face was
hidden, and the living people looked less brutal without that
terrific purified creature.

Both Violet Martin and Edith Somerville appreciated the
people's acceptance of the mystery of life, its sufferings and
sorrows. Violet Martin never forgot the words of a priest in an
Irish sermon which were repeated to her in translation: 'Oh
black seas of Eternity, without height or depth, bay, brink or
shore! How can anyone look into your depths and neglect the
salvation of his soul?' Edith Somerville ends *Irish Memories* with
an example of the simple wisdom which she loved: 'there is a
thing that an old widow woman said, long ago, that remains in
my mind. Her husband—she spoke of him as her "kind
companion"—had died, and she said to me, patiently, and
without tears, "Death makes people lonesome, my dear." '
   Yet they handle forms of comedy superbly and quite often in
the simplest way, by making us laugh. John Cronin's judgment
is a balanced one:

> They are great givers of pleasure, great entertainers. Edith
> reports of Violet that an old countrywoman said of her: 'Sure
> ye're always laughing! That ye may laugh in the sight of the
> Glory of Heaven!' The old woman went to the heart of the
> matter . . . Better than anyone else they knew the grave and
> the gay sides of their worlds.[3]

After Violet Martin's death in 1915 Edith Somerville continued
the literary partnership of Somerville & Ross, and in the same
way: they continued to chart the changing social conditions, the
decay of the Ascendancy, and to make us laugh.

Chapter I

Background and Biography

The nineteenth century in Ireland was a time of social and political upheavel which eventually led to self-government in the twentieth century. Somerville & Ross wrote of this period from a Protestant Anglo-Irish point of view. The Anglo-Irish were different from middle-class and aristocratic English writers of that time, not because the gap between them and the poorer, uneducated people was economically greater, but because there was a difference of religion, and of language too. One of the most significant factors of the Anglo-Irish culture was their Big Houses. The stern and simple adjective tells us something about the houses; few could be graced with the titles of stately homes, neither were they castles nor manor houses. They were not specially beautiful, nor were they serious attempts at withstanding siege and skirmish like the estates of the Scottish lairds—there are miles of grey stone walls bordering them but they can be scaled by anyone intent on it; and the walls add to the landscaping too. But the houses are usually in remote places; villages are not built around them and there is no attempt to blend them into the life of the country. They are not a real sign of conquest but they do show a proud independence and self-sufficiency. Each house is an island.

In the nineteenth century the inhabitants developed two strong loyalties: to the British Empire and to their own families. Both interests fostered the importance of the male: the favourite profession was service in the British Army or the Colonies; at home sons were necessary to inherit the land, to rule the tenantry and to keep the family tree flourishing. Life at the Big House was geared to the man: hunting, shooting and fishing took precedence over other activites. Daughters who did not become wives were a nuisance. If a spinster had any use at all it was to be an unpaid nurse to sick members of the family, or in a time of crisis to keep the house going until the sons returned from England or outposts of the Empire with English or Anglo-Irish wives—to whom the daughter would give her keys. Girls were George Moore's muslin martyrs until well on in the twentieth century. They were not financially independent and they usually had no means of earning money.

Edith Somerville was the eldest child of six, Violet Martin was the youngest child of fourteen; they were second cousins but did not meet until 1886 when both had begun to express themselves artistically, one in painting, the other in writing. They encouraged each other in their separate work, and when they discovered the possibilities inherent in collaborative work they considered their writing with professional seriousness, intent on making it financially profitable. The partnership was for both of them the most important relationship in their lives.

Neither formed a strong attachment to any man, though for several years Violet Martin met the minor poet Warham St Leger whenever she was in London. He was a journalist who published some of their stories when he was sub-editor of *Black and White*. Violet Martin kept his letters: their tone is light and affectionate. He poetically refers to their possible meeting as their 'twilight symposium' and fancifully promises to organise a feast of crumpets in her honour. When she goes back to Ireland he writes, 'After your departure there has been a sad relapse into the realm of slate colour and it is most difficult to believe that the afternoon on the river really took place in the present dispensation. It has rained here ever since you went away.' Charmed and attracted he undoubtedly was but the stylistic grace and whimsical tone of the letters argue against any deep involvement: 'I should like to be able to set out, like a man in a German song, and wander across England to some suitable sea port, and take shipping to Ireland, and then trudge, pilgrimwise till in some sunset I should see you, when there would be much to say.' Violet Martin presumably preferred skylarking across the Continent with her cousin. For all her singularity—'She had a spiritual reserve and seriousness that shielded her, like an armour of polished steel that reflects all, and is impenetrable'—

she was disconcertingly unconventional as Andrew Lang discovered when he took her to see St Andrews and she unexpectedly let off her unbeatable imitation of a dog with its tail caught in a door. In photographs her features have a boyish candour but the overall impression is of refinement and sensitivity; she is slim and delicate of body and dresses with extreme care. But she was far from being a weak female. In her diaries, in the midst of tea parties and church affairs are items such as: 'A rat was caught here and I brought it up to Drishane in my bonnet-box after breakfast. Patsy slew it with great precision.'

The Martins were a more literary family than the Somervilles. When Violet's father and eldest brother were forced to earn money to keep the estate going they both became journalists in London; when this was not enough Robert Martin wrote songs and verses and stories for a one-man show, inventing for himself the stage personality of 'Ballyhooley', and going around Ireland performing his own material. As a sort of forerunner of Percy French he was beloved by all, and it is as entertainer rather than as writer or political aid to Lord Balfour that he is commemorated on his tombstone:

Erected To the Memory of
    Robert Jasper Martin
Master Robert of Ross
By several of his many friends
As Ballyhooley he was
Well and favourably known
Throughout the Empire
Born June 1846
Died September 1905

When she wished to express herself and to make money it was natural for Violet to turn to the pen: her first published work was a series of serious social/political articles for *The World*; she modelled her style on Carlyle.

She was a sophisticated young woman. At the age of ten she was taken by her mother away from Ross to Dublin, and from then on her life was a series of furnished houses in Dublin suburbs, punctuated with lengthy visits to friends and relations all over Ireland and England. She was an avid churchgoer attending whichever was her parish church Sunday mornings, and St Patrick's for evensong; she went to weekly bible study meetings, and, unlike most Irish protestants, to Holy Communion on Saints' Days. When Edith Somerville first went to Ross she was impressed by the long row of heavily gilded volumes which were Sunday School prizes for scriptural knowledge. Her first entry in her first diary is the lesson and collect for the day.

This first diary, for the year 1875, when she was thirteen years old, gives us the picture of an extremely free, unregulated life for one so young. The only formal instruction was from a governess who came three evenings a week. During the day the child did lessons by herself, and went alone to weekly French and Greek lessons, to singing classes and dancing lessons. She borrowed books from a public lending library, and she made her own selection of quotations for the 'Remarks of the week' in her diary. They include Tennyson, Clough, Shakespeare, Spenser, Milton, Scott and Browning. Her mother was often away and she was left to her own devices: 'Zoe Callwell came up here this evening and cooked pancakes and omelettes,' and 'No one was here for lunch but Gertrude and me, we made toffee in the evening.' But though she appreciated this freedom and loved to read, she often seems lonely, 'I sat on the steps for hours after lunch,' and at a loose end, 'I spent the morning making snowballs.' One day she finds a stray dog, and after they have failed to trace its owner, she is allowed to keep it. Now she has a companion for walks she goes further afield than Donnybrook, to Ballsbridge, Lansdowne Road, Sandymount, and for swims in the Dodder. A typical Sunday: 'I went to Sunday School this morning and to church afterwards. After lunch I went to the hospital with the dog and then walked up and down afterwards. There was no one here at all.' As she grows older charity work replaces lessons, so that by the time she is twenty there are no lessons at all but only visits to various asylums, female orphanages and the Home for Cripples; for amusement there is bowls, tennis and turkish baths. In the 1882 Exhibition she is selling flowers at one of the stalls of the Masonic Bazaar. It was not an outwardly exciting life, but it was later to be used with point in *The Real Charlotte*.

Her preface to the 1879 diary, 'The chronicle of wasted time', shows the detachment and self-criticism which accompanies the trivial doings. The diary of her fourteenth year shows her as exacting a critic and as capable of expressing her judgment as the juvenile Jane Austen. She goes with her mother to stay with the Bishop of Cavan; her mother, her host and hostess and everyone she meets are viewed with a cool detachment and a keen sense of the ridiculous. The young curates are there for their final examination before ordination; they 'slunk in and in a terrible fright meekly swallowed a "vaste snack" . . . everyone of them without exception positively clammy with terror'. When they leave, the Bishop's children and Violet are delighted: 'Immediately after late dinner all the curates departed in flocks on outside cars, and the house was rid of their unwholesome presence. I must say I was not sorry to see them go off as I was always coming suddenly on them, wandering helplessly round the garden, and we could never play croquet or amuse ourselves in any way, without being conscious that they were watching us from behind trees and round corners. We strummed the piano all the evening in commemoration of it all being over.' No doubt the curates were just as relieved to leave the palace. The congregation of the Bishop's church she finds provincial: 'It seemed so curious after the Dublin churches, to go about shaking hands with everybody, and to feel that everybody was examining your clothes with the greatest attention.' She is never overwhelmed by position, always able to judge for herself; in church the curate comes off better than the Bishop: 'The Bishop sat in state in his big chair today looking like some extraordinary old woman in his black stiff petticoat. He read the gospel and said the blessing at the end and that was all. We had a very good sermon from the curate.' The first man of the county whom everyone calls 'the great boss', Lord Farnham, looks in at the palace and is treated to a eulogy on Violet's stray dog: 'He came over to the croquet ground and shook hands with me and began to show off a collie dog of his which he said was the finest in Ireland. I, of course, promptly gave him the lie, and gave him a graphic account of Shep. Whereat he was impressed much.'

The Bishop's children are given lessons each morning but Violet does not join them. She reads, rides about on a vicious donkey, and plays croquet with herself—her left hand versus her right hand—until they join her outside. According to her diary she and her mother are late for prayers every morning, and when the Bishop orders breakfast before prayers they are late for breakfast—ten o'clock breakfast! Violet is not a compliant visitor, she refuses to teach in Sunday School, because it is her whim to refuse, and so she sits as a grim pupil in the class of a girl she had taught in Dublin. It must have been trying for both of them. She tempts the bishop's daughters up a broken ladder into the hayloft. The ladder was about a yard below the opening and almost broken across so they could not get down again. Violet, as fearless as she was short-sighted, managed, 'and was followed by LooLoo but Kate said that unless I got up again to help her she would not get down. I got up and gave her a hand but she stuck somehow and immediately began to weep and at the same time clutched me so that I was nearly pulled down. With much ferocity I told her that if she did not go down the ladder at once and let me go I would push her down headfirst. This had great effect.' Despite her sharpness of observation and her sensitivity she was often an ordinary naughty girl, never above horse-play: 'After tea we told stories to each other in the hall, lying buried in the straw in a big packing-case. We stayed there for ages until we were hunted off to bed by Nannie Darley. When we got up to our rooms we took it into our heads to have a bolstering match. This however was attended with so much bounding and shrieking that Nannie Darley was aroused from her slumbers in the drawing room and stole upstairs upon us. We never "felt" her till she was in the room and then there was great and mighty confusion and an awful row.' Unknown to the adults she had found a pair of spurs with which to enliven her hours on the vicious donkey. Her description of one such morning, the adult reaction, and the close of the day is a typical blend of her high spirits, self-mockery, and meditative soul.

I had a long practice after prayers and then mounted the donkey. Today I had on the spurs again, but the soul of the animal rose within him and behold Violet fell. She rose and mounted, and again was she kicked off, and yet again. But by this time the soul of Violet had also risen, and after giving him flagellation I got up and spurred him again. The wily animal immediately tried to put his head down but the Violet still more wily hit him under the mouth thereby causing him to elevate it in the air. I then grasped the reins and "one tremendous welt gave him; one dig home with the spurs" and he went at a tremendous gallop. He is now quite meek. However Nannie Darley was very angry with me for using spurs and I am not to put them on again. I did not go out again until after tea when I took a long walk as it was the longest day. It was the loveliest evening I ever saw.

These early diaries are fuller than later ones when she saves descriptions of people and places for her letters to Edith Somerville or, if they are together, for their commonplace books. In this 1876 diary the novelist's sharp eye is apparent. A ward of the Bishop arrives, 'The said Harriet McIntosh is a girl of about twenty-one, rather large . . . but withal not bad looking. At any rate she holds herself very well and has nice manners and a pleasant English kind of voice. She has beautiful brown eyes with long thick lashes, but the face is rather spoilt by a thick broad hooky nose and a general heavy look.' There is a neat vignette of an emotional governess: 'I was just in time for prayers today. There was rather a sensation created by Fraulein suddenly bursting into tears and rushing upstairs in the middle of the chapter. After prayers we went up and found her in "highstrikes". I rushed to get water, somebody else got eau de cologne, somebody else got tea, in fact everybody was getting everything and doing not the least good. However she got over them pretty soon.' Her eye for landscape is remarkable in one so young, as is her ability to remember it and describe it. There is a comic description of a picnic they go on, full of the usual hazards of smoking fires and kettles which won't boil, and in the midst of it is a description of the countryside from the picnic site:

Cavan seems to be enclosed in a perfect circle of delightful looking blue misty hills which actually do seem to melt in the distance. The county itself is a beautiful succession of slopes and undulations which have a very good covering of woods here and there. It reminded me so much of the descriptions of English counties. The fields are so well cultivated and there are no stone walls, only soft looking green hedges everywhere. Here and there, there are such pretty little cottages standing at the foot of a slope in a little clump of trees, with blue smoke curling up and roses and all the other toor/al/ooral accompaniments . . .

In 1886 when Violet Martin's round of travelling took her to cousins in west Cork, she and Edith Somerville first saw each other in the church. They immediately recognised something special in each other. When Edith goes away for nine days Violet writes in her diary on the ninth day: 'Not a bad morning but nothing particular, too excited by the prospect of the return of E.Œ.S. Went to Constance's in the afternoon to try and fill up the time till 6.30 when Aylmer Coghill and I walked up the Skib. road in torrents of rain and met the Bart. and Edith.' After the more sedate life of Dublin's furnished houses Violet immersed herself wholeheartedly in the chaotic and exuberant existence of the Somerville and Coghill cousins. They were a law unto themselves in the isolated idyllic corner of Castletownshend; picnics, tennis, boating, riding, choir practice, cards, sketching, painting, photography and spiritualism were all eagerly and even passionately enjoyed. They ate large meals wherever they happened to be at meal time, and they slept wherever they ate the last meal of the day. Their estates overlapped and made one huge island in which they played and lived with absolute self-reliance and assurance. They all loved Violet Martin and from now on whenever she is free from her duties to her mother and Ross she flies to Castletownshend. Even church was fun here, with Edith, who had played the organ since she was big enough, often playing the *Te Deum* while the choir and congregation sang the *Benedicite*. That summer saw the inauguration of a new vicar: 'Edith bolted to church and by superhuman exertions got the hymns away before the third collect. Of course Hildegarde and I were late. We love being late. Mr B swore himself in with awful imprecations and an invention service. Music on a scale of unwonted splendour. (The organist said "D 3 flats" was the name of the scale.) Tea at home. Edith read Rossetti to Hildegarde and me.'

On Violet's last night in Drishane, this time, Edith has very severe toothache and they stay up to dose her with laudanum and poultices; nevertheless Violet is extremely sorry to leave: 'Had an awful bad night with that beast Edith whose face kept her and me awake all the time. They were very sorry to say goodbye to me. (Don't know anymore E. Œ.S.s)'

Edith Somerville was four years older than Violet. She was educated by a series of governesses—Welsh, English, German and French, and then a term of lectures at the Alexandra College Dublin. Mrs Somerville taught her to draw and sew, and during the governess's holidays made the children play the piano, and read Scott and Dickens aloud. Like Violet, Edith grew up a great reader but drawing was her passion. She bullied her parents into letting her go to Dusseldorf in 1881 and to Paris in 1884 to study art. In 1885 she had an illustrated essay on art studios accepted by *Cassel's Magazine of Art*; and *The Graphic* accepted a series of full-page comic strip drawings. The latter are sophisticated and amazingly masculine in the boldness of line, the complete absence of emotion and the sharp sense of the ridiculous which gives point to the caricatures. On the strength of this her family gave her a sort of coach house as a studio—known by them as 'the purlieu', Mrs Somerville had taken one look at its disgusting untidiness and said it was like 'the revolting purlieus of some disgusting town'. In Paris Edith lived on a shoe string: the longer the money lasted the longer she could stay. She could not afford the opera but she managed to see Sarah Bernhardt in *La Dame aux Camélias*: 'She didn't act. She merely was Marguerite Gauthier. The only actress or actor I have ever seen who I absolutely believed in and whose identity was really lost in her part. She even had not what mother calls "the strut".' Usually evenings were spent buying materials for the next day, writing letters, learning to play the fiddle and mending stockings. She worked in the studio from eight in the morning till five in the afternoon with an hour off for lunch. Living in a *pension* she made tea surreptitiously on a spirit lamp, and sometimes even went further: 'Had a little carouse upstairs. Beer, milk and an egg bate and boiled are very good.' She always went to worship on Sundays, on Easter Sunday going twice: to 6.30 a.m. communion at the English church, and to the

11 a.m. service at the American church. On her second visit she economises even more carefully, getting her own meals in order to eke out the money. She shares with two other girls and they pool money and divide tasks: 'Ponce cooks our dinner, Marion buys it, and my department is head scullion and bottle washer . . . we have a "regular gorge" for about three sous a piece.' They live mainly on sausages and eggs, buying lunch for one franc at the *crèmerie*. Edith's room is very different from those of Drishane: 'a convenient size, as I can open the window, or door, poke the fire, wash myself, lay the breakfast and eat it, all without getting off the somewhat limited bed.' She adores making do, and when she gets a cold doses herself on camomile tea and 'made a footbath in my bonnet box and used it successfully'. Painting is her passion and she lives for the words of her teacher; if he suggests her work is not good she feels sick, and at the words *'pas trop mal'* she rushes out delighted and treats herself to a huge lunch.

In 1887 Violet Martin was allowed to join Edith for two weeks. She did not take to student life. She mocked the momentous decision as to whether to eat a tin of sardines and a bunch of radishes *or* a couple of hard boiled eggs and a penny tart. At their favourite *crèmerie* she could see only the greasy cutlery, the badly cooked food and the sloppy service—the waitress had her thumb in the soup as she served Violet. She lacked their common passion for art—one of the girls she found such a bore that Edith had to promise not to go about with her before Violet would agree to going to Paris at all—and she was not charmed by the tattiness and lack of nicety which went with the freedom from the demands of a more formal society. Her visit was not a success but she more than made up for it at the customs on the way back into England. The officer wanted to examine Edith's huge holdall in which her fox terrier puppy was secreted; there was a moment of absolute terror for Edith (who doubtless loved the dog the more because she had nursed her through distemper in Paris, carrying her up and down the many flights of stairs 'fifty times in a day') but Violet as quick as a flash, 'crammed Patsy up her sleeves'—and got away with it.

Edith's studies in Paris were interspersed with the hectic

goings on at Castletownshend; her artistic seriousness never stopped her enjoying their frivolity.

Erected "wild and dotey" decorations all round. After an exhausting day we fed at six and received cavalry at nine. Almost everyone came and there were about sixty altogether. The room looked very nice and all our new and wild dances went very well. Especially the polonaise. The Cotillon was also extremely dotey and dancing did not stop till 6.0.a.m.! The K.O.Bs had brought their piper and we had two grand Highland Scottishes to savage strains.

On birthdays and special days they often wore fancy dress: 'Hildegarde went as Jubilee, draped in flags, Aylmer as a Chinese, the boys in the faithful old acting gear, and I as the Church, in a black robe, white choker and hair done like a wig and powdered. Egerton was awfully good as a crusader, Violet in a sheet [a Grecian lady].' They really were like a clan: 'all went down to Glen B the first thing after breakfast and were photographed by Uncle Jos in an immense group of thirty-six', and one without any responsibilities: when she forgets the diary one August she writes in later: 'In all human probability we boated in the morning and tennised after lunch.' There were frequent picnics on nearby islands: 'armed with potatoes, butter and milk. We got eggs on the island, and then boiled the potatoes and mashed them in the pot with the eggs and ate them with the simple stone implements of our forefathers. Came home to bathe and tennis.' There was certainly no time to be lonely and when she hears of the pregnancy of the girl who had been her bosom childhood friend her response is 'Heard from Ethel—Poor thing—A single life is airy.' Even the artistic life was very different from the solemnity of the studios with all her relations to bully into posing for her—and the farmyard too: 'made the goose screwed, in order to paint her, with whiskey and laudanum'. Her only cause for complaint seems to be that it was only really fine on Sundays when she was not allowed to paint: 'Very fine of course, because it was Sunday and I couldn't paint. This thing will make a Jew of me. I can't stand it much longer.' After 1888 it was not so easy for Violet to get to west Cork; Mrs

Martin decided to open up Ross once more. Violet, though twenty-six years of age, was unmarried and her clear duty was to be with her mother, even though she had just embarked on the collaborative writing with Edith Somerville. They arrived in June to find the house much dilapidated, trees and shrubs cut down, garden and avenue completely neglected. Violet worked harder than anyone at the restoration; Edith says 'the work that was accomplished by "Martin Ross" that year was small indeed as compared with the manifold activities of "Miss Wilet".' A niece's chief memory of Violet is 'seeing her about the place, slight and active; she used to carry a little hatchet and never passed a tree with ivy growing on it without cutting the ivy through at ground level.' When she had got some order outside, she tended the apple trees, raspberry canes and gooseberry bushes, and sold the fruit. Often she could not write at night because her hands were trembling too much from a day with the scythe or the shears. Indoors too the refurbishing, decorating and the management of the few servants they could afford fell entirely on her—to the detriment of her writing:

> I am writing at an article badly. I am very stupid, and not the least clever, except at mending blinds and the pump. I am tired of going down seventy-five steps to get my boots, of turning away my eyes from iniquity that I cannot rectify, of trying to get servants up in the morning—but let me be thankful, I have done somewhat, and can leave with a clear conscience. To get a kitchen chimney cleaned, the pump mended and the kitchen thoroughly cleaned and white-washed . . .

Much as she loved Ross it was always a relief to get back to Drishane. Until 1905 when her mother left Ross, almost all of Violet's literary earnings were spent on the upkeep of the house. And much as she loved her mother, who was herself well read, intelligent with a fine sense of humour and a sharp wit, living with her meant little time to write in, even when the estate and household cares gave her a few moments. One letter to Edith recounts a row she had with her mother who insisted on talking to her when she was writing, 'I would not answer her conversation' and then Violet's sister-in-law came in and not only talked to them both but began tidying the table which Violet was writing on.

In Drishane Edith Somerville's literary efforts were not treated with any more respect. After her mother's death in 1895 she took over the running of Drishane—an even more time-consuming and wearing task than Ross, for if there were more money and servants there were also many more inhabitants, more meals, more rooms to be kept up, more vases of flowers to arrange, and frequent guests. She did the book-keeping for the farm, she helped her sister with their new venture, a violet farm, gathering the tiny flowers and packing them in boxes to be sent off to Dublin. She still never refused an invitation to a dance, even though it meant travelling miles on bad roads in the dead of the night, often not getting home till five in the morning. Seeing the need for repairs and supervising the workmen all fell on her shoulders, and there was the perpetual fight with the rat race, 'The rats have turned us out of the study and have spoilt the covers of my new volumes of the Encyclopedia Britannica. They are a real plague here.' There were horses to be exercised, dogs to be walked, and she refused to drop her painting and drawing. And yet they contrived to meet their deadlines:

Monday 17 October 1898: Worked at No. 3 with Edith. It must go off by Wednesday . . . Worked in the evening.
Tuesday 18 October: Worked all the morning . . . Worked before and after dinner, up to 1.0 a.m. and very nearly finished the rough copy. Was very tired and cross.
Wednesday 19 October: Began to write at 7.30 a.m. and got the rough copy finished by 11.30. Then started in to copy. Worked till 5.15 and then got the finished MS. off by sending Jerry with the trap.

They began to learn Irish. They did work for the women's suffragette movement. They both believed it nonsense that their workmen should have the vote when they with all their responsibilities did not. They themselves were educated in political and social questions, they were as capable of rational discussion as any of the men they knew, and they were self supporting. Edith's speeches were extremely balanced: she attacks women's magazines for narrowing women's concept of themselves, and the women's columns in daily newspapers for limiting their subjects to clothes and cookery. But she always advocates moderation, women must learn to speak 'temperately, and without exaggeration or bitterness' and they must begin their rational campaigns at home for 'Everyman, consciously or unconsciously, judges women by the women he knows best, and it rests with each of us to form that opinion.' They refused to support militancy and refused to cooperate with the English suffragists for that reason. When an incursion of English women came to Ireland to preach their cause Edith Somerville went to Cork to head them off; they were 'not only coming over here to burn and destroy, but want to preach Anti-Home Rule, which things, taken together, would about finish our chance of support over here.'

As if all this were not enough Edith takes over the pack of hounds in 1903. All her literary earnings go on their upkeep. In the first years, *Slipper's A.B.C. of Fox Hunting* (dedicated to the West Carbery hounds) pays the bills. After that she just about covers costs each year; £230 a year for four horses, three men and sixteen couples of hounds. Hence she writes, 'Made up my bank book. Have £2.2.6 to face a frowning world. Haven't enough money to buy stockings but keep hounds. How very Irish!' In 1909 Edith, her sister and a brother form the Drishane House Dairy; after a year the brother whom they had decided would be manager, goes to England, so Edith and her sister find themselves looking after a three-hundred acre farm and a large herd of cows. Nothing daunted they import the first Friesians into Ireland, breed them and start a successful campaign to get them recognised at shows, and to persuade the Irish Department of Agriculture to give premiums for Friesian Dairy Bulls. Tea parties at Drishane still have sixty-five guests on the lists and somehow books get written.

When Violet was at Ross and Edith either at Drishane, or in Paris painting, frequent letters passed between them, which, like their early diaries, show them to be keen observers of society, alive to the ridiculous, the highly coloured and the sombre. There are amusing snapshots such as the woman at the tea party who was 'wearing white kid gloves, and she was eating heavily buttered teacake and drinking tea, with her gloves buttoned, and her veil down . . .' and 'Mrs De Burgh a dream of ugliness looking like a second-rate altar,' and long passages of description capturing the spirit of respective environments. Actual happenings jotted in the diaries are often written up in letters to each other, and later incorporated into stories. So that whether they were actually together or not they were collecting material for their collaborative writing, which once they had written one book together was the real centre of life for both of them. When *An Irish Cousin* was near publication Violet's diary ends the year with: 'Finished the proofs I had, with tea and trembling. The year closes on a sun-burst of Bourget and many beautiful projects built in its beams.'

Their friendship has been so much misunderstood that it is necessary to say that while their love and respect for each other could hardly have been greater, it never transgressed the bounds set by Christianity. Neither before nor after Violet's death did Edith Somerville have any orientation towards the lesbianism advocated by so many of her social equals in London. She hardly knew such sexual liberation existed, and she quite innocently went on a holiday abroad with the notorious Dame Ethel Smyth. When the latter suggested that they should embark on some sort of physical relationship Edith was shocked and horrified. Two quotations illustrate well the nature of our authors' friendship. The first is an example of the fun they shared. They are travelling, as always alone, on the night train from Orleans to Paris; the train is crowded but they have the cheek to lock themselves into the carriage, somehow fixing the door against 'possible maniacs, drunkards, and smokers of French tobacco'; eventually it is morning:

> . . . we drew forth the half bottle of Grand St Lambert that had for the last few days been carried perilously about in a bonnet-box, and with grapes and croissants began a repast that continued through stages of bovril, tea, and ginger bread biscuits till we neared Paris. The water for tea was near proving a difficulty. To get it, it was necessary to shuffle in 'night's disarray' to the buffet, and a fair amount of nerve was required to advance through the crowd of sleepily devouring men and fill a disreputable tin kettle from a carafe of water

under the very eyes of an indignant waiter. We flatter
ourselves that the most courageous man of our acquaintance
would have been afraid to do it.[1]

The second quotation is from a letter Edith wrote to her
favourite brother after Violet's death:

> There isn't much to say. Just that a life, that has always been a
> happy one, has fallen in ruins. It is ungrateful to say I have no
> future left, as there are all of you, and Cameron to be looked
> after, and all the home things, but the innermost part, "my
> share of the world", has gone with Martin and nothing can
> ever make that better. No one but ourselves can ever know
> what we were to each other. It is the only comfort I have that
> it was not she who was left behind to try and face life alone.[2]

Two tangible and lasting expressions of her grief are the
sideboard that she had engraved in gold letters to the memory of
Violet Martin and placed in the church at Castletownshend as
the communion table, and the beautiful blue and gold mosaics
on the altar floor, which she fixed herself in her own design.
Once she was convinced that, even after death, Violet's spirit
could join with her own mind when she was writing fiction, she
made herself go on with the writing even though she would
have preferred to be painting. Violet Martin's death in 1915 did
not end the literary personality of Somerville & Ross.

In the years following the Easter Rising in 1916 the position of
the Anglo-Irish in Ireland was most precarious. The immediate
aftermath was an unsettled peace in which it seemed that the
Rising had been a failure. But the climate had changed from
that of the pre-Rising years when it had seemed that the change
would come through land legislation and constitutional moves.
Periodic acts of violence became more frequent and the
Troubles began in earnest. The Anglo-Irish seemed to have a
simple choice, either they emigrated or they put up with
insecurity and isolation. Edith Somerville's letters, diaries and
essays give a clear picture of life in the south west during these
anxious years. The factors which had made life in her district
more comfortable in the nineteenth century made for the
opposite condition now: a community of landlords who could

easily be isolated from the world at large was an obvious target for the Sinn Feiners.

In 1916 Edith Somerville sympathised with the plight of the revolutionary leaders—though not of course with their wishes. Her feeling that England had no understanding of Ireland made her sympathetic to the idealists and she was horrified at the execution of the 1916 leaders. She writes, 'the fool-English shot the sincere and honourable visionaries among the rebels; Poets, dreamers, Minstrel boys who went to the war in the mantles of Wolfe Tone and Emmet',[3] and so left the gunmen to plot anarchy. From this point on she thought the British government mistaken in its handling of Ireland.

Her understanding was based on her daily experiences, which were limited to the Anglo-Irish, and the country farming and farm labouring people. She thought that most of the farmers were emotionally nationalistic and rebellious, but that their materialistic hard-headedness would keep them tied to the wealthier Britain when the crunch came. This point of view is the centre of her article 'The Intellectuals' which she wrote in 1918 in reply to an article by Susan Mitchell in *The Englishwoman*. Edith Somerville shows the farmer to be a rebel out on the hillside, but quite different in his cosy kitchen where he tells his wife, 'I think I'll carry the colt to the fair next week! I'm told the buyers are running mad buying horses for th' Army!' She did not mean the Irish army. When an increasing number of local men Gaelicised their names and began to wear green ties and caps, she comforted herself with the fact that many others gave willingly to the Red Cross collections and spoke with admiration of the men out in the trenches. She saw no danger in an Easter parade held in Skibbereen in 1918 to commemorate the Rising of 1916:

> A week or so since, there was, in a small Irish country town, a parade, commemorative of those 'giant aspirators' that failed, as at this time of spring, in Dublin, two years ago. A distressing band made night unpleasant, and local Sinn Fein, inspired by its indisputably provocative strains, broke some windows. The postman, who feeds his district with news as well as mails, was asked if anything serious had taken place.

'Is it serious?' he replied with a delicate scorn. 'The Brats! I'd have flogged them off the street myself!'

In letters to the English press she stressed that it was the farmer who was the most important person in Ireland, and that he was stalwart and reliable in his loyalty. She thought the British government was cowardly in its fear of introducing conscription into Ireland and that this cowardice had encouraged Irish rebellion. She tried to counteract German propaganda, which she thought was responsible for much of the unrest in Ireland, by persuading British officials to send cinematograph vans around Ireland. She wanted them to show pictures of the war wherever there was a wall big enough, with an informative commentary given by an *Irish* person. She knew the anger of the townsfolk but she was quite unaware of anti-British attitudes amongst the farmers and she would have nothing said against them. When a brother criticised the rebels Edith wrote back sharply; her faith in the country people she knew, and her suffragette sympathies, made her anti-Unionist:

> I do not in the least agree that Ireland is rotten, or that people should fly from her, as rats from the sinking ship. I think all this Sinn Fein business has been artificially worked up, one would really say *connived* at by the English Government. It has made me a Home Ruler; only sensible Irish men and *Women* are able to govern Ireland. England is feeble, futile, and fatuous to the extreme of Folly.[4]

The majority of people, she was convinced, did not want a bloody revolution. In an essay of 1919 she mocks the rebels, dismissing them as schoolboys who are playing games with extraordinary weapons like bell-mouthed blunderbusses and South Pacific spears stolen from Ascendancy houses. When Sinn Fein refused to allow any more fox hunting until Britain released all political prisoners, she ignored the threats. She believed that the local Sinn Feiners, who were countrymen, would never stoop to poisoning hounds. They did not. Her confidence in the loyalty of the Irish people lasted till 1920, but the letter she wrote in June of that year is the last sign of this faith. It was written to an English newspaper:

Sir, at a moment when every law-abiding hand has a stone in it to cast at Ireland, may I whose hand, tho' law-abiding, has no stone in it—offer a general observation, the statement that some houses are made of glass? In the *Bab Ballads* it is said

> The terrible avenger of the Majesty of Law
> Was far less like a Hatchett than a dissipated saw.

The Majesty of Law in Ireland is in much the same case. The Police are standing back to back trying to defend themselves. The British Army provides the raiders with service-rifles. There is scarcely a country-house that has not been proved vulnerable, since all have been successfully raided for arms and left with absolutely no means of defence. In Ireland law and order continue to survive solely by the sanction of the people. Yet, sir, when I read of the murders and the burglaries that occur in other more favoured lands, I cannot but feel that if I am to sleep with my dining room windows open and my silver on the sideboard, I should choose rather to do so in west Cork than in London.

She was horrified at the importation of the Black and Tans. Its effect was like the execution of the 1916 leaders; it provoked Irishmen into joining Sinn Fein. In the English press she continuously condemns the policy of reprisals pursued by the Black and Tans. Such a policy only made rebels of the people when the houses of quite innocent people were set on fire. It also meant that the Republicans were not caught because the Black and Tans were too busy burning farmhouses to chase them. She wrote with anger of the way in which the Black and Tans actually stripped people and made them run naked through the streets, and she tried to show English people that such barbaric behaviour only antagonised Irish people and made them fervently anti-English. The Black and Tans were offering no protection to Loyalists, and they were potential murderers to the rest of the country. Local men were bullied by Sinn Fein into destroying bridges by night, and then commandeered by the Black and Tans to rebuild them by day. In Cork the Black and Tans burned the City Hall and most of the shopping district as a reprisal; the big shops were mainly owned by Loyalists.

So that while she lost her faith in the loyalty of most Irish people, she was equally saddened by the behaviour of England. Like most of the Anglo-Irish she felt quite deserted by England. They had remained loyal but England offered them no protection. She was antagonised by the English press which she thought dismissed the plight of the Anglo-Irish far too easily. Boxing, tennis and golf were given columns of report compared with a few words telling that another Big House had been destroyed by fire. She describes vividly the horror of having one's house burned out in the night, and of suddenly discovering that all one has in the world is the nightclothes one is wearing. If anyone notices the brief newsclip their reaction is usually, 'They want more troops in Ireland!' More troops means more reprisals and more Loyalists emigrating to England in borrowed clothes. Such emigration meant also that the many people employed in Big Houses were without work or wage. Their plight was little better than that of their ex-landlord now, 'a broken and bored old man' who will 'be doing his best to forget also his own people and his father's house in the thrills of a daily potter round the Suburban golf-course.'

By May 1922 Edith Somerville is writing, 'The scum and the dregs of this wretched country are now in power,' and, 'I don't know where my old, dear Ireland has gone. The friendly, kindly people who you could trust and who trusted you.' But when her English friend replied in a similar vein condemning the Irish, Edith writes a furious letter supporting her countrymen, and then an apology: 'I am sorry. Ireland is so awfully near me. I can't see it dispassionately, and I suppose my skin is unreasonably thin.' She admits her disillusionment, 'I suppose I have been a romantic and a fool all my life, and made excuses or shut my eyes to facts', but it does not qualify the resentment she feels towards England:

> I am tired of English volte-faces. They have blackened *our* face anyhow (I mean the faces of people like us, who have tried to reassure waverers that England would never desert them etc.). And then Irish gentry are derided and despised because in the past, instead of joining the aggressively disloyal agitators, they continued to send their sons to the English

Army and Navy, and were true to their traditions of fidelity to
the Crown. Personally, I know, I have been all wrong. You
can hit *me* as hard as you like. I am not going to be anything
any more—neither Optimist or Pessimist, or Loyal or Rebel.
Nothing—except an indifferent painter, a writer whose one
subject is justly discredited and unpopular, and a breeder of
good horses that no one will buy![5]

The nearest conflict of appreciable size to Edith Somerville
was the Battle of Skibbereen, 3–5 July 1922: the Republicans
tried to seize the barracks. They took over the Post Office, the
Corner House, and the Bank of Ireland. They cannoned the
barracks for two days, and took it over on the third day. Only
one man was killed, a Republican who was minding a cannon
gun on the top of a nearby hill. The bank manager told Edith
Somerville how they set up a big gun in his bedroom which faced
the barracks; they first knocked holes in the wall to fire their
rifles through and then turned to the big gun:

> Firstly they put in some handfuls of black powder, and then a
> handful of tow. Then they had some more powder, and then a
> tin-can of broken iron, and then some more powder. Then
> they said they'd fire it. 'Well come out of the room and fire it
> with a wire so' says I, 'if you value your lives,' says I. They
> were said by me then, and they came down the stairs, and let
> it off. I thought the roof was gone. After a while they went up
> to the room. 'Good God!' says they 'Where's the gun?' The
> ceiling was down, and the windows were blown out and one
> wall was on the floor, and the rest shaking, and not a bit of the
> gun was in it larger than your two fists.

The incident ended with a farcical dénouement of mistaken
identity: on the day of the funeral of the Republican who was
killed, a brother of Edith Somerville arrived home. Because the
roads were impassable he was dropped at Castletownshend by a
destroyer. The Republicans, awaiting the funeral, saw the boat
draw near and a rumour started that the destroyer had six
hundred Free Staters on board who were landing. The Republican leader immediately set off to blow up the barracks and to set
fire to Liss Ard where five hundred barrels of petrol were stored.

The local Free State leader, on hearing the rumour, rushed to Castletownshend to welcome the army of supporters. The villagers were terrified, and piled beds, clothes and food on their donkey carts, bicycles and wheelbarrows and left the village quickly. The priest saved the barracks by fending off the angry Republicans by words alone. Both sides were disgusted when they realised their mistake; their leaders were reported to have fought a battle of fisticuffs that night. Edith Somerville's sympathies were with the villagers:

> They fled with their children, and their poor little household things, . . . flying they knew not where—'back in the country', out of the line of fire anyhow. Our nice good postman's wife and children were among these wretched creatures, and the poor man broke down when he was telling me of it all . . . I know you don't sympathise with the decent ones of 'No courage, No public opinion' etc. All quite true, but No one who has not been in their place (or as near it as we have been) can be expected to understand their position, and how very far back, and at whose feet, the blame should be laid.[6]

Castletownshend escaped Republican occupation mainly through the efforts of Father Lamb, the priest who had saved the barracks single-handed. At the end of July a party of Republicans arrived to take over the Coastguard station. They made local men help them destroy the two quays and the Castle bathing-house landing-place, so that there was nowhere for the Free State troops to land. Father Lamb charged at the Republicans even though they were all armed, and they dispersed before his rage and courage. He would not pander to Loyalists either. Later that day Edith Somerville and a brother went to the village meeting:

> As we came, Jim Brown said 'I object to the presence of Colonel Somerville!' Father Lamb said 'I don't want Colonel Somerville, or any other Colonels here! This is *my* business!' C. and I retired at once. Afterwards we heard that Father Lamb had begun by marching with his own party into the guard room and seizing four rifles. Then he said with a loaded

rifle in his hand, 'Now, if you won't listen to me and obey me, I'll shoot one of you first!' He pulled out his watch. 'I'll give you five minutes to make up your minds to quit this damned work. . . . If you won't do it, I'll shoot!' They gave in.

In August, however, another party of Republicans arrived and burned down the Coast Guard station, despite Father Lamb's efforts to stop them. Edith Somerville noted with horror that when the Republicans did not burn down the houses they took over, they wreaked havoc: carpets were ruined, photograph frames smashed and bits of glass used as darts, with even a Rembrandt painting used as a dartboard. Books were used to barricade windows, and lorries were driven across tennis courts and lawns. When Edith was confronted by a party of Republicans at Drishane who had come to demand saws and crowbars, she gave them a sermon on their wickedness. She reported afterwards that they were most respectful, but said if they did not obey their orders to get the tools they would be shot.

The Somervilles' position was typical of that of the Anglo-Irish in the south west who stayed; they were surrounded by lawlessness and physically cut off from the rest of the world. Once the road to Skibbereen was blocked by blowing up a bridge, their only way out was by sea. Once the Coast Guard station was destroyed, they could make no contact with the outside world until they arranged to make light-signals to the British destroyer. This was against the laws of neutrality but they had a system of signs arranged with the navy in case of an emergency. When the Free State soldiers were stationed in Skibbereen the Somervilles acted as go-between for the soldiers and the navy. The Captain went to Drishane for croquet and tea.

Edith Somerville was well aware of their danger when she wrote to a friend in England telling her that in the last week there had been twelve murders of politically inoffensive men whose sole crime was being Protestant. One was eighty-three years old, another sixteen, and such reprisals continued long after the Black and Tans were withdrawn. But she refused to leave her home. She looked upon those who left as 'bolters', and, although she offered various reasons for staying such as not being able to afford to move and having to look after a brother, it is clear that she remained because of her passionate love of Drishane and because she believed it was her right. Drishane was her home and Ireland had been her family's country for 300 years; nobody was going to shift her. Because her brothers were abroad it was her duty to keep the home fires burning. Lady Gregory's love of Coole Park was the same, and she too stayed there alone throughout the Troubles for the sake of family and posterity. 'I would be quite satisfied to keep Richard's home a resting place in this stony and uncertain and broken-up world. . . . If there is trouble now, and it is dismantled and left to ruin, that will be the whole country's loss.'[7] Similar spirit was shown by Edith's brother Hugh when he was at home for a short time. He got through to Cork City, and on his fourth determined visit to the Post Office he contrived to wrest forty-three bags of detained mail, which had been allowed to moulder, from the office despite official red tape. He made a visit to the Free State General to inform him that the Republicans had put bombs on ships in the river so that they could block the channel to Cork, the only opening left between Castletownshend and the rest of Ireland. The General claimed that he could do nothing without orders and refused to accept responsibility for taking any action, so it was Hugh Somerville's initiative that stopped them from being cut off by sea as well as by land. He got into a motor launch and went out to the blockade and cut the boats adrift, then went on board the boats and disconnected the bombs. Although snipers shot at him throughout the operation, he returned home unharmed.

Despite all this, life went on very much as before. In June 1921, Edith Somerville wrote to an English friend: 'It is a curious world I live in, and I often marvel at the way we all sit calmly on the lid of a very seething pot, and play croquet and make hay—as if we were in Kent or Surrey.' She wrote in 1922: 'Well-well. What use is it to cry? Ye might as well be singing and dancing! and I play with my two absurd puppies in between the miseries.' And later that summer: 'We have each other to tea, and play a little tennis, and a little croquet, and talk about the last rumours that Jerry the postman or Paddy the baker's messenger has brought from Skibbereen.' In the toughest times when her morale was low Edith Somerville's resolution to stay was strengthened by a message from Violet Martin, who told her that she, Edith's father, uncle and other relatives, were spending all their energies on building a cordon around Castletownshend and influencing the rebels so that they did not harm the Somervilles or Coghills. Edith believed and drew courage from this: 'Absolutely *nothing* else explains our immunity from robbery, incendiarism and worse.' Her fortitude was commendable. One night she awoke to hear the shouts and knocks of the rebels and, after waking her brother who lighted the red lamp in Edith's bedroom which was the signal to the destroyer, she went downstairs and checked all the windows to see if they were shut. The next day she wrote to friends, 'It would be shabby to bolt . . .'. She only admitted that 'We all find ourselves waking suddenly and starting up in bed if a door bangs or a window rattles! Such a nuisance.' Similarly Lady Gregory faced the raiders at night, and when threatened showed the same indomitable courage which Yeats writes of:

> Augusta Gregory seated at her great ormolu table,
> Her eightieth winter approaching: 'Yesterday he
>   threatened my life.
> I told him that nightly from six to seven I sat at
>   this table,
> The blinds drawn up'[8]

When Edith Somerville heard of a Republican plan to raid Drishane for blankets and men's clothes, she alerted the Navy and spent a frantic hour packing, tying and labelling the contents of the two other houses which she was storing, as well as the Somervilles' own, into six enormous bundles. The bundles were carried by a donkey and cart to a field precipitous to the sea. Then the giant loads were rolled down to the shore where the Navy collected them. Edith Somerville was composed enough to enjoy the sight: 'the grand bluejackets staggering over the rocks with the bundles, looking like those spiders with bloated tummies and brief legs'.

The murder of Michael Collins was an encouragement to the local young men to volunteer for the Free State Army, but there were not enough rifles for them and there was no time to train them to use what weapons they had. The civil guard was unarmed. There were no police and no courts of law. Groups of disbanded Republicans who were armed raided and looted houses and shops, often in daylight. When they were caught they claimed they were students and were let free again. Free State soldiers were sent to protect Skibbereen, but their presence did not improve the daily conditions: they were billeted on people who could ill afford to keep them and nobody was given compensation. One man, a widower with several children, told Edith Somerville that he had been given six soldiers and had used up a lifetime's savings in five weeks of housing and feeding them. There was no training and very little discipline; officers and men got drunk together. The effects of civil war were visible in the empty shops, dirty streets, and small groups of distressed people who whispered together on street corners. Even when fairs could be held, sale prices were bad: cattle worth £20 two years before fetched from £4–£7. There were no trains, no posts or telegrams, and travel by road was impossible for more than a few miles because of ambushes and the continual blowing up of bridges. Food was very scarce and farms began, if they could, to grind their own wheat. Priests who denounced their flock were scorned by young people striding out of chapel. Father Lamb shouted from his altar: 'I will put down looting and robbery in this Parish! I will put it down, and you can shoot me if you like! It'll be a small thing you'll have to boast of when you've shot me!' Personal morality was inevitably on a par with political, and the sentries on guard at the banks in Cork City are reported to have sat in armchairs out on the pavements fooling around with girls on their knees.

Much pointless vandalism was committed, such as the way Castletownshend woods were burned down and young apple trees ripped up by the roots and left to die. In September Edith Somerville wrote:

> I am tired of all this. It isn't 'on the nerves' in the least, it is only that I am sick of it all, and am beginning, for the first time in my life, to wish I were 'a happy English child'. Everything is so troublesome and humiliating, and dangerous, and so maddeningly inconvenient.[9]

And in November: 'I never *never* would have believed Ireland would have come to this if I hadn't lived through it.' In the new year she wrote that to be angry with those you have loved worked like madness in the blood, and that she was getting more furious each day. People refused to accept the verdicts of their own courts; she told of two cases where the loser had gone personally and revenged himself on the opponent, beating and wounding and burning. One of the many incidents concerned an elderly Miss Dobbs. Her story illustrates the spirit of the Loyalist ladies and the climate of the time. Her house was raided on the eve of her departure for England. She swiftly pocketed her travelling money, £20, unseen, under the eyes of the raiders, poured them out whiskey, and slipped away. She hid behind a pillar in the hall until the way was clear and then walked five miles to the Free State garrison. The commandant wanted to wait till morning to take action, but she insisted they go then. She went with them and directed the proceedings: making them leave the trucks and creep up the avenue so that they could and did take the Republican raiders by surprise. As the servant had also left, she spent the remainder of the night alone in the house. The next morning as she walked to the station in solitary defiance, an old woman cursed her: 'Cromwell's breed!' Similar are the experiences, which Edith collected, of a Mrs Crowe. This seventy-five-year-old woman was pulled out of bed in the middle of the night and asked to sign a cheque for £200. When she refused, at gunpoint, they asked her where she would like to be buried. She said anywhere would do. After a week as a prisoner in a rat-ridden shed she did write the cheque, but by that time the government had captured eleven of the men and threatened to shoot them if Mrs Crowe were not released. Edith says, she 'came out unbroken, and worked in her garden the same day'.

In February the rebels issued an edict that all ploughmen, postmen and schoolteachers who went to work were to be shot on sight. In the same month Sir Horace Plunkett's home was destroyed. He was a man who had worked diligently and selflessly for Ireland, and Edith's anger gave way to sadness: 'I only love very few of them now. Mike, and Mrs Kisby, and Father Lamb. Really I don't think I *thoroughly* trust any others.' Nevertheless Ireland was her country, and when an opportunity came to return to some kind of normal life with those around her, she seized it. This was in August, 1923. Her brother Cameron, who was president of the local branch of the Farmers' Union, was asked by the local people to stand as one of the three candidates for West Cork. Fortunately, so far as the family was concerned, for he had neither the talent for public speaking nor the money to live in Dublin, the Farmers' Executive in Cork refused to endorse his candidature because of his Anglo-Irish background. But the gesture of peace had been made, and the people had shaken hands with the Somervilles. Edith wrote to her brother in London:

> It shows a wonderful change of heart that they should ask a gentleman, an ex-soldier, ex-Landlord, and Protestant, to be a member! They did so with enormous panegyrics of the Somerville family for all generations. . . . It is of course, a very great compliment to Cameron, and the family.[10]

She worked enthusiastically for the election, and on polling day drove to and fro with voters in a pony and trap through a day of torrential storms. Encouraged by this she began to organise an organ and violin recital to help pay some of the church debts. The recital was followed by a Fancy Goods sale and tea party where she collected twenty-four pounds.

Politics receded into the background, and she once more tried to paint and write amidst the ordinary social demands. She earned badly needed money dealing in horses which she trained and sold to America. The farm could not be neglected and there was always something: fallen trees, cows calving too soon, flooded drains, insurance agents for the workmen's cards, many letters to be written. Her bitterness towards England did not fade quickly. She wrote angrily to Longmans when they failed to mention the *Irish R.M.* stories amongst their list of successes, 'I suppose, in literature, as in life, this is the treatment Irish Loyalists now must expect from England.' In 1928 she wrote an article for *Time and Tide* rebuking the the BBC for a sloppy presentation of the Armistice service. She told them about the way it was done in Ireland. Poor people gathered around a statue of 'The Maid of Erin'—commemorating the 1848 rebellion. 'And in the front rank, beside the tall officers, are four little old poor women, with thin old faces, and thin old clothes. They hold up their heads, and stand as straight as any soldier of them all. One can see how conscious each is of the glory of the medals that shine on her breasts.' She then describes England's effort at honouring the dead:

> Beginning as it did with lugubrious bromides of that machine-made type of music which may be summarised as Bandmasteries, proceeding to a part-song, stale as it is sugary, Pinsuti's 'In this hour of softened splendour,' evoking in some listeners, incredulous of the testimony of their ears, memories of a village tenor bleating a nasal entreaty to his lady to hear him while he 'tells all his love'. And this followed by that venerable—one had hoped long since perished of old age— travesty of the Return of the Prodigal Son, a dirge-like strain with every accent misplaced:
> 'I—will—arr—rise. I—will—arr—rise,
> and—go—to—my—Fa—a—ther!'

When one brother demurs about wearing the shamrock she sends him for St Patrick's day, saying he does not feel very Irish, she is furious. He had been to school and college in England, had spent his life abroad serving in the British Army, and had lived in London since his retirement. But she writes to him about this 'nonsense about being "English"! I don't mind your saying "British" if you like, but the only pallid trickle of *English* blood in your veins comes from *one* marriage, when Hester Coghill married Colonel Tobias Cramer, a *pure-blooded Hun*—if not Jew! You might just as well say you were German!' So far as she was concerned there was no bewilderment about national identity, 'My family has eaten Irish food and shared Irish life for nearly three hundred years, and if that doesn't make me Irish I might as well say I was Scotch, or Norman, or Pre-Dilavian!'

At the same time there was much that she disliked in the new Ireland. She was antagonistic to compulsory Irish in schools; she refused to fill in any forms in the Irish language that the Government sent her. The murder of her seventy-three-year-old brother, Admiral Boyle Somerville, by 'Nationalists' in 1936 increased her aversion from the new order. His offence had been

telling Irish boys who asked his advice how to apply for posts in
the British Navy, and sometimes writing references for them.
The newspaper reports infuriated her with their cheap emo-
tionalism and the suggestion that the Somervilles were leaving
Ireland

> I think less of them than ever now when for the last three
> weeks, I've seen one lie after another being published about
> Boyle. Especially about poor gallant Mab. How she 'col-
> lapsed' was 'unable to speak coherently', 'fainted'—Boyle's
> 'last words: Be brave my darling'! It makes me sick. And now
> these foul journalists are selling 5/- paragraphs, saying that
> 'The Somerville Family are sorrowfully obliged to leave
> home' &c &c ad nauseam.[11]

But events did not diminish her love for Ireland for long, and she
still maintains, 'I will not regard those dirty little sneaking
assassins as representing Ireland. Ireland is my country, not
theirs, and when I look out over Reen, or away to the Bantry
mountains, I don't and won't associate all the beauty that I have
always loved, with those sneaking half-bred curs.' And still
neither her English friends nor those of her family who live in
England are allowed to criticise Ireland without getting a sharp
reply. 'You really should not be so sweepingly violent about
Eire. There are far more decent people than blackguards . . .
And thousands of nice country people. Why damn us all in
heaps, because of old Dev and the I.R.A.?' She supported
Ireland's neutrality in the Second World War, saying that if
they had not been neutral Germany would have bombed them
to bits, and England could not have helped them:

> Also, you might remember that the soldiers *we* sent over were
> volunteers, not conscripts, and there's hardly a house round
> about here at all events—that hasn't a sailor or a soldier or a
> nurse in the War. I know one little house in Rineen that has
> sent three sons and two daughters to help in the trouble.
> Anyhow *we've* not produced 70,000 miners to take England
> by the throat and stop her coal supply, only because they
> wanted more than £5 a week wages.[12]

She is glad to be Irish and she always stands up for her beloved country, but there is sadness there too at the tremendous changes she has seen in her lifetime. In 1945 she was persuaded to chair the Bi-Centenary celebrations of Dean Swift, and her regrets for the past days are clear in her comment on the day:

> Hildegard and I felt *deep* sorrow for Old Times, but they were all awfully kind and friendly, and I autographed dozens of Menus &c, &c; at last, all was over, and the Prophet having had far more Honour in her own country than she ever expected, departed, and we got home by 8.20 p.m. and weren't too tired.[13]

Ireland had begun to see Somerville & Ross as more than upper-class patrons of the comic. In 1932 Trinity College, Dublin had given her the degree of Doctor of Letters, and she became a founder member of the Irish Academy of Letters. She was at this time increasingly worried about lack of money. All she had earned writing went on the hounds and what she earned from horse dealing went towards the upkeep of the farm, which merely accumulated debts due to the fall in animal prices and the rising cost of employing men. There was a movement to get her a British pension and she responded wholeheartedly saying that 'Between 1920 and now I could have invested about £2000 only for the farm.' But when she saw the form sent out by the Royal Literary Fund she refused to apply saying that she would gladly accept a literary reward but not charity, a pension but not a donation. 'I would rather earn my living without doles.' The editor of the *Times Literary Supplement* persuaded her to change her mind; and she was awarded £300, £100 more than their highest donation. She paid off her personal overdraft and managed to raise enough money to take over her brother's overdraft and so stop the bank from selling the estate. The next year she was forced to sell all the pigs because of the increase in price of pig food. In 1941 she notes in her diary, 'received my Bank book which gives the intelligence that it contains £1 on the credit side. Accepted this fact with the frigid tranquillity enjoined by Dr Johnson.' The death of the brother whose pension had maintained Drishane hit Edith and her sister hard. They struggled on with the farm for another four years, helped by financial gifts from another brother. Then the compulsory farm labourer's wage bill which meant that each man must have more than £100 a year as well as a house and milk, forced them to sell up. All of their stock, including the carefully bred and cared for Friesian cattle was auctioned. The two elderly ladies were heartbroken. Edith wrote in her diary, 'The three men, Richard, John Connell and Dinny Crowley, came for a formal farewell, gave them respectively £25, £15, and £10, and (after their withdrawal) our tears.' Nobody seemed to understand how they felt and she wrote sadly to a brother that people 'keep on congratulating us for a fact that brings us near tears. But a £2,000 debt *must* be wiped out, and with this sale and the savings that we've put aside, I believe we shall do so. Then we sink ignobly into being Villa Residents, without as much as an Ass butt.' Later that year, 1946, they moved into the nearest establishment she ever got to a villa, when her nephew, heir to Drishane, and his wife, arranged for her to live in the ironically named *Tally-Ho*.

But though plagued with ill-health and fading physical powers, she was never despondent for long. Her sense of humour never deserts her: when the Count de Suzannet begins to buy their MSS. she writes with attractive modesty,

> I feel that my shabby old manuscripts have been treated with far more honour than they deserve. It makes me think of a story of a vulgar mother and daughter who, somehow, achieved invitations to a 'Drawing-room' in Dublin Castle, in the old days, when Dublin was still a place where one met ladies and gentlemen. The mother was heard to murmur to the daughter—
> 'Mary! Mary! Aren't you the lucky divil to be here?' And the daughter replied solemnly and with deep feeling, 'Mamma, I am!' Thus my manuscripts to one another.[14]

When she can no longer see to read and her handwriting is reduced to little more than a scribble she has no self-pity. In 1948 she manages to scrawl to Geraldine Cummins, 'I am unable to read or write, and only wish some kind lady would take me up and send me to a well-run ragged-school and get me taught. It is very depressing sitting in bed with nothing to do. Like Mooney's goose full of play, but no one to play with.' And the literary judgments in her letters are as precise and to the point as ever: she reads *Villette* for the first time:

> It seems to me very unequal—masses of it admirable stuff, but she goes mad in hatred of 'the errors of Rome', and is very boring about them. And the end of the book boils up into purple absurdity. The two chief characters lose continuity, and then, suddenly, she infuriated me with a sort of kaleidoscopic Happy Ending. But in spite of quite absurd coincidences and a most senseless and superfluous and badly done sham ghost story, I was immensely interested . . . its great descriptive power impresses me into forgetting what I can't ignore.[15]

She chooses material and has curtains made, goes for rides in the pony trap and insists on holding the reins herself. It is the time for stock-taking, reading her old diaries and Violet Martin's, Violet's letters, their old commonplace books and manuscripts. 1886 is always there as the changing point of her life: in 1937 she writes 'Fifty-one years today since "when first she came".' Violet's birthday, 11 June, was always a special day of remembrance. She re-reads her youthful letters to her brothers: 'Until Martin came my sense of humour was very undeveloped, but I was a very light-hearted girl.' She is amazed at how they wrote *The Real Charlotte*, 'All our writing done in casual scrapes. We had no consideration for ourselves and still less did anyone else show for us,' and at their 'entire want of method and system'. She was lonely and she was ready to die, but it was no desolate bitter waiting. It had been a good life and her repentance is likely the right one:

> We talked of whether we would care to live our lives over again on earth. She said that she would certainly like to relive hers and did not wish to make any alterations save in giving a great deal more time to painting and a great deal less to hunting.[16]

Chapter II

The Collaboration and the Use of Dialect

The collaboration of Somerville & Ross is remarkable, because nowhere in the work they wrote together is there evidence of two separate hands. Attempts to distinguish their different talents must be based on outside evidence, texts which we know they wrote separately. The subject matter tells us a little: we know that the Dublin life described in *The Real Charlotte*, both in the early chapters and the later scenes in Bray, must have come from Violet Martin's experiences. But there is nothing in the style of these passages which could establish that she wrote them alone. Dr Cresap Watson in his unpublished thesis on their collaboration decided after a detailed analysis of their style that Edith Somerville's was the more colloquial and that she relied more on the visualisation of objects. He sees her technique as 'dramatic pictorialism', and he thinks her content both more representational and more superficial than her cousin's. He suggests that Violet Martin used more elevated and abstract diction, darker themes, more profound thought, less robust and more wistful comedy. He sums up their respective gifts as 'painter and poet', a fair conclusion. Edith Somerville herself said much the same:

> I believe I am right in attributing to my cousin the more subtle and recondite adjective, the more knife-edged slice of sarcasm, the more poetic feeling for words, and a sense of style that seems to me flawless and unequalled. And I believe that possibly my profession as a painter, has helped and developed my feeling for colour, and a sense of form . . .[1]

It is possible to find passages which illustrate their separate individual styles. In one essay for example, Violet Martin describes a scene which is notable for its effective communication of a sombre mood, a mood which is not just evoked by the visual description:

> The air was dead and cold; the sense of suspended weight, of huge force, of indifference to the human creature, was oppressive. At length the opening became feasible only for a lizard or an eel, and after that for the water, moving in unimaginable stealth through the veins of the rock.
>
> We turned and worked back towards the daylight, lost to us for some minutes; the darkness seemed desirous to keep us, and created a childish horror of its dominion.
>
> Then the sane, firm radiance of outer day was born, the trodden grass, and the grey January sky; it seemed a new heaven and a new earth.[2]

It is typical of her style that rhythm as much as image conveys the emotion:

> A sea fog has begun to cling about the expanse of heather and bog, and the white rocks show through the greyness like touches of foam on a wide and gloomy sea. The desolation behind is wrapped in a more mysterious desolateness; the sense of remoteness is quickened, till something is felt of the true value of distance, of the old fashioned significance of it to those whose world still lies within their longest walk.[3]

The visual experience here is not important for its own sake but for the feelings of loneliness, isolation and restriction which it conveys. Compared with these passages Edith Somerville's writing is much more visually orientated:

> Halfway up this harbour the cliffs give way, the channel takes a sharp twist, and an irregular horde of grey, slated cottages struggles up from the yellow, seaweedy shore. About midway up the steep hill they pull themselves together and agree to form a street, though from the water their roofs, gleaming from the midst of trees, look more like the steps of a huge moss-grown staircase.[4]

Here the vitality of the passage is due to the images and the full use of personification. The description is from an essay written to try to tempt painters and artists to use west Carbery as a sketching ground, so she was trying to give a convincing picture, although the way she does this is of course still literary.

The difference between the two writers is really one of vision. Violet Martin wanted to express thoughts and feelings which need the moodiness and gentle rhythms of her prose: ideas, often intangible to the factual mind, necessarily blurred and inarticulate, are given form in her descriptions. Edith Somerville is usually deeply interested in the thing which she is describing, but she uses words not to paint a picture of it but to capture the look and feel of it. She catches the essence of a thing in a few sharp words: '. . . a little she Peke, a perfectly odious little brute, that attacks my poor dogs, who think it is a sort of cat, and daren't retaliate . . . It weighs about three pounds and looks like a possessed yellow ostrich feather.'

But it is equally easy to find passages which they wrote separately but whose authorship it is difficult to identify. The following passage is such a one; it is in fact by Violet Martin and it illustrates one of her foremost literary skills, the way in which she can move from standard English to dialect so smoothly. This is not a matter of mere technique, it is her ability to grasp and express two different ways of thought. The story's charm is in the interaction of two women who have quite different backgrounds and yet are able to communicate with each other despite this:

> 'Sure, I wasn't in the place at all, but whatever was in it, the Lord save us, he seen the woman, and he knew well it was meself, and she coming to him, and she in a valley, and it was the fall of the evening, in harvest-time.'
>
> Her heavy face had not changed, and the rhythm of her quiet speech had neither hastened nor slackened, yet the reaped fields and the dust must have been before her eyes, must have seemed inevitable to the story. Better than 'dusk' or 'twilight', or any other motionless word, was 'the fall of the evening'—the dew was in it, and the gentleness and the folding of wings . . .
>
> I asked her presently if she had heard of a priest, renowned for his preaching, who had lived in the village forty years before.
>
> 'I did to be sure, though I was only a little girl, the same

time. He was a great priest, and after he died, it's what the people said he went through Purgatory like a flash o'lightning; there wasn't a singe on him. Often me mother told me about a sermon he preached, and I'd remember a piece of it, and the way you'd say it in English was "Oh, black seas of Eternity, without top nor bottom, beginning nor end, bay, brink nor shore, how can anyone look into your depths and neglect the salvation of his soul?"'

The translation came forth easily, with the lilt of metre and the cadence of melancholy. Anastasia looked into the fire and said, after a pause. 'Twas thrue for him.'[5]

That extract comes from a story which has been praised as her best, but it is not so very different from the following passage written by Edith Somerville in 1933. The way in which the prose flows from one character's mind to another without jarring the reader, the poise of the whole, makes it similar to the previous passage:

It was during the last days of Shraft, before Ash Wednesday had forbidden all such wordly affairs as Matrimony, that I was paying a visit to a young country-woman, a widow, and the subject of marriage, as was appropriate to the time, came under discussion. I remember that she told me of the recent grand wedding of a rich elderly cattle-buyer, and when I asked her how he had made all the money, she replied with a laugh:

''Tis what the people say he does jobbing in widows! This now is the third one he's got for himself!'

We were standing on the verge of the western cliffs, looking away across a rough grey sea to Cape Clear. The clouds were low, but not implacably low, there was a pale light over the horizon, and through a high rift in the cloudy roof a thin screen of silver reached from sky to sea, ending in a long dazzling streak. Seventy feet below us the sea was growling in the heart of a long cave, conquered in its onslaught by the iron rocks of that fierce coast. Every now and then a sullen boom, like a blast in a mine, followed by a puff of white spray, told where an imprisoned wave had burst its way out of a cleft in the cliff that faced where we were standing. My widow owned a small farm that went back from the cliffs to the hills. A lonely place; the small house and farm-sheds were down in a hollow below a high bank, on which some alder bushes and a few miserable wind-thrashed ash-trees tried to give protection from the south-westerly storms. She had a half-dozen of hungry little cattle and a handful of 'mountainy' sheep; her bare fields were islanded by a waste of rocks and furze; she lived a life as solitary as Robinson Crusoe's save that the parts of Man Friday and the parrots were played by an old father and three little children.

She was a hardy, handsome creature, fair and weather-beaten, big and bony. She stood beside me in the sea wind, on the heathery ground over the cliff, firm as a tower, with a pair of a men's big boots on her feet. It was easy to think of her tramping about her narrow fields, working like a man, the thought of her three children and the old man all dependent on her, always in her mind. Perhaps she guessed at what I was thinking, for she said the times were hard enough, and it wasn't easy for one that'd be alone.

So I asked her whether she thought a married life or a single one was the happier.

She considered a moment, her sea-blue eyes remote and thoughtful. Then she said:

'Well indeed it is what I think, once ye'd got over the disgrace of it, a single life'd be the more airy. But faith!' she added with a laugh, 'if ye get marri'd or if ye stay single, it's aiqual which way it is, ye'll be sorry!'[6]

Here the writing is crisp and controlled, it is as if Violet Martin had gone over it with a blue pencil; for the sloppiness of some of the writing in *Mount Music* and *An Enthusiast* does suggest that Violet Martin was the more restrained in their use of adjectives.

More is known about the collaboration in practice. The book in progress was talked into existence; the sentences were spoken, its phrases played with by both of them, and then the sentence written down by whoever happened to be holding the pen. The first draft was written on the right hand page of the exercise book. Corrections were made later, often separately. If it was a matter of altering a word or two the changes were written in above the original words; if whole sentences were to be introduced or subsituted for others, they were written on the facing left-hand page. These new sentences were marked alphabetically and their identifying letters were inserted in their respective places in the text opposite. When the entire manuscript had been checked in this way, a second draft would be written incorporating all the corrections. This draft was usually in Edith's hand. She writes later, 'Such manuscripts as I have are complete, and are in my autograph, almost, if not quite, exclusively, as Miss Martin's sight was not good, and she preferred to dictate to me from our first rougher copy. In this way we were able to put a finishing polish on our work.' This clean copy was sent to a typist. The typed draft would be checked against the clean copy before going to the printer but no changes were made at this stage.

In *Happy Days!* Edith Somerville gives an account of how the Irish R.M. stories originated which also provides a clear description of the manner in which all the collaborative work was done:

> . . . Gradually we talked and argued into existence one after another of the little group of men and women . . . One after the other of Major Sinclair Yeats' friends and neighbours came effortlessly to our call. It seemed as if we had always known them. I can truly say that in order to identify an actual representative of any of them, it would be necessary to tear each of them to pieces, and, collecting the fragments, resume them into a sort of human rag bag. . . . There, prone on the yellow sand, we lay and talked and wrote, bit by bit; . . . And Great Uncle McCarthy's ghost, with its 'fumbling hand and inebriate shuffle' materialised, and Flurry Knox and Slipper began to assert themselves. We found ourselves on the threshold of a new world, that was yet our own old Province of Munster, peopled with unknown yet entirely familiar beings.

So characters came first and incidents followed. No doubt in writing the characters do transcend their original concepts of them, but the first ideas were often based on people they knew. The first few notes to a novel often merely give names of characters with the names of real people in brackets to denote who and what the characters are. Violet writes about the parent of a heroine: 'a mother would be a nuisance, but have her instead of a father if you like—a Speranza would be too like Mama. I don't want to describe Mama—especially as Aunt Marian's there . . .' The actions of the characters would be jotted down before they actually began writing, so there was plotting first, but they refused to submit plots to their agent before they had written a novel. Violet says to do so would make them feel unduly restrained because normally they altered so much in the course of writing. In *Happy Days!* Edith continues describing how a particular story 'Trinket's Colt' was written:

> Then, one morning, I remembered that my grandmother had had a legendary mare of fabulous beauty, and that her name had been Trinket. Then we endowed Trinket with a colt of equal beauty and knew at once that in 'Trinket's Colt' we had an inspiring title to hand, and incidents began to rise in our minds like bubbles in champagne.

They were on holiday in France at the time and the arrival of some relations bent on holiday-making meant that the story was written amidst the usual sort of interruptions.

> Thus did Martin Ross and I employ any of the idle moments that happen in holiday times; moments of waiting while the painter stretched a canvas; of waiting for Madame Lá-Lá's kettle to boil at the tea-party she was giving for our guests; or of waiting while the Dean caught and harnessed the donkey. . . . During one of these chance intervals one of us would scribble the haunting notion that had tormented us—a half-remembered saying of Slipper's, an elusive adjective that had evaded us. Somehow scrap by scrap, the story unfolded itself for us, and I think we enjoyed its culminating instant as much as did old Mrs Knox.

While I do not doubt the last statement for one minute the story was perhaps less fluent in its birth than she might suggest. The ending does seem so absolutely right that one might suspect that it was the only one. But this is not so and in their rough plotting it was quite otherwise. Yeats goes to Flurry for lunch and to see how the colt is shaping up; while he is there Slipper arrives saying that the police are searching for the colt and on their way there. Flurry has the bright idea of burying the colt in a ditch:

> All hands fall to work, and Yeats goes back to the house to keep out of the way. He lurks in dining room, and to his horror sees the old grandmama drive up. She asks servant for Flurry. Yeats listening in agony. Servant says that Flurry was in the house a while ago—She comes in to see whether he is now at home—Yeats hides under the table. Servant goes back and says Flurry is out—old lady comes into the dining-room and waits. Yeats remains sweating under the table—old lady reads over the fire. Just as Yeats determines to try to crawl out behind her back enter the police, to say the horse cannot be found. Yeats lies within an inch of his own sergeant's boots. Slipper—[7]

The manuscript, which is in Violet Martin's hand, ends at this point, but it is an example of how much they did change the plot in writing.

Some of their books were written when they were together for only a part of the time; *An Irish Cousin* is such a one. They wrote the first half of it together; Edith corrected this by herself, sending it to Violet for her approval, assuring her that where the corrections were drastic she had kept the original. Violet then made her comments on the corrections. The letters which they wrote to accompany the MS. were full of apologies, hesitations and downright conviction: 'I have always felt something like this here—don't say it's premature it isn't—and I do think that that kind of thing seems probable. Of course add if you like, but I would not sweep or modify . . . Please goodness we will have many a tooth and naily fight next month—but don't let's combat by post, it is too wearing.' They were together to plot the second half, but apart before they had finished the first draft. So they wrote separately sending the chapters to each other for approval and rewriting. Each of them read aloud to their relations what they had written and they did pay attention to the response. Even when they were together they read their work aloud to selected members of their families; the first seven chapters were read to Edith's and she records 'it took two hours. Felt generally depressed when it was over.' Mrs Somerville loathed the book; she 'liked improprieties' and thought there was too little love making. Edith records gloomily, 'Our families declined to take us seriously, but none the less offered criticism incessant, and mutually destructive.'

After Violet's death Edith Somerville goes into far more detailed preparation before she starts writing. Intricate family trees are worked out as well as maps of the locality. For *The Big House of Inver* there are several maps of the neighbouring countryside, the sea, the nearby towns. The family trees are balanced against the kings and queens of England; incidents in the novel are dated and compared with a list of actual political and social happenings. The action of the 'last week' of the novel is written out as if it was the diary of events.

At all periods of their writing there was an initial stage of paralysis, which they grew used to, and learnt to cope with; after that they wrote swiftly if it was a story or travel sketch, but far more laboriously if it was a novel. *The Real Charlotte* was begun in 1889 but not finished until 1893. Usually the gaps in writing were due to the demands made on their time and energy by their families; but sometimes they stopped novel writing in order to earn quick money by journalism. It is clear from remarks in diaries and letters that journalism took precedence over more serious writing on two accounts: they needed the money it brought them, and it demanded less concentration. When hordes of relations and an enforced social whirl made novel writing impossible they could still turn out stories and sketches in free moments. A novel demanded consistent work over a long period of time and they often, reluctantly, just could not commit themselves to it. Pinker, their agent, found a ready public for their short stories and because of this they never attempted another full-length novel of the seriousness of *The Real Charlotte* during Violet's lifetime. In 1897 they began a proper novel, *A Man of the People*, immediately after *The Silver Fox*, but the huge success of the Irish R.M. stories in 1898 meant that they shelved the novel. Sadly, Pinker encouraged them writing in 1899 when they were eager to write a novel: 'From the literary point of view I think it would be a mistake. I think your happiest work is in this semi-sporting vein . . . If you and Miss Martin can give us more work like the *Badminton* stories'. They agree to try and write a 'semi-sporting' novel, much against Violet Martin's better judgment. After her serious hunting accident this year it does seem to them that a serious novel is out of the question for some time. A year after the accident the semi-sporting novel has not reached its deadline: Edith writes to Pinker, 'Miss Martin is not at present nearly strong enough for the sustained effort and strain of writing a novel . . . I am afraid that the state of her health absolutely and unavoidably precludes our having the novel ready . . .' Six months later, June 1900, the contract is cancelled. *A Man of the People* is later chopped up and bits of it used in various Irish R.M. stories. In 1911 they complete the semi-sporting *Dan Russel the Fox*. Two years later they tell Pinker that they would love to write a novel but that the long time it entails without any financial return makes it impossible at the moment. Two years later Violet Martin is dead.

It is a mystery why their collaboration worked so well, and how they managed to produce together work superior to anything either of them produced independently. They shared tastes, distastes and a fine sense of the ridiculous; theirs was a common inheritance and environment; somehow they were catalysts for each other and the result was literature. Edith Somerville thought that close scrutiny of the collaboration was impertinent. After E.V.Lucas had written an article about them in *The Spectator* she wrote to a brother:

> It is *impossible* to apportion general responsibility in our writings but even to have said '*hardly*' a 'paragraph, a phrase etc.' was written single-handed by either of us would have been an exaggeration. Even in the quotations Mr Lucas gave, some were hers, some mine . . . Already various journalists have been tearing at me to write, to give them data for articles, anything, to try and make money out of what is to me a sacred thing. It distracts me: this prying greediness in raking up any scrap of personal detail . . . If you get a chance say [to C.L.Graves] how abhorrent is to me all the senseless curiosity as to 'which held the pen' . . .

To her it was a gift from God that they were able to collaborate:

'How does *anyone* write if it comes to that? How does any artist or maker do anything that is not actually manual? If I tried for a month I couldn't tell anymore than I have told, nor could Martin either . . . Why don't they ask me how I write by myself? I could assure them it is much more of a 'mystery' to me how I do it.' It is as much a mystery how the collaboration continued after Violet Martin's death. Speculation about the nature of that collaboration will never result in 'proof' that will convert the sceptical. Edith Somerville wholeheartedly believed that it was possible for Violet to go on working with her, influencing her thoughts as she had done when she was on earth:

> . . . our reliance on one another, whether on this plane or another, is what never can be explained. There have been many empty moments, long spaces of silence, both grappling with the same intangible idea. Sometimes the compelling creative urge would come on both, and we would try to reconcile the two impulses, searching for a form into which to cast them—one releasing it, perhaps as a cloudy suggestion, to be caught by the other, and given form and colour, then to float away in a flash of certainty, a completed sentence.[8]

The daily automatic writing in which Violet spoke directly to her, and the plentiful evidence from professional mediums, convinced her not only that when writing fiction she was still receiving help from Violet but that she was often little more than an earthly secretary taking down dictation!

Their first collaborative effort, a dictionary of their families' speech, indicates their immense interest in words. They knew that because they were Anglo-Irish they spoke the English tongue differently from the English as well as from the Irish. When Edith Somerville refers to the dictionary—which does not seem to have been preserved—she shows strongly this feeling of the otherness and even superiority of her race. Their families' speech she says was 'the froth on the surface of some two hundred years of the conversation of a clan of inventive, violent, Anglo-Irish people, who, generation after generation, found themselves faced with situations in which the English language failed to provide sufficient intensity, and they either snatched at alternatives from other tongues or invented them.'[9] The speech of the Irish people around them was to them even more fascinating, because it was more colourful and poetic. When they began to learn Irish in 1897 it was not in order to study ancient texts but to illuminate the things they heard said around them every day. They carefully preserved trial reports from local newspapers for the amazing dialogue recorded: 'I did not say that I would keep her between the gate and the pillar until I would squeeze the decay out of her.'

Their advantage over many of the writers of the Irish Literary Revival was that they did not live in Dublin but in daily contact with the people of the West of Ireland. The Ireland which their contemporaries visited to collect folk tales was their ordinary environment. They did not romanticise the peasantry nor exaggerate the unspoilt nature of their lives because they knew only too well the squalid conditions in which many of them were forced to live. And although there was always the tremendous barrier of the Big House and the differences in education and religion they still *knew* the country people. They went to their births, marriages and deaths, and attended them in sickness; they worked with them in stable and garden, and they met them at horse fairs, agriculture shows, races and hunting. Necessarily in a rural community there is more mutual dependence and helping each other than elsewhere. They knew the country people with an intimacy quite different from the observation— however sympathetic—of an outsider. And so they had the immense advantage of knowing another way of life and another way of speech.

After their survey of their families' speech they began to collect sayings and phrases of the Irish around them; their scant knowledge of Irish was no drawback because it was the particular English dialect the people spoke which was their joy. Violet Martin continued to work in the gardens at Ross, long after it was strictly necessary, in order to listen to the speech patterns and stories of an aged gardener. She had a good ear and memory and Edith says that she would 'justify herself of her idleness by repeating to me at length, one of his recitals'. If Edith was not there the speech was written in a letter to her, and the letters contain many sayings which appear later in the stories and novels. Edith Somerville always claimed to be delighted when the people she was visiting were out and she could sit and talk to the servants instead. After a local wedding she complains that she has nothing to say because she was prevented from sitting in the kitchen with those whose talk was 'all pearls and diamonds'. Both of them were persistent eavesdroppers, and recorded the conversations they overheard on trains, at fairs and in cafés, and most of these found their way into print too. Letters from tenants and servants were carefully filed away, and soon their family and friends began to write them letters about the sayings which they had heard. Edith Somerville's sister writes to tell them the words of a woman who was describing to her the death of her six-year-old mentally retarded son: 'He made no sound—I'd never seen Death before. I gave him a hot bath, and he white in the face. He died, Lady Coghill, like a fish. The mouth open. I having him under one arm and the little girl alive under me other arm. God took him. God knows best. I hope he's happy.'[10]

It was partly because this was not their own language that they were so well aware of its uniqueness. The words were mostly the same but they were put together in such a different way, and they expressed a whole range of thought and emotion that was the opposite of trivial. It was a new world which yet could reflect the ways of thinking they themselves had inherited. The sense of being away from someone you care about, and who might need you, is poignantly captured in the following letter of entreaty from a poor woman whose husband is in hospital and who has no food for the children: 'I'd take a day's work only for the youngest one I have, and he only two years. When I'd rise early and go out I'd feel him very far back from me.' Sometimes the strangeness is in the sentiment rather than the words; in the old man's response to the new railway from Oughterard to Galway: 'Ye used to have plenty of time, driving in, to be talking and enjoying yourself, and now ye wouldn't hardly have a pipe smoked before ye'd be in Galway'; or the reply of a horse dealer when Edith Somerville commented on the man's extravagant eulogy of his horse 'Well, he doesn't look like it,'—'No, Miss, he does not. He's a terribly deceitful horse.'

Often the attraction is in extravagant images juxtaposed with startling contrast: 'The Lord God of Heaven never put the breath of life into cut throats the like o' them Driscolls', sometimes a quaint fancy, 'He was that small he'd have to stand upon a thrippenny bit to see into a duck's eye.' The extravagance is often of Elizabethan magnitude, such as a man's expression of how much he liked Edith Somerville: 'Tell her she might ride through our standing corn. And it ripe.' There is an ability to put abstract concepts into concrete images which foreshadows the language of O'Casey's plays: 'High gintory does be jumpin' mad for lodging in this village', and 'The walls were that thin ye'd hear the people in the next house changing their minds'. There are hundreds of examples of personification, especially regarding food: a pudding has 'a jocular shape', the saucepan is 'simpering' on the fire, until it is brought to the 'capering point'; and the cook promises, 'I'll use my influence with the pudding, ma'am.' There are many examples of the logic which lies behind the Irish bull: 'The Black and Tans are gone, and the soldiers are gone, and now the polis is going and the boys can fight in peace,' and the explanation of what happened in a strike: 'Well now, there was a settlement but no one would agree to it.'

The most organised of the commonplace books giving such examples is the one divided into sections according to subject matter. This huge notebook is an attempt to bring together some of the more haphazard jottings of the end pages of diaries and exercise books. They refer to it as *Stock Pot Irish Memories* and intended it to cover the whole period of their writing: the title page reads 'V.F.M.—E.Œ.S. Collectors. From January 1886 to 19—'. The contents page is as follows: 'Hunting; Dogs; Letters; Trains; Horses; Racing; Beggars; Domestic; Medical; Abuse and Exclamations; Blessings and Commendations; Cookery and Food; Matrimonial; Social and Religious; Weather and Agricultural; Fishing; Boating and Shooting; Drink and Fighting; Idioms; Unclassified; Supernatural; Phrases (partly obsolete); War; Prayers'. When an entry is used in a story or novel it is marked with a cross; occasionally the title of the work in which it is used is written beside the cross. In the following short survey the dialect of two novels has been checked against the notebook. In *Mount Music* the main character speaking in dialect is Mrs Twomey, the Coppinger Court's dairywoman. Almost all her words can be traced to actual sayings recorded in the notebook. Some of it is direct transcript from actual speech: 'Ye'll not see a fat face or a red cheek on one of thim that come back [from America]', and 'Look! When I'll be dead, let ye tell the car-pennther that he'll make the coffin a bit-een too long, the way the people'll think the womaneen inside in it wasn't altogether too small enthirely!'

Most of her dialogue had only slight changes:

NOTEBOOK	NOVEL
Rich as you are, you couldn't put a penny into the mouth of every man that's saying it.	As rich as your Honour is, you couldn't put a penny into the mouth of every man that's sayin' it.
Sure a little thing like me'd tell fibs like I dunno what!	Sure a little thing like me'd tell lies as fast as a hen'd pick peas.
I'm the same owld three an' fourpince, an' will be till I die! (a screech of laughter) An' I won't be long dyin'! (another screech) An' it won't take many to carry me to Castlehaven! (final screech).	'I'm the same owld three and fourpince, and will be till I die' triumphed Mrs Twomey, with another screech of laughter, . . . 'An' I won't be long dyin'!' another screech; 'an' it won't take many to carry me to Cunnock-a-Ceoil churchyard!' A final and prolonged burst of mirth succeeded this announcement.
Ah those people are very suspeecious. Give them a smell and they'll do the rest.	Give them a smell, and they're that suspeecious they'll do the rest!
I had to put the height of the house of curses to it before Mary would believe me.	Didn't I have to put the height o' the house of curses to it.
Look! Tell him there's always one foolish in a family, and what it is with Masther Jack he's too give-ish, that's what he is.	Tell him there's always one foolish in a family, and what it is with Masther Larry, he's too give-ish.
Indeed I don't know how I got it, but the same you'd get a stitch over a churn. [On falling in love]	One day it'll sthrike ye all in the minute—the same as a pairson'd get a stitch when they'd be leaning over a churn!

And why wouldn't she be fond of him. Let me alone now! Sure the dog'd be fond of him!	And why wouldn't she be fond of him? Sure the dog'd be fond of him!
God of Heaven! She has a rag on every bush.	Sure didn't I tell him it was what it was he had a rag on every bush.

In *The Big House of Inver* most of the dialect can be traced to the notebook; it is not confined to mainly one character. Some of it is again direct copy of actual speech: when Jimmy Connor is in the beer tent at the races he repeats words which Edith Somerville overheard at Oldcourt races, 'I'd never had anny taste for singin', but if I'd be cot in a corner of a shebeen I'd sing! I'd sing all around me! That's my way, an' I don't give a dam' if it's good or bad! Me heart, d'ye see, is as big as wings!' The judgment later made on Jimmy is again an exact copy 'I know his carackther. He couldn't face you to look at you, there's something bad standing always between his eyes.' Remarks shouted to stop a fat and drunken man from riding a horse at a fair are also straight from the notebook of recorded speech: 'No, John! Do not, John! You're too weighty entirely, John! Oh, you're a very weighty man, John! Very weighty entirely.' When variations are made they are not significantly different:

NOTEBOOK	NOVEL
She intherfares most confoundedly in front, and she's no betther behind. She have the emblems of owld marks on her knees.	Ah, he intherferes in front, and he's not much better behind. He has the emblems of old marks on his knees . . .
They have all the thricks as good as any in London. If you picked forty holes in a horse they'd have fifty pegs to put in them.	Ah, them country-fellows have all the thricks as good as any old dealer in Dublin. If ye pick'd forty holes in a horse, they'd have fifty pegs to put in them.
Write! If that owld cock had a pen in his paws he'd write as good as him.	If me wife's old cock had a pen in his paws he'd write as good as him!
Why then I was late and I was all in a glee to get down to Harry Mahony's for a grain o' tay.	Jimmy's all in a glee to go.

If ye was to boil down Danny B—'s bones a man might get nicely drunk on the broth.	They used to say of me in the Regiment that no man ever saw Jas blind, but if you boiled down his bones, a fellow would get drunk on the broth!

Clearly the dialogue in the novels is closely related to actual speech. It is more naturalistic than most of the dialogue in the plays of the Irish Literary Revival, or in the prose work of many other Irish writers. At the same time it works as literature and rings true; they convince us that they have captured the spirit of the people as well as being strictly accurate in their representation. The dialect does become a strain when it is not dispersed amidst narrative and dialogue of a more conventional English, as in 'A Patrick's Day Hunt' which is all dialect. The words are tiresome to read on the page, and they seem exaggerated and unreal even though, as Violet Martin was at pains to point out to justify the story, they are quite authentic. They prized accuracy and quarrelled with the editor of *The Strand* over his refusal to print the 'God help yous' and 'Oh God' in case he should offend his nonconformist readers. Violet Martin protests to Pinker that Irish people use a stronger language than English people without any profane intention, and that they will not alter what they know to be true in order to conform to English taste.

They thought that English as it was spoken in Ireland was especially rich because of the interaction of two cultures which had given rise to the speech: '. . . the talk of the men of quality, bred in the classic tradition, enriched the vocabulary of the peasants, while the country gentlemen, themselves Irish speakers, absorbed into their English speech something of the vigour and passion, the profuse imagery and wilful exaggeration that are inherent in the Gael.' The speech of the educated classes of the time was varied, according to their rank in society; and in their writings Somerville & Ross capture these grades of speech within the middle and upper middle classes. The English spoken by the Catholic middle classes differed in the same way from that spoken by the peasantry, and there were many in-between grades, sharing only the raw materials. English spoken in Ireland was 'a fabric built by Irish architects with English bricks, quite unlike anything of English construction'. In their estimation it was ideal for literature, 'a medium for poets and story-tellers that is scarcely to be surpassed, a treasury of idiom and simile meet for the service of literature'. In their remarks on the way writers used dialect they always judged according to the rhythm of the dialogue. They praise Maria Edgeworth for capturing the jogtrotting beat of Thady's talk, and Gerald Griffin for expressing dignity and pathos in his work. They select from *The Collegians* to illustrate his rhythm: 'I'm ashamed o'myself to be always this way, like an owld woman, moaning and behoning among the neighbours, like an owld goose, that would be cackling afther the flock, or a fool of a little bird, whistling upon a bough of a summer evening, afther the nest is robbed.' They condemn Thackeray for giving stage brogue to Captain Costigan, and Kipling for relying on peculiarities of spelling to give Irish quality to Mulvany's speech. They accuse Carleton of inauthentic rhythm and a grotesque spelling which wearies the eye without informing the ear. Lady Gregory's dialogue in the plays they thought veered on the chant-like and the monotonous with its frequent 'I to be' and 'he to be' which failed to capture the fine sense of metre of the people. Some of Synge's dialogue they also thought too monotonous and lacking the fire and spontaneity of Irish talk. Violet Martin perceptively recognises that Synge's ideas demand the rhythm, but in her eyes his ideas are too narrow, and often deny all the quickness of repartee, the ability to argue and the sharp humour of the Irish people. They thought that one must either aim for ideality as Yeats does in plays like *The Countess Cathleen* or else copy the speech almost verbatim. The twists of thought, the imagination and vision of the Irish people was known only to themselves. In one review Edith Somerville tells readers to *listen* attentively to the prose, not to the sound of separate words, but to the rhythm of the whole, so that they can respond to the emotion in the sentences.

They knew that failure to perceive speech rhythm meant more than artistic failure. It was 'want of knowledge of the wayward and shrewd and sensitive minds that are at the back of the dialect . . . the shape in which thought is born, the point of the mental attack, the moment in the metre of the sentence where the weight must fall. These can scarcely be set down, yet they govern all.'[11] Much of the speech of the country folk was a translation not just of Irish names but of Irish *thought* into English, and to change that almost literal translation was to change the thought. Any falsification of idiom and twist of phrase meant changing the way of thought that lay within the words. Only through the speech of the people could they ever come near those minds which were so different from their own. Somerville & Ross handle dialect flawlessly in all its rich variety.

Chapter III

An Irish Cousin—Naboth's Vineyard—Through Connemara in a Governess Cart—In the Vine Country— Beggars on Horseback—In the State of Denmark

When the 1889 *An Irish Cousin* was revised and reprinted in 1903 the revisions were not drastic nor interesting enough to merit discussion here, but as the later edition is more easily available that is the one used here. It is a sombre book despite its many comic scenes. Contemporary critics found it too gloomy, but Edith Somerville believed that it owed its success with the public to the very fact that it was 'first in the field of Irish country life which did not rollick'. The gloom is not simply that of the sensational gothic sort—though there are elements of that too, but emanates from the mists and rains and winds sweeping in from the Atlantic over the desolate West of Ireland, so that the lonely inhabitants are driven almost mad by the natural conditions and their own isolation. It is still a polite society and their indulgences are hid beneath a veneer of manners which makes the sins more awful as well as more interesting. So secret are some of the sins however that the reader is never quite sure of the truth. Uncle Dominick's plotting to get the house and estate from his elder brother is clear enough, but his relationship with Mad Moll is not. She believes herself to be the illegitimate daughter of an uncle of Dominick—that is, his cousin. This claim seems to have been respected by the family; she has been allowed to live in the house as a kind of housekeeper. Unfortunately she becomes Dominick's mistress. When he marries she is turned out and married to a tenant. Dominick's wife dies in childbirth and Moll, who has given birth to a child at the same time (presumably Dominick's?) becomes the child's foster mother. Moll's own daughter falls in love with her foster-brother (and presumably her half-brother) and during the course of the novel marries him. The somewhat intricate plot is unrolled somewhat shakily with a few creaks, by way of a brass memorial plaque in the church, reminiscences of old tenants, the discovery of a diary and the revelation of an unposted letter.

Although the tale and characters are uncannily similar to Sheridan Le Fanu's *Uncle Silas*, the novel is more worthy of attention because it is more serious. It is not just a supernatural tale written for effect. There are phantom carriages and hauntings but there is also social and psychological realism. It began indeed as a 'shilling shocker' and what turned it from that into a novel is extremely interesting. It was an experience which was in itself, ironically, sensational—much closer to Catherine Morland's than Jane Austen's idea of reality. It is also the first appearance of the subject which is to interest them for the rest of their lives as writers, and to provide them with endless material for stories and novels:

> The sunset was red in the west when our horses were brought round to the door, and it was at that precise moment that into *The Irish Cousin* some thrill of genuineness was breathed. In the darkened facade of the long grey house, a window, just over the hall-door, caught our attention. In it, for an instant, was a white face. Trails of ivy hung over the panes, but we saw the face glimmer there for an instant and vanish.
>
> As we rode home along the side of the hills, and watched the fires of the sunset sink into the sea, and met the crescent moon coming with faint light to lead us home, we could talk and think only of that presence at the window. We had been warned of certain subjects not to be approached, and we knew enough of the history of that old house to realise what we had seen. An old stock, isolated from the world at large, wearing itself out in those excesses that are a protest of human nature against unnatural conditions, dies at last with its victims around its death-bed. Half-acknowledged, half-witted, wholly horrifying; living ghosts, haunting the house that gave them but half their share of life, yet withheld from them with half-hearted guardianship, the boon of death.[1]

In the novel this kind of distress is made vivid and put into perspective by the point of view: everything is seen through the eyes of a Canadian cousin who is in Ireland for the first time. She is quite unaware of there being Irish and Anglo-Irish: 'In fact, had my uncle and cousin met me on the pier, clad in knee-breeches and tail-coats, and hailed me with what I believed to be the national salutation, "Begorra!" I should scarcely have been taken aback.'[2] Ireland to her is a remote corner of the British Empire and she arrives saying 'I am thankful to get back to Great Britain again!' Through her eyes we see a countryside of a sad and wild beauty made ugly by man. The nearest village, Rathbarry, is the first of many similar villages in their work, a single street of low, dirty cottages interspersed with grubby shops. In the vicinity there are three Big Houses: the O'Neills' home, Clashmore Hall, where life is orderly and things are looked after and cared for; the Jackson-Crolys' house where dirt is swept under the carpet; and Durrus, the Sarsfields' house where there is never any sweeping done at all. Durrus is overrun with rats, its walls furred with damp, thick layers of dust and cobwebs settled over everything. When Theo finds her hair-brush used to support the window because the sash is gone she finds it 'eminently characteristic of the slipshod manner of life at Durrus'. When a latch is broken on a gate, a stone is used to prop the gate shut; nothing is ever mended. Peach trees grow out through the broken windows of the greenhouse. The rest of the kitchen garden is a wilderness with unpruned trees, overgrown paths and lichen-covered bushes. But, there is nothing charming or romantic about this neglect:

> Certainly I had never before seen anything like the mixture of prosperity and dilapidation in these solid stone buildings, with their rickety doors and broken windows. Through the open coach-house door I saw an unusual amount of carriages, foremost among them the landau in which I had driven from Esker, with a bucket placed on its coach-box in order to catch a drip from the roof. A donkey and a couple of calves were roaming placidly about, and, though there was no lack of stable-helpers and hangers-on, everything was inconceivably dirty and untidy.

In such descriptions the setting transcends gothic gloom; the physical decay of the house and environs expresses the moral degeneracy of its inhabitants. When Moll, struck dumb by some nameless horror, pirouettes before the house at night, with curtsies and dumb prayers as she kneels motionless, hands crossed on breast, pale face beseeching the sky for justice, or peers through the ivy covered window, and creates such an effect that the whole countryside seems to catch her agony, 'the patches of grey lichen on the trees repeated in the growing twilight the effect of the grey face at the darkened window' we are in the realm of popular Victorian fiction, but always intermingled with these scenes is mundane carelessness, ordinary slackness and dilapidation that inject life into the book.

Night and the weather are used poetically to reflect the suppressed guilt and subconscious fears of the characters. When Theo and Dominick confront Moll, indoors, 'It was getting darker, and the rain came driving in from the sea in ghost-like white clouds'; as the human suffering increases so the storm comes inland to them. It rushes in from the Atlantic hurling down trees, throwing itself against the Big House with such force that they cannot open the shutters in day time: 'I sat in the semi-darkness of the library, trying to read, and looking from time to time through the one unshuttered window out onto the gravel sweep . . . A great sycamore had fallen across the drive a little below the house, and the other trees swung and writhed as if in despair at the long stress of the gale.' When Willy allows himself to be blackmailed into marrying his foster sister and so gives up all hope of making anything of his life, his misery is in tune with the gale: ' " It's all over now," he said. "Everything's gone to smash." A rush of wind shivered through the laurels, and shook a quick rattle of drops from the shining leaves.' When Dominick commits suicide, nature is a fitting backdrop:

> There was weight in the air, the sky was low and foreboding, and a watery streak of yellow lay along the horizon behind the bog. A rook rustled close over my head with a subdued croak; I dully watched him flying quietly home to the tall elms by the lodge; he was still circling round them before settling down, when a long, wavering cry struck upon my ear, a sound that once heard is never forgotten, the cry of a woman keening.

The tenantry play an important part in this novel. We see

them and the Anglo-Irish through Theo's eyes. She goes to the birthday party the tenants hold for Willy and comes upon quite another way of life. Instead of Corelli and Schubert played on piano and violin, there is a hunchback on a donkey playing jigs on his bagpipes, which to her strange ears sounds like 'a succession of grunts and squeals of varying discordancy'. Surrounded by men in knee-breeches and tail-coats who are drinking porter she feels for the first time since she has been in Ireland a complete foreigner: 'in spite of my Sarsfield blood, a stranger in a strange land'. When she goes to the town with Willy she finds her horse the focal point for beggars and groups of women who discuss her lineage and looks as if she were deaf or an inhabitant of a different planet. The Irish funeral on the Strand of the Dead again makes her feel her otherness: she watches the boats arrive with the coffin, sees the women beating their breasts and chanting and keening. With the burial over they go to their own family graves to pray and tell their beads; she looks at them in their blue cloaks, with the grey headstones the pale blue sky behind them as if they are in a picture. When they talk to her it is with a pleasing mixture of ease and formality; lively talk which ends graciously, 'Good-evening to your honour, miss. May the Lord comfort your honour long, and that I may never die till I see you well married.' The townspeople, on the other hand, are far more constrained— Willy and Theo are expected to want a room by themselves for tea in the hotel, and the traveller already in the dining room leaves at a word from the boots as soon as they enter.

Sweeney's cottage is a realistic picture of such an abode. There is the proverbial hospitality and good manners side by side with the barbaric cruelty to animals: Mrs Sweeney is busy plucking a live goose when they arrive. When Willy talks to her he automatically adopts an accent and vocabulary close to her own. He remembers the names of her children and their various ailments but he does not patronise her and she does not pander to him. He tells her she is 'a greater fool than I thought you were' and that her senile father-in-law has more sense than she has. When she says goodbye to them, she gives them a bowl of eggs and tells Willy to carry them home for Theo's breakfast, and then gives him a hearty slap on the back: '"Och, there's no fear

but he'll mind!" she said, winking at me. "He'd do more than
that for yourself, and small blame to him!" ' The difference
between the two Irish communities is not ignored but one is not
held up to ridicule more than the other. We do laugh at the
servants sometimes, as when Theo's dress is inspected by the
Durrus servants as she leaves for the ball. To her astonishment
she finds them lined up in the hall: ' "Well, miss," began Mrs
Rourke in tones of solemn conviction, "ye might thravel Ireland
this night, and ye wouldn't find her aiqual! Of all the young
ladies ever I seen, you take the sway!"

"Glory be to God! 'tis thrue!" moaned the kitchen-maid in
awe-stricken assent.' This is more good natured perhaps than
the comedy of the Jackson-Crolys' annual dance. The master of
the house stands at the foot of the stairs to welcome his guests, 'a
small, bald-headed gentlemen, moving in an agitated way from
leg to leg, and apparently engaged in alternately putting on and
taking off his gloves.' The style of dancing is aggressive,
consisting of couples trying to knock each other over, a mode
which one of Theo's partners explains by saying the one he's
trying to bump is his cousin Kate. She reflects, 'There seemed at
the time nothing very incongruous about this explanation.
There was a hilarious informality about the whole entertain-
ment that made it unlike any I had ever been at before. Every
one talked and laughed at the full pitch of their lungs.' At supper
she overhears one lady saying, 'Now, captain, if you say that
again, I'll pelt me patty at you!' When the popular 'Sweethearts' is played on the piano the pianist and all the dancers sing
the refrain together:

'Oh, lo-*ove* for a year,
A we-*eek*, a day,'

The chaperones take it in turn to be pianist, and are applauded
according to the vigour with which they bang the piano. At
supper-time the doctor goes in two or three times, each time
working his way down the table like a mowing machine. The
social comedy veers on the savage as Theo sees: '. . . a convivial
party of lunatics . . . Mob-caps, night-caps, fools'-caps and sun-
bonnets nodded in nightmare array round the table.' The
description of the ball struck Sir William Gregory as a little too

realistic. He admired the book very much but wrote to Mrs Martin that Violet should be reprimanded for that: 'By the way I ought to scold her for giving the idea that our Irish county balls are of the ramshackle nature described—though I should not be surprised if my narration of one in this County may have lingered in her mind. But what will Co. Cork folk say?'

The language in the book is precise; adjectives are used with discrimination, and images though rare are witty. When Theo meets Mrs Barrett she finds, 'a monumental old lady, who having been established by Willy in the most reliable chair in the room, remained there in mammoth silence, motionless, save for her alert eyes, which wandered from face to face, and suggested to me the idea of a restless intelligent spirit imprisoned in a feather bed.' Dominick's nature is apparent in the phrase which describes his manner as 'glacial geniality' and his voice as being 'of a mellifluous not to say alarming propriety'. Willy's nature and state of education is captured in the description of his speech as 'ungrammatical gallantry'. Theo's self-contained coolness is always present in her style: she reports the palmist who says she has 'no sense of humour, and homicidal tendencies combined with unusual conscientiousness'; and she describes her feelings about the sea-sickness she has recently suffered as: 'But for me it has only two aspects—the pathetic and the revolting; the former being the point of view with which I regard my own sufferings, and the latter having reference to those of others.'

The poised narration is Theo's personal tone of voice; each of the other characters has his own voice. Dominick's English is almost eighteenth-century in its politeness; the rector of Rathbarry has such a strong Cork accent that Theo can hardly understand the sermons. Mimi Burke, a fearless hunting lady, with a deep voice which breaks out in 'booming cadences' has a sort of half-way speech. Her accent is basically Co. Cork but Theo says no system of spelling would give any idea of it; briefly, ' "fie" she pronounced "foy", and "Sarsfield" in her sonorous tones became "Sorsefield" '. Her speech is sprinkled with imagery which makes it more colourful than that of most of the Anglo-Irish characters; it is closer to the peasantry. She tells Mrs Jackson-Croly: 'Why, you're a grand woman! We'd all be dying

down with dullness only for you!' Mrs Jackson-Croly's snobbery
is reflected in her speech as she tells how she has to take her
daughters to Southsea (where the military are) to stop them
from getting an accent: 'I loathe a Cork brogue! My fawther
took me abroad every year; he was so alormed lest I'd aquire it,
and I assure you, when we were children, he used to insist on
mamma's putting cotton wool in our ears, when we went to old
Mr Flannagan's church, for fear we'd ketch his manner of speaking.' The speech of the tenants is lively and authentic,
depending as much on the rhythm of the sentences as on the
vocabulary.

The main characters are Dominick Sarsfield, the two cousins,
and Nugent O'Neill. Dominick shares many characteristics
with Uncle Silas: he is a gentleman; he speaks with the greatest
courtesy; he is a snob and he is utterly self-engrossed. Where
Uncle Silas is a secret opium addict, Uncle Dominick imbibes
more than a bottle of brandy a day. Selfishness is responsible for
his neglect of his son Willy. He lacks the money to send him to an
English public school, so he lets him grow up with a level of
education far below his own. Unable to provide Willy with any
companions of his own standing he lives in dread that Willy will
disgrace himself by befriending the young girl in the lodge, but
he is too lethargic to think of any alternative. At the first
mention of the pretty lodge girl, Moll's daughter, he flares up,
'When people in that class of life are taken out of their proper
places they at once begin to presume.' His classic speech about
the breakdown of the class system is as fiery as it is because he is
involved personally, through his fear of what Willy will do:

> 'I cannot believe that any sane person can honestly hold
> such absurd theories. What! do you mean to tell me that one
> of my tenants, a creature whose forefathers have lived for
> centuries in ignorance and degradation, is my equal?'
> 'His degradation is merely the result of injustice,' said Miss
> O'Neill, coolly adjusting her *pince-nez*.
> 'I deny it,' said my uncle loudly. His usually pale face was
> flushed, and his eyes burned. 'But that is not the point. What I
> maintain is, that any fusion of classes such as you advocate
> would have the effect of debasing the upper while it entirely

failed to raise the lower orders. If you were to marry your coachman, as, according to your theories of equality, I suppose you would not hesitate to do, do you think these latent instincts of refinement that you talk about would make him a fit companion for you and your family? You know as well as I do that such an idea is preposterous. It is absurd to suppose that the natural arrangement of things can be tampered with. This is a subject on which I feel very strongly, and it shocks me to hear a young lady in your position advance such opinions!'

In his eyes it is far worse for Willy to marry the lodge girl than to take her as his mistress; the latter is possible without taking her out of her class. When Willy disobeys him, his malicious spite is singularly well conveyed; he speaks slowly: ' . . . the words falling from his lips like drops of acid. "You mean to say she is your wife?" ' His fury is inflamed by his own guilt and fear of exposure as well as his snobbery and cold sense of rightness; his expression of it is exact in the mixture of controlled hatred and sarcasm: ' "And your bride? May I ask if she has done me the honour of coming here?" He wiped a thin foam from his lower lip with trembling hand. "Or is she perhaps at her father's residence?" ' Icy sarcasm alternates with animal ravings as he decides that his son shall be cut off penniless rather than let his new bride profit by her marriage. But, convincingly enough, he is polite to Theo even when at the height of his alcoholic ravings; she is a lady. He is passionately determined to get a door opened; she cannot do it, and his reaction is the elegant: ' "No, my dear, I see it is no use trying tonight. You are tired, and so am I."—he sighed deeply, and put his hand to his chest—"this oppression that I am suffering from tries me terribly. I will go to my room and see if I can get a little rest. I need rest badly." ' When his mind gives way, the mellifluousness of tone, and the grammatical propriety is kept. It is a most convincing picture of a mad old gentleman: Theo tells him he looks tired.

'Do I? Well, to tell you the truth, I have been quite unable to sleep lately. I am so much disturbed by these hackney carmen who make it a practice to drive past the house at all hours of the night; I hope they do not annoy you? I have told them several times to go away but they simply laugh at me. And the strange thing is,' he continued, leaning over the rail of the corridor, and looking suspiciously down into the hall, 'that though I gave orders that the lodge gates should always be locked at night, it does not stop them in the least—they just drive through them. Well, goodnight, my dear,' he said, nodding at me in a friendly way.

Willy is the Irish cousin of the title, but the centre of interest is shared between him and the narrator, Theo. She is an unconventional heroine. At the start of the book she is suffering from seasickness; as for looks, we are told that when she has a riding hat on she looks just like her father did when he was a boy. She is often muddy from playing with wet dogs; she goes ferreting; the rats in the house do not bother her at all; she wraps an old carriage rug around her shoulders and puts on a cap of her cousin Willy's when she goes for a walk. She prides herself on being clear-headed and sensible, and though she is romantic about Ireland and the new life it may hold for her, she is not hoping to fall in love. She never deceives herself about Willy, whom she finds such an excellent companion. He is immense fun but she notes, 'he could not be said to be either very cultured or refined.' Her naïvety makes her shock at finding out Willy's love for her very credible: she is so upset that he is suffering and that all their good times are over, and yet she is made to recognise that much as she likes him and sorry as she is for his sorrow, nothing will make her feel differently. Time will not change her: 'every feeling in me rose in sudden revolt at the idea with a violence that astonished myself'. She is equally surprised at the suddenness with which she recognises she is in love with the arrogant Nugent: 'I could not understand how this improbable, this incredible thing had come about.' Like the usual heroine she turns to her diary to see when she began to notice Nugent, but there is nothing there: only one entry after a day's hunting, 'Mr O'Neill piloted me. Dull and conceited.' Nugent is the silent stiff man of principle.

Nugent, the heroine's choice, is not easy to like; like Darcy he will not flirt, nor try to please: when Theo tries small talk with him he gives perfunctory answers; he is not a polite man. And he is patronising, 'I have always heard that Canadian young ladies had a very gay time,' and 'ladies do not generally get on very well without shops and dances'. He only begins to be polite when Theo shows an interest in music. Again there is Mr Darcy's kind of superiority—when Theo offers to accompany him, ' "Oh, thanks very much; my sister always accompanies me," he responded coolly.' Theo finds his deliberate self-possession extremely exasperating. He has 'frigid, uninterested civility'. At the dinner party when he has to entertain Theo he annoys her by being so unexcited, so quiet, and yet with a humorous turn to his sentences which she finds interesting despite herself. He is utterly poised and self-contained. When Willy petulantly intrudes on a speech of Nugent's the latter ignores Willy until he's finished his sentence, 'Then, with a tolerating smile . . . asked him what he had said.'

Willy is a delightful portrait of a young man full of potential who is the victim of circumstances: his father, and the isolation of Durrus. 'There's no sound I hate like that row the ground-swell makes out there at the point. If you're feeling any way lonely, it makes you want to hang yourself. . . . I tell you you've no notion what this place is like in the winter. Sometimes there's not a creature in the country to speak to from one month's end to another.' All the responsibility of the house and farm falls on him. He runs it all. He is well-dressed, amiable, eager to please and to make his cousin feel at home: he sees that there is a fire in her room and puts pen and paper there for her letters; he gives her tea as soon as she arrives. Theo finds him an excellent host, 'He plied me with everything on the table, eating his own breakfast, and talking all the time with unaffected zest and vigour, and I began to feel as if the time I had known him could be counted in months instead of hours.' He has the seemingly feminine ability to sit over a fire and talk for hours about nothing in particular; he adores gossiping, but without any malice; and he has as well 'quite a special gift of recounting small facts with accuracy and detail'; indoors and out he is an excellent companion for Theo. When he falls in love with her his already sharp observation and sensitivity to others is even heightened so that he 'appeared to be able to take in my doings with the back of his head.' Nothing is too much trouble for him, and throughout the novel *he* is the charming and amusing young man, not Nugent. In an episode similar to the necklace one on the day of the ball in *Mansfield Park*, our sympathies are with Willy not Nugent. The latter sends Theo a gorgeous spray which he has made himself out of splendid yellow chrysanthemums and feathery maidenhair fern. Willy goes out in the pouring rain to look for the first violets, and gives her a bedraggled little bunch. Like Fanny Price she solves the predicament by taking both; she wears the violets and carries the bouquet, but feels 'somehow Willy's bunch of violets had taken away most of my pleasure [in the hot-house flowers]'.

Through Theo's relationship with her Irish cousin and Nugent O'Neill the authors begin to explore the nature of romantic passion, giving it a background of alcoholism, murder and suicide. All Willy's goodness is vanquished when Theo tells him that she cannot love him 'like that'; he flings her flowers into the fire; he grabs hold of her and forces kiss after kiss upon her. As if he knows his case is doomed he always unerringly chooses the most unsalubrious place to talk to her of his feelings for her. First a dreary, tasteless study, then the dark, dank hole of the commercial room in the local hotel, where the tea is red and 'the bread and butter and the china were alike abormally thick', these things being somehow an image of what life with Willy would be like. Nugent talks to her in the midst of music and potted plants, elegant drawing-rooms and pleasant perfumed conservatories. If there is any kind of rationale in her choice of Nugent it is simply that she is too fastidious to accept Willy, much as she likes him. The scenes of passion are well done: Willy, having been blackmailed into marrying the lodge girl, comes to say goodbye to Theo and still cannot leave her if there is a chance that she has changed her mind. When she kisses his cheek he misunderstands and will not let her go until she is forced to say, 'I meant that I was fond of you, but I never was in love with you.' Before he goes she is in tears and then so is he: 'He snatched my hand again, and kissed it many times; he was crying too. "God help us both!" he said. "Goodbye."' Willy's suffering is brought on by this unrequited love, but it is deepened and made entirely hopeless because of his earlier affair with the lodge girl and his father's sins of greed and sexual

exploitation. Willy is not strong enough to overcome the dis-
advantages of his environment. His voluntary exile to Australia
is the only attempt at putting things right he can make. Theo
might be able to inspire passion in others, but she is not capable
of it herself. Without Willy's complications her falling in love
with Nugent would be entirely sweet and creditable.

Naboth's Vineyard was commissioned in 1889 for a literary
magazine which was intent on publishing writing of various
political and religious opinions. But the commissioner, Langbridge, changed his mind and decided to publish it in a 'cycle of
newspapers' as he feared it would lead to partisan feelings over
the Land League question. Somerville & Ross refused to let it
appear in newspapers, so Langbridge bought the copyright for
£30, and brought it out as a novel in 1891. To the authors'
amazement it was treated as a serious work about the political
situation, and given solemn reviews by *The Spectator*, *The Times*
and the *Saturday Review*. Later Edith Somerville was always
derogatory about the book: 'I have long realised that Martin
and I made a very great mistake in writing *Naboth's Vineyard*. Not
a bad plot, but quite unreal characters.'[3] She said that the
characters were 'ladies and gentlemen who talk in brogue—
quite a good brogue, only that "Judy O'Grady" has "the
Colonel's lady" under *her* skin . . .'[4] She really did believe that
one could only write about the social class one belonged to! As it
is, the characters in this book are very uneven, and most of them
are stage Irish figures. Ellen Leonard is a stock colleen of the
Irish melodrama, pretty, simple and innocent. The stock villain
is there in the gombeen man who is also the president of the local
branch of the Land League; hence he is able to use his position
there in order to better himself and grab more land. Rick
O'Grady is the conventional hero, the returned emigrant, who
has made his fortune in the States and returned in time to shelter
the distressed colleen and perform acts of bravery for her sake:
he breaks the boycott, swims a brimming river, puts out a
farmyard fire single-handed, and marries her in the end. Even
the landlord is the traditional absentee who is hated because of
his absence; when his woods are on fire the men will not stir
themselves, 'If he wouldn't live in the counthry and mind his

place, let him lose it and be d—d to him!'[5] The half-idiot boy, Dan, who is eaten up with two passions, love for Ellen and hatred of the gombeen man, does belong to the melodramatic: there is the macabre scene where he sees the gombeen man's corpse in the river, and bends to shake hands with him to say farewell and then as he bends suffers one of his epileptic fits:

> He tried to shake the hand up and down, but it felt as heavy as lead. It seemed to him as if it were pulling him down; blackness came before his eyes and he screamed. But the hand still drew him down, and he fell forward and lay, face downwards, in the mud.
>
> There was great quietness after this, and before long the startled sandpipers and curlews were hopping and running about, and digging their long bills into the mud, not twenty yards from where the two figures lay.

The easing of the facile emotion with the description of the natural life reasserting itself does slightly mitigate the macabre, but it is still magazine stuff. Better are the scenes of Dan's wooing of Ellen; he cannot think, but is motivated by simple emotions of desire or hatred, and he is embarrassingly pathetic in the love scenes. Ellen's mother is partly the stock widow with the pretty daughter whose virtue she must protect, but she is given some vitality by her passion for her land. She is a woman of fierce determination who will take on the gombeen man and the whole Land League to keep her land. And it is not for the sake of her daughter. 'If there wasn't a one left in this house only meself and the Lord Almighty I'd stay in it if the town of Rossbrin came to put me out!'

It is however with the other strong woman, Harriet Donovan, wife of the gombeen man and old girl friend of the hero, Rick O'Grady, that they transcend stage Irish characters. Harriet is the first of their women characters who is motivated by both good and evil impulses. She has married for money instead of waiting for the man she loved to come home, and she has to stand by and watch him fall in love and marry a much younger girl. Because her emotions have never become involved with her husband she cannot see that her relationship with Rick is completely different from what it was before she was married. She still loves Rick and because of the strength of her emotions she believes she has every right to love him. She cannot see that she has changed and that instead of the gentle soft girl she was seven years ago when Rick went off to make his fortune, she is a ruthless married woman, eaten up with frustrated passion and thwarted desires. Throughout she has a commonness which is consistent: it was that which made her marry Donovan for comfort and security and then made her incapable of accepting her lot. Her first words are full of irritation and pent-up emotion: when her husband asks her why she has come out into the countryside, even though she *is* guilty of an ulterior motive she cannot resist getting in a jibe about the disagreeable house she has to live in, 'What'd keep me in the town? I came up here to get out of the smell of them beastly fish!' Their horrible married life is clearly depicted; his rough desire for her and her hatred of him: jealous of Rick, he tells her that Rick fancies the girl Ellen. Harriet's loathing is vivid: 'She felt she could kill him as she looked down on him, stretched out in sodden comfort before the fire, with an egotistical smile on his heavy face, and his fat hand caressing his tumbler of whiskey and water.' There is an awful scene when he discovers that she has invited Rick to the house; husband and wife glare at each other like wild animals, and he attacks her with his stick and then manages to stop himself and breaks the stick in half before rushing out; she, undaunted, is still spitting her malicious remarks at him as he goes. So wrought up is she that with Rick she cannot be sensible. She has no idea of playing her cards carefully. She knows that he condemns her malice and dislikes her for it, but she cannot help herself. Jealousy gets the better of her and when there is a chance to belittle the young girl she takes it. She sneers at her for wearing a shawl instead of a hat; she pretends that the village idiot is engaged to be married with the girl.

At the height of her jealousy she is driven into the forest in a storm, grappling with the question of whether Rick loves the girl or not. The furious storm matches her own inner turmoil, and in this heightened emotional state she lets her husband fall to his death when she could have saved him. This almost-murder is again to be used in later books to show the kind of evil which a very ordinary person can be guilty of. Harriet has a moment of choice, her first impulse is to save him but, 'before her lips opened some devil's messenger of a thought shot lucidly through her mind' and she obeys it. 'Her husband's step was on the bridge; she became rigid and numb, and all things seemed as unreal as a dream.' She lets him fall and then rushes to the bridge, too late of course: 'She turned, and, not knowing what she did, fled away through the woods.' Throughout the action she is living on two different levels of knowledge. In her heart she knows that Rick does not love her any more and is attracted by the young girl, but she cannot bring this knowledge into her daily mind. She convinces herself that Rick befriends the girl out of a mixture of personal and political motives, 'out of antagonism to her husband and a high-handed contempt for authority'. She persuades herself that she lets her husband die partly out of a desire to protect Rick, turning the awful deed into an opportunity for self-advancement in the field of passion: 'She would call to him and stop him; he would know how true she had been to him.' In a final painful scene she throws herself about Rick's neck saying, 'I forgive ye, Rick . . . they'll never know it, and you and me that loves one another will be happy in the end.' The conventionality of the ending—her retreat into the convent—is slightly mitigated by her lack of repentance. Even now she cannot subdue her passion; she spends her last night 'kneeling at her bedside, her remorse and penitence put by for a future day, weeping fierce, unsatisfied tears, with Rick O'Grady's photograph pressed to her lips.' It is their first picture of a woman at the mercy of her passion, their first study of the triumph of evil.

When Longmans thought of reissuing *Naboth's Vineyard* in 1916, Edith Somerville was not enthusiastic 'The subject is very tragic and, just now especially, I doubt whether a Land League story would be popular. Undoubtedly people just at present prefer stories of a cheerful character.' *Naboth's Vineyard*, like *An Irish Cousin*, is potentially tragic not because of its picture of the political situation but because of its depiction of a life in which evil predominates over good.

By 1889 Somerville & Ross had made their mark in the London literary world and in that year they were approached

about a guide-book for the West of Ireland. They were under no
illusion about the value of such a project.

> . . . you chuck in your interesting writing and at the end of
> each chapter place the facts of hotels, distances and so forth *à
> la* Baedeker. The present guide book is a most paltry thing,
> called *The Emerald Isle*—So now,—if we had $20 to spare
> what fun it would be to go round—and get our facts—that is if
> we had an order from Cook's in our pockets. There was a
> much more intolerably vulgar guide to Connemara pub-
> lished last year by the people in Dublin—written as it were in
> description of the tour made by a party of people. Jack—very
> manly, the young ladies—very lady-like, a kind and humorous
> mother, etc. Jack was very much the most revolting. The
> informant of the party gave many interesting facts about the
> disappearance of the Martins from the face of the earth.

When Edith Somerville is enthusiastic, Violet Martin goes
about the tour in her usual businesslike way. She writes to Edith:

> Now as to Cook—it would be charming—but I haven't the
> money—I shall all the same try and work Cook himself and
> see what the chances are what the terms might be. We might
> at all events manage Connemara, from here and take in
> Sligo—Lough Gill being a sort of small Killarney . . . it
> would be a good idea to get a few people to write to Cook,
> complaining of the dullness and smallness of his guide—one
> or two would be enough—One thing is certain my finances
> are not at their highest, but on *certainty* of repayment I could
> borrow the money requisite.

They do not persuade Mr Cook but the *Lady's Pictorial* signs a
contract for ten articles.

These articles, which together make up the first of the travel
books, set the style for them all in so far as it is deliberately
unconventional in its presentation both of the countries they
visit and of themselves, the tourists. They mockingly set forth the
list of necessities they carry with them: spirit-lamp and kettle in
a tin hat-box, potted meat, Bath Olivers, Bovril, Burgundy, a
rubber bath, a rusty revolver—the cartridges in an 'Easy Hair

Curler' box, a change of clothes and a gingham umbrella. In the tours of Connemara and France, Edith is the narrator with most of the laughs on Violet, while in the tours of North Wales and Denmark the tables are turned: we giggle at Miss O'Flannigan, the artist. Of them all, the Irish tour is the most unsuccessful. It is flat and the tone is often offensive. They cannot get over their class consciousness and their feelings of superiority to everyone they meet. Because of the nature of the tour they are looking for laughs too; they want to be amused and other tourists, fishermen, and clergymen are only viewed as copy—which reinforces the detachment between the authors and their subject. Connemara did not in fact live up to their expectations. It was neither amusing nor dirty, nor full of outrageous incident. Their diaries are dull and consist of their honest responses to the hotels they stayed in with remarks such as 'unexpectedly civilised'. So they invent.

Two years before the tour an angry beggarwoman had turned on Edith Somerville in Lismore and told her, that she 'knew me and me owld mother when I was thravelling the roads in a pack on her back, pucking at every hall door in the counthry begging spuds'. In the tour it is said to have been said to Violet by an old one at Tully fair: 'Aha! I knew ye, and yer owld mother before ye, the time ye were thravelling the country in a pack on her back, puckin' at every hall-door in the counthry beggin' spuds!'[6] The lively episode of the Widow Joyce's cottage where they are given 'the Major's sheets . . . that not a one ever slep in but himself' and share the bed with millions of fleas, warding off a huge grey goose, is purely imaginary. That night was in fact spent in 'O'Grady's Hotel' which was 'A Land League place, but clean and cheap'. Equally invented is the mad bulldog episode, where the dog takes fright when they fire the gun at it and throws himself on to the lips of a cow so causing the whole herd to stampede. The only time they actually used the gun was to shoot at stones and a bottle which they did out of sheer boredom. Edith seems to have been responsible for these two pieces of invention for Violet wrote to her saying that she has read the Widow Joyce chapter to her mother and brother Robert and they like it but think it too short; but that she 'weakened frightfully on the bull-dog—It seemed to want point'. It does want point, but it stayed, presumably to shock the English ladies of the *Pictorial*.

The best parts of the book are the descriptions of the countryside and the visits to Ballynahinch and Renvyle. The wild and untrammelled landscape is shown to be very different from the 'offensively sleek and primly-partioned pastures of England.' It is a misty July and the soft white mists sweep by like 'a procession of ghostly balldresses', and the mountains look as if they have 'with one accord taken the veil and retired from public observation'. Warmth goes quickly in the day—'the invalid sunshine had already swaddled itself again in cotton wool and retired for the night,' and people are few: 'the only human creature we met on the road was a grey old bagpiper, who looked as though he might have lost his way among the hills some time in the last century'. Equally simple and genuine is their response to Ballynahinch castle, which turned out not to be a proper castle at all, and their disappointment after they have romanced about the home of the 'Princess of Connemara' the heroine of Lever's *Martins of Cro' Martin*. At Renvyle they meet Mrs Blake, an upper-class Widow Leonard, who fought boycotts single-handed and managed to hold on to her house and land. Their very real joy of finding themselves in civilised comfort once more is present in diary and book: 'Under the influences of dark mahogany panelling and a low Queen Anne window we became mellow and thoughtful, and sank into soothing reflection on our natural affinity to what is cultivated and artistic.' They have achieved a nice tone of self-mockery but with it goes a facetiousness which is objectionable. The good things in the book are the ones based on actual happenings, things actually seen, but at this stage they do not have the confidence to write solely of them. But they certainly produce an alternative to the 'Jack—very manly' kind of guide book, and Bord Failte would not employ them today.

Two years later in 1891 the *Lady's Pictorial* commissioned another series of articles—on French vineyards. They are given £20 to cover expenses, an introduction to Gilbey's, and told 'to write about people as well as the vintage'. They buy a Kodak, accept an invitation to Gilbey's château, and set off from Dover to Calais on 30 September. The sense of adventure which it was

impossible for them to work up on a tour of the West of
Ireland—even when it was done in a jennet and cart—inspires
them throughout here. They are also more confident of their
ability to interest simply by telling the truth, and in the book
there are no incidents which did not take place in fact. It is there
just as it happened from the first night onwards:

> *Diary:* Got to Hotel Bergère at about seven. Had coffee and
> eggs and sat out in a hot stuffy courtyard till bed time. Small
> hot room, beds packed with fleas.
> *Book*: We cannot pretend to say we slept well in our opera-
> box. Everything in the hotel seemed to stay up all night,
> including a small but devoted party of fleas; and the
> atmosphere, even when diluted with as much courtyard air as
> the windows would let in, was heavy and hot.[7]

The hilariously funny scene where they try to buy a mosquito
net without knowing the French for it, and end up being draped
in black lace by the saleswoman, who tells them how becoming
it is, while they are doubled up with laughter, is as it actually
happened. Their command of French is good enough to get by
on, except when it comes to a polite tea party. Edith's studio
slang is all right for the rural folk, but does not stretch to the
upper middle-class conversations. As late as 1946 she writes to a
French count: 'If you would do me the honour of writing—
especially about Art and drawings—in French, I should be so
delighted. I could *never*—alas—speak French—except to coolies
and slaves.' In restaurants whenever the menu is too much for
their French they fall back on *'œufs sur le plat'*. Unlike in
Connemara, when they criticise here, the criticism is always as
much against themselves as the country: *they* do find it hard to
get up so early, to drink their coffee with *hot* milk and to have to
put up with impregnable shutters. They do go armed with their
spirit-lamp, kettle, teapot and half a pound of English tea in
their hat box. They are unconventional in their dislike of the
tourist attractions—the mummies in the church of St Michel,
Bordeaux, which they are expected to find fascinating, bore
them, 'awful little brown things, propped round the walls of a
dark cellar. Saw also the rather dull cathedral'. And it is the
ordinary daily lives of the people which they enjoy most. They

have the nerve to do what they could not make themselves do in Connemara, they go and spend a night in a peasant cottage. They do it deliberately—the diaries tell us, 'Went, in pursuit of copy to Jeanne's cottage. Fed there, very well . . . Good bedroom, but fleas awful. Scarcely slept at all.' In the book they change the name of their hostess, and they pretend that they broke down nearby and were forced to spend the night there. They also stress the strangeness of the meal. They were given *cèpes*, 'which resembled sweetbreads and cut rather like tough custard pudding. It was fried bright brown, but the inside was yellowish white, and the whole thing was swimming in hot oil . . . a dreadful taste, as though rotten leaves and a rusty knife had been fried together in fat'.

The Queen Anne house which they relaxed in in Connemara is replaced here by the châteaux in which they are instantly raised from literary tramps into serene ladies of quality. The descriptions of the 'English managements and comforts' plus 'the aromatic flavour of French surroundings and the vivid pageant of the vintage' are idyllic. Bouquets of roses and heliotrope are given them, they take baths, play the piano, and 'civilisation is re-established'.

In 1893 they made their last two tours for travel books: to North Wales and then to Denmark. Violet takes over as narrator and much of the fun is at the expense of her cousin, Miss O'Flannigan: Violet must pose when she has a streaming cold because 'Miss O'Flannigan did not see it, but when painting she sees nothing but values. Ordinary humanity does not see values any more than fairies, but Miss O'Flannigan and other artists do.'[8] The Welsh tour was commissioned by *Black and White*, who cancelled the series when one of the articles was lost in the post, and it was eventually published by Blackwoods. The tour is even closer to fact than the French one was. Nothing is invented and the narration follows the diaries day by day, just as it happened. They made a conscious endeavour to be true to life—one letter Violet writes for example, 'I am toiling at No.10. I find it very hard to remember the road between Llanberis and Bell except in small spots.' The only obvious change is in the names of the hotels—if they are making adverse comments. They mock themselves, describing their attempts at economy which lead them in a village shop to ask for, 'A very bad umbrella—the worst kind you have got'. And they are well aware of the ridiculous figures they cut on the two small ponies setting off in the pouring rain for Bettws-y-Coed.

> Swaddled, like cabmen, in comforters and capes, we came forth and mounted. During the process of sorting the reins, the umbrellas, and the tips for the two ostlers, we could not be unaware of the guileless enjoyment of the hat department opposite, and the more critical but equally unaffected interest of the circus ladies and gentlemen at the window of a ground-floor sitting-room. As we unfurled the pink parasol and the tent-like gingham and went down the street like a pair of fungi on four legs, the chorus that broke from the ground-floor window was acutely audible:
> 'Oo're ye goin' to meet, Bill?'
> '*Ave* ye bought the street, Bill?'
> 'Larf?—why, I thought I should '*a died*—'
> Our riding-canes were in the hold-alls, but we kicked the Tommies to a trot and fled.

They had set off in a heatwave, 'Our heads swam, our throats were as dry as the traditional lime burner's wig . . . All we desired was a cool death—"something lingering", with icebergs in it,' and are plagued by flies, but it very soon reverts to the more usual torrential rain and fog. The summer solstice is invisible on Snowdon. The book is enlivened by their anti-romantic comments: they don't know which of the mountains Snowdon is. When they find out they nearly die of the walk up it. In fact they found the Summit Hotel, 'the foul little shanty hotel on top . . . loathingly got into filthy bed in tiny room with all our clothes on'. In the book this is not toned down much. The hotel is like 'the cabin of a fifth-rate coasting steamer' and the bed described as looking as if all the previous occupants had slept in their boots. When they do get a 'view': 'The world was obviously meant to be regarded *en profile*, and not to be stared at, flat-faced, from above . . . it seems to us that a beautiful view is not a mere matter of miles seen from a great height.' For a guide book they are amazingly frank, 'Corwen is a dingy, mean town, in spite of the wooded cliff at its back.' Their sense of the ridiculous sends them into irresistible maniac laughter at entirely the wrong moments. When they have collapsed, half-dead with exhaustion, on the way up Snowdon, they ask their Welsh-speaking guide, Griffith Roberts, about eagles. 'Oh yess indeed,' is his reply, which they realise means he doesn't understand what they have asked him.

'Eagles! Big birds, you know!' screamed Miss O'Flannigan.
The guide shook his head, and again said, 'Oh yess.'
Miss O'Flannigan got up from her boulder. 'Big birds?' she repeated, 'with beaks like this'—she put her forefinger to her forehead, and described thence a brilliant outward curve—'with big wings'—she flapped her arms violently—'big birds who steal lambs!'
'Ah,' said Griffith Roberts, 'ze *fahxes*. Oh yess, many fahxes.'
Miss O'Flannigan sat down again, and I laughed a great deal.

There are no Big Houses nor châteaux in Wales and they only have the preaching and the ponies to take delight in. The strangeness of the sermons was what most impressed them; they hardly seemed Christian at all. The preacher speaks, 'With the monotony of a mountain wind, with the swinging cadence of a belfry, the minor periods rose and died. It might have been the sombre prophesying of a Druid, chanted beneath the oaks in days prior to Gregorians.' They admire the mountain ponies which they encounter on a narrow pass:

They turned all at once, as if blown by a wind, and floated down the green valley side, whose steepness we had scarcely cared to look at, with heads up, manes and tails streaming, and shoeless hoofs flicking the turf in bounds that seemed headlong, yet never went beyond control. In the bottom of the valley they swung to the right with the incredible oneness of a flock of birds, and halting, looked up to us and neighed defiance.

But mostly they are not favourably impressed with either the scenery or the people. They do like the deep wooded glens near

Bettws, but the sight only leads them to think of the time when they were highways for London, when 'the best that Ireland had to give swung along this road towards London to the tune of sixteen hoofs'. They go to Llangollen, but the place only makes the two ladies who retired there seem even more eccentric than they had thought them before. It holds no beauty for them. They sum up the two weeks in Wales as a time of 'the leisure and independence, the fatigue and inconvenience, the life expanding unintellectually in long solitudes'. When they get back to Holyhead and find that their luggage is lost so that they have to let the boat go without them, there is just blank melancholy as they face another night in Wales 'and the rain began to fall'. Edith Somerville's later fears that 'these amateur gypsy tours' may seem more enjoyable than in fact they were is needless over the Welsh one.

The Danish tour was commissioned for the *Lady's Pictorial*. They went by boat from Liverpool to the Hook of Holland, and then by train through Holland and Germany to Hamburg. Violet Martin has the usual laughs at her cousin: she describes her talking French at a very grand dinner party 'with a gesture whose Parisian *abandon* had yet in it some unconscious touch of the Skibbereen apple-woman'.[9] She tells of Edith's confident assumption that she knows how to ask for a boat-trip in Danish and going up to the row of boatmen demanding loudly, 'I want a bath. Can you give me one?' She is also of course able to laugh at herself, and their terrifying adventures become comic material. At Hamburg Edith goes to register luggage while Violet stays on the train. Without warning the train moves off. It gathers speed and rushes through the night with Violet aboard without any luggage, ticket or money, and without any German apart from the declension of adjectives. The train stops at the station where they were to change trains for Denmark; she descends, even her self-possession shattered. Eventually Edith, who had been tearing about Hamburg in taxis from station to station, gets a message through to the station where her cousin is stranded. Violet has been sitting lost in an office:

Had an official come in and assured me that I really did not exist in Altona, and that I should presently find myself sleep-walking in Galway, I should have believed him, so little individuality has the ordinary human being when torn from its accustomed surrounding. The official came, but it was to beckon me forth to a private room in the station, where a large, stern man sat before a machine that clicked. He did not speak, but taking from the table strip after strip of paper, began to read along their length in the voice of the ghost in *Hamlet*. I felt it to be appropriate. In these fateful accents he proclaimed to me my story, told by my cousin at Hamburg, how an English lady, without tickets, money or German speech, was possibly at Altona, or possibly far on her way to Denmark. I found the description pathetic, and realised that if I had shed tears throughout the difficulty it would have been advantageous, and what might have been expected.

They did not take Denmark to their hearts much more than they had Wales; it seemed to them rather like England only without the beauty of antiquity, 'A mild, unhistoric land', where the cleanliness and order was at the expense of vitality. The fair days are too well mannered with the Danish farmers sitting in neat rows in the refreshment tent, 'decorous . . . with reasonable eyes' compared with the Irish ones they loved; even the cows seem religious in character, a singular contrast to the 'nimble and free-thinking herds of Galway'. The sights leave them quite unimpressed as usual. When they force themselves to visit Frederiksborg castle, the huge doorways and magnificent ceilings, parquet and pictures 'swam before our eyes, and admiration, however genuine, could not but be aware of aching legs, and of the faint yet pursuing chill of a building in which no fire is ever lighted'. How many of our own feelings do they echo when they admit that 'it seems a casting away of a singularly royal residence that it should now be merely destined to undermine the constitutions of tourists as they wander, half appreciative and wholly exhausted through its immensities'. And then there is the description of how one falls at the end of a guided tour, weakened by cold, tiredness and hunger into the eager hands of the seller of photographs of all the things which have exhausted one. Their judgments are refreshingly honest:

from a distance the castle does remind them of the Kensington workhouse, and the Houses of Parliament seemed like an income tax office from the outside, and like the saloon of an ocean liner, with all its white and gold, from the inside. Their boredom with being tourists who do the proper things is never disguised and the tone of the diaries, 'Spent a noble but exhausting day in sightseeing', is maintained in most of the article. In the cathedral at Aarhus they say they have to restrain each other from damaging a bas-relief with their umbrellas, under the very eyes of the curator, 'such pressure on the brain does sight-seeing induce in those by nature unfitted for it'.

Here, as in the other tours, it is the personality of the narrator and her cousin which makes the articles of interest. They are self-reliant and intrepid wherever they are; they have absolute confidence in their own perceptions and judgments. What might seem like individual unconventionality is usually the result of this Ascendancy dash and often it borders on arrogance. One Sunday in Copenhagen they go to a Danish church, but annoyed with the Danes who whisper throughout the service, and finding the hymns too long and wearing, they leave before the sermon. They go on to the English church where they enter in the middle of the General Confession. Nothing daunted they walk to the front for seats and find themselves sitting behind the Princess of Wales, Queen Alexandra and her daughters. In comparison with the royalty they say they feel 'hulking, superfluous, and ill-dressed'. But they certainly did not feel overwhelmed, because suddenly feeling very hungry just as the sermon is about to begin once more, they get up and go out. This time, however, they do not get away so easily. They mistake the door and find themselves in the vestry, with the choice of entering the church once more, or staying, hungry, in the vestry, or climbing some railings to get out. In full view of the Princess of Wales' coachman they start to climb the railings. The church warden, however, who was doubtless alerted by the vestry door which had 'a clanking ecclesiastical latch' followed them: he silently unlocked the gate and thrust us forth, and the worst feature of the case was that we laughed'. They continue to amuse themselves by drinking cherry brandy with their lunch, which tickles them as a fall from grace after such a burst of church-going'. A rather daring visit to the night club, the Café-National, leaves them cold; in their eyes the serpentine dancer and friends are merely 'elderly ladies, in tights and two or three coats of paint' who 'danced with creditable activity'. They sum up the evening, 'If a regular attendance at music-halls is considered fast and fashionable, then, as Falstaff said, "God help the wicked".'

In Denmark, as elsewhere, they begin to appreciate the country once they leave the hotels and tourist spots for the houses of the Danish people. They are fortunate enough to have letters of introduction to charming intelligent people who live in stately homes where, of course, they feel immediately at home. In one palatial house they find, 'an old lady with white hair and dark eyes and straight brows, and a welcome whose kindness and unconventionality made us aware that great ladies are of the same pattern in every country'. Here they find an intellectual life which was so much missing in Wales. They spend hours discussing books, meet friends of Ibsen, have great talks about his plays and come to the conclusion that 'there appears little attempt to claim for him a meaning beyond the simple reproduction of character and action'. They eat exquisite formal dinners and leave feeling very impressed with Danish aristocracy; appreciating more than anything else the ultimate kindness of those who came to see them off on an 8.30 morning train—giving them a basket of fruit and bunches of roses.

Edith Somerville tells us that they were under certain limitations when they wrote up these tours: 'We were given editorially to understand that the events, be they what they may, were ever to be treated from the humorous point of view. "Pleasant" is the word employed, which means pleasant for the pampered reader, but not necessarily for anyone else.'[10] She need not have feared that they distorted things in order to make them pleasant. And as for the humorous, after the Irish tour there is never any discernible effort to amuse the reader. The tours on the whole are pretty unpleasant, and only their high spirits and innate sense of the ridiculous and propensity for the *fou rire* make them in any way tolerable. The reader can imagine that they had fun but would not wish to emulate them. They do not pander to the English ladies who were meant to be reading them either. The discomforts and boredom far outweigh the pleasures. Except in the most painful moments, such as when they were separated in Germany in the middle of the night, they always make a point of telling foreigners that they are not English. Telegramming in distress, Edith Somerville calls Violet Martin an English lady as a sort of shorthand for Ascendancy female of the British Empire; at other times they are Irish. And they tell us that people respond with immediate warmth, especially the French, once they learn that our authors are not English. They also steer clear of English tourists, especially those with the English voice. In one country they hear it 'asking with easy patronage whether there was "anything to see, about here?" . . . the tone caused a sudden vivid insight into the feelings of dislike, contempt, and respect which our countrymen inspire in other lands; and we so felt, for the hundredth time, the real touch of greatness that lies in the self-esteem of the Briton.'

What the tours did do was give the cousins confidence in their ability to write about ordinary things truthfully. Beside *An Irish Cousin* and *Naboth's Vineyard*, the articles are simple and realistic. Nothing much happens on the tours but they make good reading, and they showed the authors that they could be writers without sensational subject matter.

Chapter IV

The Real Charlotte

Somerville & Ross started writing *The Real Charlotte* in 1889; it was not finished until 1893. *Naboth's Vineyard, Through Connemara in a Governess Cart, In the Vine Country,* and many short stories and articles were written and published during this time. This is not because they thought little of the novel, on the contrary they thought so highly of it that they would give only their best to it. The other things were written when, owing to ill-health or family pressures, they had not the peace of mind for their novel. And once they had conceived of the novel, the time spent not writing it was a period of gestation. Edith Somerville has said that once they had thought of the characters they were hardly ever out of their minds, whether they were writing other things or making tours or playing. Francie especially 'was taking a hand in what we did, and her point of view was in our minds'.

The first mention of the novel is on 6 November 1889: they are working at '*The Welsh Aunt* as we now waggishly call the successor to *An Irish Cousin*'. They spend five days plotting it and then leave it to write *Naboth's Vineyard*. The next spring they return, 14 April 1890, 'Made a fresh start at writing *The Welsh Aunt*' but it is premature, and nothing comes of it until 8 May that year, 'Made a fresh start at *The Welsh Aunt*.' The slowness of the early chapters was mainly due to Violet Martin's poor health. It was her experiences they were drawing on and Edith could not write on without her. The usual round of summer engagements and the influx of people from England made writing impossible for the rest of the summer, and in July they tour Connemara for the travel book. It is 29 October before they return to the novel, 'Wettish. Made a start at *The Welsh Aunt*.' They work steadily each morning and within a week have written four chapters, by 20 November five. Then they must start writing up the Connemara travel articles. Then the usual bouts of winter colds and fevers begin. There are the starving peasants west of Castletownshend to be looked after, hunting and shooting are time-consuming distractions. In February 1891 Edith goes to stay at Ross, and 'Begin again at *The Welsh Aunt*.' But almost at once Violet takes to her bed with acute indigestion. When she recovers, Edith falls sick. When they are both up, they need the relaxation of the woods and there are bright frosty days so they ramble about with guns looking for pheasants. Slowly they return to work, 13 March, 'a good day's work. Seven pages—our best record', 14 March, 'good bit of work. Are only in chapter XI just the same'. They settle down to regular morning writing and by 4 April the first volume in sixteen chapters is finished. Edith returns to Drishane and begins reading it aloud to their friend Ethel Penrose.

By May Violet is in Drishane ready to start on the second volume, but by 21 May they are only as far as the second chapter. Violet is too bilious to work, and Edith starts spring cleaning, decorating the house, buying new curtains. When Violet is fit they fall to, and for the first time they work all through the summer, giving only the afternoons to their demanding relations and their games of golf and tennis. By July they are writing for an hour before breakfast as well. The comings and goings of the many visiting members of the Somerville and Coghill families meant that Violet Martin never knew where she was sleeping. She fitted in wherever there was room. Their work was seen by everyone else to be merely self-induced duty which kept them from joining in the fun, or from the real duty of entertaining visitors and paying visits. July was the worst month: 28 July, 'were hunted from place to place like the Vaudois, seeking in vain a cave wherein we could hold our services unmolested. Did one poor page.' 29 July, Edith, aged thirty-three, escapes from her mother, who is determined to take her visiting, 'by adopting the extreme measure of hiding in Hildegarde's dress cupboard'. 31 July, 'Martin and I hid about in the sheepfield and did a bit more work.'

They persevere until September when they make the tour of France. After they have written up the French tour they are back at the novel without a day's break, but they have lost the rhythm. Not until March do they write regularly. By 26 March, 'Finished chapter seven of volume three.' Exercising the hounds, hunting and ill-health make their usual demands but by 19 April, 'only about 11,000 words more'. By the beginning of May the end of the story is clear, 'Arrived at violent conclusion with regard to final course of the plot.' For the next month they work each morning and whatever evenings they can make free; when they go to Lismore for a week they take the work with them, and write in bed before breakfast. On 8 June they leave Lismore and, travelling by train together as far as Mallow, they wrote 'feverishly' all the way, and 'succeeded in finishing off Francie'. This is not tantamount to finishing the book; that was done at Drishane. Edith Somerville tells us 'There is a place in the orchard at Drishane that is bound up with those final chapters, when we began to know that there could be but one fate for Francie. We felt her death very much . . . It felt like killing a wild bird that had trusted itself to you.'[1] She told a nephew that both she and Violet were in tears as they wrote the death scene. In the diary it is 'this vile chapter 50', which is so reluctantly written; they hated killing Francie but felt that it had to be done. The Autumn is spent clean copying, doing illustrations for *In the Vine Country*, and coping with heavy colds. Not until January 1893 are they getting it ready for the publisher. In February it is sent to Bentley, his offer of £100 is rejected, and they sell it to Ward & Downey for £250 and half the American rights.

The authors were resting in Paris when the novel was published. Mrs Somerville kindly wrote and told them the family's opinion: 'All here loathe Charlotte.' She protested against the realism, the nastiness, the vulgarity of the characters; the weakness of Christopher and the fact that Pamela did not marry Cursiter. Her comment to an aunt of Edith's deserves to be quoted because it has been echoed by modern critics: 'Francie deserved to break her neck for her vulgarity; she certainly wasn't nice enough in any way to evoke sympathy, and the girls *had* to kill her to get the whole set of them out of the awful muddle they had got into!' One of Edith's brothers wrote to them angrily, 'Such a combination of bodily and mental hideosity as Charlotte could never have existed outside of your and Martin's diseased imaginations.' A cousin on being appealed to amused them by stating firmly and calmly, 'I do not like the book. It is all curses and dirty kitchens.' But, Edith says, although they could laugh at the adverse comments, nevertheless, 'a certain depression was inescapable'. Back in Drishane she wrote gloomily in her diary, 'No one here likes *Charlotte.*' Her brother Cameron seems to have been the only relation to recognise their amazing achievement in the book, and he becomes the confidant of both women. Violet tells him that she cannot sympathise with the demand for extra charm in a heroine, 'I think she ought to be in some way striking or in some way typical of her type, but not necessarily with leanings towards perfection.' And Edith shares with him her sadness at their family's philistinism, 'It shows a failure of understanding that is awful in the light it sheds on the gulf between our and their mental standpoints . . . My feeling is that any character is interesting if treated realistically. They care for nothing but belted earls or romantic peasants.'

Several characters in the novel are based on real people. Charlotte is modelled on one Emily Herbert, an enemy of the Somerville family, who had grasped an inheritance meant for them. Edith's diary tells us that Emily got everything but 'about £500 to the Somervilles of which Papa and I get £50 each. It is a curious instance of the power of Will—Emily's will in particular.' Later that year, 1886, Emily rented one of the houses in Castletownshend and Edith writes, 'Emily Herbert has taken the Mall. Agony, rage and despair.' Emily Herbert had died before they wrote the novel, and while they were writing it her spirit communicated a message of such vehemence and hatred that Edith's only reaction is, 'Hell holds no fury like a woman scorned.' They actually forgot this incident until two years later when an old lady who had been intimate with Emily Herbert asked Edith how she knew about Emily's 'love affair', which had been such a closely guarded secret. To Edith's astonishment she went on to tell her about Emily's lifelong passion for an attorney. 'He had had a wife, a little nonentity, to whom, as in the book, Emily had paid every court, and when she died Emily had made a hard fight to secure him, but failed. Also she *had* been known to steam open letters! I think it is most uncanny . . .' The character was closer to life than they had thought, the very characteristics which they had consciously imagined turning out to be the real Emily Herbert.

James Canavan, the Dysarts' retainer, is based closely on James Tucker who fulfilled something like his role in the Ross family. Tucker was a hedge schoolmaster with a gift for poetry who had gone to Ross during the Famine to help with the school which the Martins had started for the tenants' children. He stayed on for the Martins' own children: Violet's memories of Robert Martin include an account of Tucker:

> He taught us the three Rs with rigour and perseverance, he wrote odes for our birthdays, he was controller-in-chief of the dairy . . . Tucker was slightly eccentric, a feature for which there was always toleration and room at Ross; he entered largely into the schoolroom theatricals that sprang up as soon as Robert was old enough to whip up a company from the ranks of his brothers and sisters. The first of which there is any record is the tragedy of *Bluebeard* adapted by him at the age of eight . . . Tucker was stage manager, every servant in the house was commandeered as audience. The play met with much acceptance up to the point when Bluebeard dragged Fatima (a shrieking sister) round the room by her hair, belabouring her with a wooden sword, amid the ecstatic yells of the spectators, but at this juncture the mistress of the house interrupted the revels with paralysing suddenness . . .
>
> There remains in my memory a play got up by him [Robert Martin] when he was about seventeen, in which he himself, despising the power of his sisters, took the part of the heroine, with the invaluable Tucker as the lover. A tarletan dress was commandeered from the largest of the sisterhood, and in it, at the crisis of the play, he endeavoured to elope with Tucker over a clothes horse draped in a curtain. It was at this point that the tarletan dress, tried beyond its strength, split down the back from neck to waist; the heroine flung her lover from her, and backed off the stage with her front turned firmly to the audience, and the elopement was deferred *sine die*.[2]

These two incidents are combined in the coach house play in the novel. It is Garry Dysart's birthday and family and servants have been bullied into attending the performance: 'nightmare snatches of *Kenilworth*'. James Canavan is Queen Elizabeth, dressed in the cook's shirt, a gold paper crown, and a ham-frill ruff to hide his whiskers. Amy and Leicester ride away on a clothes horse, and the wildness of the Ross plays is there when Canavan dances on Amy Robsart's grave until the lid of the trunk gives way and he is knee deep in the 'tomb' still dancing on the girl's body. Garry comments the next day. 'You never know what he'll do next. I believe if mother hadn't been there last night he'd have gone on jumping on Kitty Gascogne till he killed her.'[3] This eccentricity which belonged to James Tucker also comes out in the scene where Canavan in his black-tailed coat and tall hat looks meditatively at the young rat which Garry wants to have as a pet. Then, in front of the child, Canavan picks up his stick 'and balanced it in his hand,

> "Voracious animals that we hate,
> Cats, rats, and bats deserve their fate,"

he said pompously, and immediately brought the stick down on the rat's head.'

Lady Dysart shares many characteristics of Mrs Somerville, and the places in the novel are rooted in actual places. The neglected squares of North Dublin and the little back streets of Bray are unmistakably represented; so is Christ Church Bray, the Protestant church on the hill, as well as the pier at Kingstown, the St George's Yacht club, the Royal Marine Hotel, and many of the streets and details of Dublin. Bruff, both in its setting—with its own lake in front, and its architecture— the broad limestone steps, is modelled on Ross. The countryside around is County Galway. But the small town life is closer to Castletownshend, and the church at Lismoyle and choir practices are those of Castlehaven church, Castletownshend.

The story is told from the point of view of an omniscient narrator who sees and understands far more than any of the characters in the story. The tone is detached and uninvolved, allowing the characters to reveal themselves through action and dialogue. Usually the reader knows more than the characters, and judges differently. Thus Lambert is showing us his shallowness when he condemns Christopher: 'A fellow that'd rather stick at home there at Bruff having tea with his sister than go down like any other fellow and play a game of pool at the hotel!' Because the authors presume there is a common attitude between them and the reader, they usually leave us to make our own judgments. There is little of the clumsiness of George Eliot's crude interpolation. And when they do comment on the characters it is never to explain something which they cannot *show*, and the narrative does not jar:

> It was almost pathetic that this girl [Francie] with her wild-rose freshness and vivid spring-like youth, should be humble enough to think that she was not worthy enough of Mr Hawkins, and sophisticated enough to take his love-making as a matter of common occurrence, that in no way involved anything more serious. Whatever he might think about it, however, she was certain that he would come here today, and being wholly without the power of self-analysis, she passed easily from such speculations to the simpler mental exercise of counting how many hours would have to crawl by before she could see him again. She had left the avenue and she strolled aimlessly across a wide marshy place between the woods and the lake . . .

In this quotation we can see the movement from direct comment to a description of Francie's state of mind, to an exposition of her level of awareness, to a description of the countryside. Throughout the novel there is this flexibility in the prose. In the following passage Francie's reactions to poetry are narrated but so clearly that we know her perception and sensitivity in all their limitations: Christopher is reading a Rossetti poem to her.

> Francie's attention, which had revived at the description of the Queen, began to wander again. The sound in Christopher's voice told that the words were touching something deeper than his literary perception, and her sympathy answered to the tone, though the drift of the poem was dark to her. The music of the lines had just power enough upon her ear to predispose her to sentiment, and at present, sentiment with Francie meant the tender repose of her soul upon the thought of Mr Gerald Hawkins.

Letters are used to reveal character. Francie's letter to her girl friend in Dublin shows her egoism, the superficiality captured in the slang, the clichés, the slack grammar and careless adjectives:

> Although I'm nearly dead after the bazaar I must write you a line or two to tell you what it was like. It was scrumshous. I wore my white dress with the embroidery the first day and the pink dress that you and I bought together the second day and everybody liked me best in the white one. It was fearful hot and it was great luck it was at the flower stall Mrs Gascogne asked me to sell.

The dialogue in vocabulary and rhythm is that of the social grade to which the character belongs. Sometimes a character is given more than one voice—Francie adopts an English accent in place of her Dublin one after she has returned from her honeymoon in Paris. Characters with two or more voices cannot always control them. Charlotte and Lambert both lose control of theirs when they are in a passion. Christopher would normally be treated to Lambert's most impeccable English, but when Lambert is jealous of Christopher's relations with Francie his accent astonishes Christopher: 'During this recital Mr Lambert's voice had been deficient in the accent of gentlemanlike self-importance that in calmer moments he was careful to impart to it, and the raw Limerick brogue was on top as he said, "Yes, by George! I remember the time when she wasn't above fancying your humble servant!"' The various voices reflect the characters' lack of single-minded sincerity. Lady Dysart's utter inability to distinguish one Irish accent from another is an indication of her obtuseness. Even in reported speech or thought the individuality of the character concerned is kept. Here is Hawkins's crudity, selfishness and triviality:

> As he reflected on that escapade he felt that he would have given a good round sum of money that it had not taken place. He had played the fool in his usual way, and now it didn't seem fair to back out of it. That, at all events, was the reason he gave to himself for coming to this blooming menagerie, as he inwardly termed Mrs Beattie's highest social effort; it wouldn't do to chuck the whole thing up all of a sudden, even

though, of course, the little girl knew as well as he did that it was all nothing but a lark.

The language is sharp: the discomfort of the superfluous women at the tennis party is caught in the phrase 'midge-bitten dullness'. The subtle changes in consciousness as Francie slowly responds to Christopher's care and goodness are delicately and comically expressed: 'as a sea-weed stretches vague arms up towards the light through the conflict of the tides, her pliant soul rose through its inherited vulgarities, and gained some vision of higher things.' When imagery is used to describe a character it is amusingly appropriate. The clergyman follows a major's denunciations of English politicians 'but chastenedly, like an echo in a cathedral aisle'. Nance the Fool is described as 'a bundle of rags with a cough in it'. Adjectives are used with wit such as Christopher's 'platonic philandering' and the 'Arcadian industry' of the young girls who gather rosebuds in their prettiest clothes hoping that they can attract Christopher's attention.

Dialect is as lively and colourful and exact as it is in any of their work. The amazing metaphors come tripping off the tongue: 'sure, Louisa tells lies as fast as a pig'd gallop'; and of the tailor's poor apprentice, 'when he came here he hadn't as much rags on him as'd wipe a candlestick'. When the Tally Ho household moves to Gurthnamuckla not all of them appreciate the social climb it represents. Norry the Boat sadly misses the beggars' visits, 'Ah, God help ye, how would I hear anything? it'd be as good for me to be in heaven as to be here, with ne'er a one but Nance the Fool comin' next or nigh me.' The long passages of dialect are just as convincing: Mary Holloran tells of her mother's quarrel with John Kenealy.

> ''Twas last Tuesday, Lady-Day an' all, me mother was bringin' a in a goaleen o'turf, an' he came thunderin' round the house, and every big rock of English he had he called it to her, and every sort of liar and blagyard—oh, indeed, his conduck was not fit to tell to a jackass . . . is it bring me mother into court!' says I, 'sure she's hardly able to lave the bed,' says I, 'an owld little woman that's not four stone weight! She's not that size,' says I—Mary Holloran measured

accurately off the upper joints of her first two fingers—'Sure ye'd blow her off yer hand! And Kenealy sayin' she pelted the pavement afther him, and left a backward sthroke on him with the shovel!'

The natural background is realised graphically and poetically. The ride from Lismoyle to Gurthnamuckla is a changing panorama as sleek pastureland gives way to limestone rocks and shrubby bushes—the land between the Big Houses which is fit for goats alone, bog land with rushing streams; and then suddenly the deep lush fields of the manor house. The natural beauty of the West contrasts sharply with the squalor of town life, so that even Francie is affected by it. She does not see the landscape clearly but she feels its quietness and grows gentler herself. The reader sees as clearly as the narrator. 'In the sunshine at the other side of the wall, a chain of such pools stretched to the broad blue water, and grey limestone rocks showed above the tangle of hemlock and tall spikes of magenta foxgloves. A white sail stood dazzlingly out in the turquoise blue of a band of calm, and the mountains on the farther side of the lake were palely clothed in the thinnest lavender and most ethereal green.' The magical charm of the many small islands which are floating on the lakes and sea is vividly conveyed. On Innishochery is a glade in the woods:

> It was a glade that had in some elfish way acquired an expression of extremest old age. The moss grew deep in the grass, lay deep on the rocks; stunted birch-trees encircled it with pale twisted arms hoary with lichen, and, at the farther end of it, a grey ruined chapel, standing over the pool that was the birthplace of the stream, fulfilled the requirement of romance. On this hot summer afternoon the glade had more than ever its air of tranced meditation upon other days and superiority to the outer world, lulled in its sovereignty of the island by the monotone of humming insects, while on the topmost stone of the chapel a magpie gabbled and cackled like a court jester.

The changing seasons give an emotional harmony and pattern to the novel. The main action starts in June, and

Lismoyle unfolds in long hot days of picnics and tennis and a relaxed peacefulness. Francie leaves there in September, but it is December before we really get to know the little house in Bray, and it is 'a damp dark December, with rain and wind nearly every day'. There is heavy cloud, a bleak coldness which reflects Francie's inner desolation and bleakness. It is May when she returns to Lismoyle, as Mrs Lambert, and it is as beautiful as ever:

> Spring, that year, came delicately in among the Galway hills; in primroses, in wild bursts of gorse, and in the later snow of hawthorne, unbeaten by the rain or the wet west wind of rougher seasons. A cuckoo had dropped out of space into the copse at the back of Gurthnamuckla, and kept calling there with a lusty sweetness, a mist of green was breathed upon the trees.

Francie and Hawkins are neither of them strong enough to do anything but partake of the spell of the spring:

> Walking there the glitter of the lake came up brokenly to the eye, through the beech-tree branches, that lay like sprays of maiden-hair beneath them; and over the hill and down to the water's edge and far away among the grey beech stems, the bluebells ran like a blue mist through all the wood. Their perfume rose like incense about Francie and her companion as they walked slowly, and ever more slowly, along the path. The spirit of the wood stole into their veins.

The weather is used similarly to mirror the emotions of the characters and the mood of the action. The old aunt dies in a howling east wind. When trouble is coming for Francie it is always heralded by a change in the weather. As Lambert's jealousy gets a hold of him and he loses himself in his obsession for Francie, the tension is conveyed to us through the impending storm:

> Late that afternoon, when the sun was beginning to stoop to the west, a wind came creeping down from somewhere back of the mountains, and began to stretch tentative cats' paws over the lake. It had pushed across the Atlantic a soft mass of

orange-coloured cloud, that caught the sun's lowered rays, and spread them in a mellow glare over everything. The lake turned to a coarse and furious blue; all the rocks and tree stems became like red gold, and the polished brass top of the funnel of the steam-launch looked as if it were on fire.

As the human passions rise and catastrophe is unavoidable so the storm sweeps over the lake reflecting some of their agony for us:

The lake had turned to indigo. The beds of reeds near the shore were pallid by contrast as they stooped under the wind; the waves that raced towards the yatch had each an angry foam-crest . . . and hissed and effervesced like soda-water . . . A few seagulls that were trying to fight their way back down to the sea, looked like fluttering scraps of torn white paper against the angry bronze of the clouds, and the pine trees on the point . . . were tossing like the black plumes of a hearse.

When Francie and Hawkins are stranded in the boat their emotional state is revealed to us by a description of the weather and lake. The heavy hypnotic sexual passion drugs them into a kind of deep slackness: islands look 'seductive . . . in the yellow haze of the lowered sun. There was not a breath of wind, and the launch slid her way through tranquil, oily spaces of sky that lay reflected deep in the water, and shaved the long rocky points so close that they could see the stones at the bottom looking like enormous cairn-gorms . . .'.

Whenever Francie is in disgrace or despair the sun never shines; always, unobtrusively, the tensions are reflected in the seasons and weather until the fateful day when she has to decide whether to stay with her husband or go off with Hawkins. A storm is in the offing but it does not come and the tension increases as we wait for it: 'The expected rain had not come, though the air was heavy and damp with the promise of it. It hung unshed, above the thirsty country, looking down gloomily upon the dusty roads, and the soft and straight young grass in the meadows; waiting for the night, when the wind would moan and cry for it, and the newborn leaves would shudder in the dark at its coming.' All is strangely static and waiting as Francie rides to her death, 'the shadowing greenness had saturated the daylight with its gloom, but out among the open pastures and meadows the large grey sky seemed almost bright, and, in the rich sobriety of tone, the red cattle were brilliant spots of colour.'

Social events are used to carry the plot and reveal character. Tennis parties, tea parties and picnics are purposely arranged to do this as well as to be representative of the kind of society they are actually portraying. Less formal gatherings are used in the same way. The chance meeting of Lady Dysart, Pamela, Hawkins, Lambert and Francie on the railway station at Kingstown is amazingly rich. Dublin's proprieties are much looser than those of Lismoyle and it is ironical that in Lady Dysart's eyes Francie's behaviour is shocking whereas to her aunt and uncle it is perfectly acceptable. Lady Dysart shows her disapproval in the only way possible to her with her standards of politeness. There is simply no 'geniality' in her manner towards Francie. Pamela reacts with her usual sensitivity and kindness; she sees her mother's coolness, she senses Francie's anguish at meeting Hawkins, and she gently communicates her compassion to Francie in the only way open to her—in the tone of her voice. In the midst of her turmoil at meeting Hawkins again, Francie is sensitive enough to recognise Pamela's concern and she is moved by it. Francie has never felt more confused and upset, but social conventions demand that she behaves with propriety. She forces herself to be polite and to behave with decorum under Lady Dysart's eyes, and for once she sees the value of such conventions; keeping them saves her from breaking down. For the first time in her life she acts differently from how she feels, and she is amazed at how ordinary her voice sounds when her heart is breaking. Hawkins meanwhile tries to avoid all conversation by busying himself arranging rugs in the carriage. The whole scene lasts only a few minutes but a lot of information is given.

The plot is carefully constructed with events which seem ironical on a second reading, but which at first only add to the feeling of inevitability of the action. When Lambert stops the milk-cart horse which is bolting with Francie on board in the first chapter she responds with 'Botheration to him! Why couldn't he have been somebody else?'—a thought which is to return to her countless times in the future. His ominous reply also foreshadows future situations, 'We'll be friends, and I won't tell on you this time.' There is irony in Lambert's casual remark to his wife, 'God help the man that's got to fight with Charlotte anyhow!' The first two chapters form a prologue to the main action which is framed by two rides, both in June, both to Gurthnamuckla. Each time Billy the beggar, who terrifies Francie, is there, his very presence threatening her. On the first ride Francie is flirting with Lambert and catches a glimpse of Hawkins; on the last ride Lambert is the husband she wants to run away from. On the first June day he gathers up the reins of her horse and says to her bitterly, 'Some day you'll be breaking your neck, and then you'll be sorry.' The death by horse is foreshadowed from the start when the milk horse bolts with her, and echoed with the stampeding horses at Gurthnamuckla.

The Real Charlotte covers a much wider social range than the two earlier novels. None of the main characters is taken from the lower classes but they are very vividly there, if in the background. Ferry Row cottages where the washerwomen live are graphically described:

> The clouds of steam from the cauldrons of boiling water ascended from morning to night, and hung in beads upon the sooty cobwebs that draped the rafters; the food and wearing apparel of the laundresses and their vast families mingled horribly with their professional apparatus, and, outside in the road, the filthy children played among the puddles that stagnated under an iridescent scum of soapsuds.

But outside of the servant class the other grades of society are all Protestant, Anglo-Irish; there are no middle-class Catholics in the novel. What we do see is the variety within the Anglo-Irish. Only the Dysarts live in a Big House, the rest are all part of a highly mobile society; often their positions are the result of mixed marriages, and they are all very ambitious. With the exception of the Dysarts and Julia Duffy — who is on the downward path—everyone is out to grab as much land as they can get. Their fight for position and wealth is every bit as determined as the tenants' political struggles. The political movement is very peripheral; we hear merely that the Dysarts' tenants are attending Land League meetings, and that the priest has written to tell the Dysarts that their tenants have joined the Plan of Campaign. Lambert is perhaps typical of himself, rather than agents in general, when he welcomes the political disturbance to cover up his own misdemeanours as he pockets what rent is paid. 'A certain amount of nominal disturbance' is useful when he is secretly committing fraud. The intricacies of the new Land Acts are of interest in the novel not for themselves, but because of what they tell us about the characters: neither Christopher nor Lambert can understand them, and we are told that only Charlotte could. Politics does not play an important role in the novel because the characters are not interested in them. This is of course a criticism of the characters. They are generally complacent and only interested in themselves. Charlotte treats her plumber as if he is a rebellious teenager, keeping him immersed in cold water up to his waist until he sings *God save the Queen*. There is no ill-nature in this and she is thoroughly good hearted when she tells the story but it was hardly tactful.*

As a group, the Anglo-Irish are seen to be politically unaware, mercenary and snobbish; the agent, who is a cad, is the head of the Lismoyle visiting list by virtue of good looks, a wife with money, and a new house at least a mile from the town. It is a disgrace to be poor, and when Julia Duffy can no longer afford new hats she stops going to church. There is an emphasis on the houses these people live in, which adds to the picture of the materialistic society even while it tells us about the characters. Each house in the novel shows forth the moral and psychological state of the inhabitants.

The Fitzpatricks' social descent to Albatross Villa is a part of their general inability to make anything of life. The squalor of the house is at one with their moral slackness as their young daughters have illicit affairs and nobody has the energy to care. The kitchen sink is perpetually blocked, the chimney smokes,

*Edith Somerville herself does a similar thing two years later: 'They decorated Nelson's Arch yesterday in honour of Trafalgar day, and Dan Neil had, much to his fury, to stand holding the Union Jack over the laurel wreaths while a photograph was being taken—When it was over he hurled the flag to the ground and roared "God save Ireland!" I must chaff about it when I seen him next.'

the tablecloth is badly stained, clean plates have coal-dust finger-marks on them; domestic economy means saving on soap and scrubbing brushes and a diet of strong tea and cheap bread in order that the daughters' hats may be as smart as the neighbours'. The contrast between this house and Bruff, the Big House, is similar to that which Jane Austen depicts between Portsmouth and Mansfield Park. Instead of the warmth of affection and the vitality of a family of children, there is disorder, noise and a callous lack of respect for one another. The mother is exhausted, the father is embittered and the maid is drunk. Gurthnamuckla, the noble country house of Julia Duffy, is a mixture of the elegance and solidity of Bruff and the sordidness of Ferry Row cottages. Julia is the daughter of a hard-drinking Protestant farmer who married his Catholic dairywoman. She cannot keep Gurthnamuckla up but she refuses to get out. The rotting hall door is held together with a beam of wood which is itself rotting beneath a shroud of cobwebs. Rags are stuffed into the broken window-panes, hens and turkeys live undisturbed in the kitchen. What was once a levelled lawn is now a field. The house is at one with Julia who dresses like a Dublin tinkerwoman, and is absolutely filthy but retains a voice 'carefully genteel'. Tally Ho reflects Charlotte Mullen's personality: the rooms reek of cats, cupboards are stuffed with dirty old rags, and everything is ugly and slightly unclean. She is on the way up just as Julia is on her way down, and we mock Charlotte's efforts at grandeur. Her attempt at a tea-party, that specially English institution, is farcical: the maid sets the table as if for breakfast with two egg-cups in the slop basin; when the teaspoons are eventually tracked down (nobody dare ask where) they have to be cleaned before they can be used; and the cake turns out to be one from the village grocer, the usual 'conglomerate of tallow, saw-dust, bad eggs and gravel'. The food in Tally Ho is kept locked up, and there is no end to Charlotte's meanness. She really thinks she is fulfilling her aunt's dying wish that she should look after Francie, when she says to the cook: 'You might give her a jam dumpling—use the gooseberry jam that's going bad. I've noticed meself that the child isn't eating, and it won't do to have the people saying we're starving her.' The Lamberts' suburban house is clean but it is of all the houses the one most tastelessly furnished and decorated. When Francie marries, one cannot imagine her penny fans on the walls to be any improvement.

Bruff is a going concern, an eighteenth-century house which they have the taste to keep as it was and the money to keep comfortable. Of all the houses in the books of Somerville & Ross it is the one most approaching Pemberley or Mansfield Park. There is order, tranquillity and harmony, and to Francie it is blissful—once she has forgotten how unfriendly and imposing it can be too.

> The long, unusual leisure of the afternoon passed her by like a pleasant dream, in which, as she sat in a basket-chair under the verandah outside the drawing-room windows, illustrated papers, American magazines, the snoring lethargy of the dogs, and the warm life and stillness of the air were about equally blended. Miss Hope-Drummond lay aloof in a hammock under a horse-chestnut tree at the end of the flower-garden working at the strip of Russian embroidery that some day was to languish neglected on the stall of an English bazaar; Francie had seen her trail forth with her arms full of cushions . . . No wonder, she thought, that Pamela wore a brow of such serenity, when days like this were her ordinary portion. Five o'clock came, and with it, with the majestic punctuality of a heavenly body, came Gorman and the tea equipage, attended by his satellite, William, bearing the tea-table. Francie had never heard the word idyllic, but the feeling that it generally conveys came to her as she lay back in her chair, and saw the roses swaying about the pillars of the verandah, and watched the clots of cream sliding into her cup over the broad lip of the cream jug, and thought how incredibly brilliant the silver was, and that Miss Dysart's hands looked awfully pretty when she was pouring out tea.

For Francie it is a well-earned rest, but time lies heavily on Miss Hope-Drummond who is just sitting about waiting for Christopher to propose to her. Lady Dysart is a comic character; she is amusingly judged: 'She was a clever woman, a renowned solver of the acrostics in her society paper, and a holder of strong opinions as to the prophetic meaning of the Pyramids.' She discharges her social responsibility with two annual tennis parties. A poor judge of character, she is wrong about Charlotte, Francie and Christopher. She has married for money and social position. Her ignorance at gardening is remarkable.* Gardening was taken seriously by Ascendancy ladies; Lady Dysart happily spends the morning planting a whole bed with the chickweed which her gardener has just pulled up. Pamela, her daughter, is a gentle portrait of a self-effacing girl, the mainstay of tea parties, old ladies and the Church. She is absolutely credible in being almost too good to be true. She speaks with a 'pleasant, anxious voice', and disregards men and clothes, and has no malice in her. She is friendly to everyone, and she never sees Francie as any worse than she is. She is never bored and she gives whoever she is with her full attention. Her brothers wonder how you can be as good as her and live. Her only real love is for her dogs.

Christopher has a nominal post in the Diplomatic Service but nothing at all to do at home. When he inherits the title and estate, his hopes that he has found some *raison d'être* come to nothing. The structure of things, with Lambert (who hates Christopher and is jealous of him) as agent, would take a much stronger man than Christopher to break into. Like Pamela he is quite without ambition, so after signing his name a few times he is back on the lake pottering about. The traditional ways of wasting time as a country gentleman are closed to Christopher as he neither shoots, nor hunts, nor fishes; he is too serious to make flirting a hobby. The things which do attract him— photography, painting and writing poetry—he is too good a critic of to spend his time doing; he knows he will never be first rate at any of them. Compared with Lambert he is a first-rate man, and Hawkins is a cad beside him. He is honest, intelligent and self-aware; he is as much a gentleman as Mr Knightley or Mr Darcy, but he lacks their determination. He is the effete side of the Anglo-Irish, terribly nice, and utterly straight, but somehow

*The back pages of Edith Somerville's *Diaries* are often covered with lists of plants to be sent to friends, and other lists of plants to be taken from friends' gardens. Then details of what she intends to do such as: 'To be done in rock garden: Shift Ayrshire rose from corner wall. York and Lancaster do. Substitute ramblers for Clematis. Transplant broom seedlings. Get calicanthus praecox and do. Florida . . .'

lacking in purpose. He is much sharper than his mother and he sees through Charlotte, and never can bring himself to like or trust her. He sees Francie rightly, recognising her zest for life, her gaiety and her innocence for what they are. He can see beneath the vulgar chatter; but then, unlike Knightley or Darcy, who continue to see in proportion, he romanticises her. His love for her is good, and he is right to see her potential, but he too is judged, and we see his romanticisation for what it is: 'He had idealised her to the pitch that might have been expected, and clothed her with his own refinement, as with a garment.'

He presumes her to have a depth which she has no inkling of. He reads her poetry which she cannot hear, he shows her beauty which she cannot see. He takes her to the point of his estate from which the lake is at its most beautiful, but she is blind to the natural beauty. She is of course honest and she does not feign a response, but she only sees Hawkins in a boat on the lake.

Bruff enables Pamela and Christopher to be free from selfishness, and to have the security and time to dedicate themselves to other people, but it does not give them enough guidance. Life is aimless there, and the peace is too often merely the absence of noise and disorder. Much of its value is traditional and not a reflection of the present generation of Dysarts. Sir Benjamin is, after all, gaga and confined to a wheel-chair, in which he hides in doorways waiting to trip up his young lady visitors with the crook of his walking stick.

Lismoyle is a polite society where behaviour is fixed, and to be accepted means to observe the customs. There is a spiteful comedy of manners as the selfish and trite women each have to exercise their base emotions within fixed limits. When Francie returns to Lismoyle as Mrs Lambert there is great consternation. The ladies of the parish have a tea party in order to discuss what their attitude to Francie is going to be, and how she is shaping up as Mrs Lambert. Even with a common enemy, Francie, whom they are all jealous of, they are still bitchy to each other. The rector's wife pretends she has called on Francie, not out of inquisitiveness, but because it was her duty as a clergyman's wife to call. Mrs Baker, the bank manager's wife, does not believe her of course but she seizes the opportunity to emphasise how low in the social scale the Church is:

'Oh, of course we know clergymen's families can't pick their company,' went on Mrs Baker, dismissing the interruption not without a secret satisfaction that Carrie Beattie, who, in the absence of Miss Corkram, was pouring out tea for her future mother-in-law, should see that other people did not consider the Rev. Joseph such a catch as she did. 'Only that Lambert's such a friend of Mr Baker's, and always banked with him, I declare I don't know that I'd have gone at all. I assure you it gave one quite a turn to see her stuck up there in poor Lucy Lambert's chair, talking about the grand hotels that she was in, in London and Paris, as if she never swept out a room or cleaned a saucepan in her life.'

'She had all the walls done round with those penny fans,' struck in Miss Kathleen Baker, 'and a box of French bongbongs out on the table; and oh, mamma! did you notice the big photograph of him and her together on the chimney-piece?'

'I could notice nothing, Kathleen, and I didn't want to notice them,' replied Mrs Baker; 'I could think of nothing but of what poor Lucy Lambert would say to see her husband dancing attendance on that young hussy without so much as a mourning ring on him, and her best tea-service thrashed about as if it was kitchen delf.'

This sort of scene which works through comedy and dialogue is a dramatic portrayal of the triviality and snobbery which pervade the society described. Francie is an outsider, ignorant of their ways, and not even aware that there are accepted modes of behaviour, taste and dress. She is utterly carefree, tasteless and beautiful, and the Lismoyle ladies detest her as much as their men adore her. Francie is made slowly aware that there is value in discretion, subtle colours and simple lines. She recognises that her scarlet and bright yellow silk gloves are crude, she learns to dislike what has been her favourite dress, a pink one covered with large pink horse shoes. And she realises that it is not done to invite a young man to tea when she is in the house by herself; nor to hide with him behind the piano when she hears a carriage draw up. Her whole affair with Hawkins is a series of similar incidents each of which offends against the modes of behaviour accepted in Lismoyle. Francie's naturalness is however preferable to the deceit and hypocrisy of Charlotte and Lambert, and to the superficiality of those who hold on to the limits of convention and manage to be beastly within them. When Francie stays at Bruff the conflict between her ignorance of how to behave and the code of conduct of the society is brought into the foreground. Lady Dysart sets the tone and at first she goes out of her way to make Francie feel at home. Francie goes on in her own natural way and delights Christopher by her freshness and originality. Her table manners are quite inadequate but though we laugh at her mistakes we endorse the butler's judgment. He recounts her behaviour to the rest of the servants and then, 'gave it as his opinion that Miss Fitzpatrick was as fine a girl as you'd meet between this and Dublin, and if he was Mr Christopher, he'd prefer her to Miss Hope-Drummond, even though the latter might be hung down with diamonds.' And although the visit ends in disgrace for Francie, with Lady Dysart glad to see the back of her and saying as she goes, 'never, no never, have I seen a girl so abominably brought up . . . and of all the man-eaters I have ever seen, she is the most cannibalistic!' our judgment is not Lady Dysart's. The common understanding which we share with the authors is made through the comedy. Francie is not guilty of anything else than going for a ride in Hawkins's boat and missing dinner because the boat gets stuck on a mud bank. The episode is comic with the dignified, indignant butler striding up and down the edge of the lake beating the dinner gong, to the amusement of all the cattle of the estate who gather round bellowing in reply. Lady Dysart's solemn vocabulary as she thinks that Francie has 'transgressed beyond forgiveness' is mock heroic. So is the description of Francie's return when the men leave her on shore 'to face her tribunal alone'.

The Real Charlotte is a study of the individual in society and it works mainly through comedy. They make their judgments on the action by making us laugh. Comedy holds the characters in check. Like Jane Austen in *Mansfield Park* they are concerned with the role of the Church in this nominally Christian society. This too is done through comedy. Francie has all her life attended Sunday School. The early chapters show how in Dublin this is a useful institution for amusing the children while the parents sleep off the large lunch. Their idea of Sunday peace is to lie 'in mountainous repose on the sofa', their rhythmic snores are 'the last expression of Sabbath peace and repose'. For the children the Sunday School is a place of social excitement where they can show off their best clothes. In Lismoyle the church is the centre of life, it unites all the Protestants, and they meet for choir practice during the week as well. But we see a congregation which is entirely irreligious, except maybe Pamela Dysart. Comedy makes the point, here we see through Christopher's eyes:

> There was nothing suggestive of ethereal devotion about Pamela's neighbours. Miss Mullen's heaving shoulders and extended jaw spoke of nothing but her determination to out-scream everyone else; Miss Hope-Drummond and the curate, on the bench in front of him, were singing primly out of the same hymn-book, the curate obviously frightened, Miss Hope-Drummond as obviously disgusted. The Misses Beattie were furtively eyeing Miss Hope-Drummond's costume; Miss Kathleen Baker was openly eyeing the curate.

Francie, even though she is herself a Sunday School teacher, can make nothing much of Christianity. She knows the Bible stories but has no understanding which makes religion in any way applicable to her own life. The failure is as much Francie's as it is the Church of Ireland's, but it *is* a failure and it is seen as such. At Bray it is Christmas Day and Francie is driven into the church by the bitter cold—and habit, 'the day's done for now, it's as good for me to go up to the four o'clock service as be streeling about in the cold here'. Unable to follow the special psalms which the choir are singing Francie 'felt her religious duties to be for the time suspended' and she falls into worrying about the bills she owes for the dresses she bought to take to Lismoyle.

In her pocket was a letter from a Dublin shop, containing

more than a hint of legal proceedings; and even if she were able to pay them a temporising two pounds in a month, there would still remain five pounds due, and she would not have a farthing left to go on with. Everything was at its darkest for her. Her hardy, supple nature was dispirited beyond its power of reaction, and now and then the remembrance of the Sundays of last summer caught her, till the pain came in her throat, and the gaslight spread into shaking stars.

The service went on, and Francie rose and knelt mechanically with the rest of the congregation. She was not irreligious, and even the name of scepticism was scarcely understood by her, but she did not consider that religion was applicable to love affairs and bills; her mind was too young and shapeless for anything but a healthy, negligent belief in what she had been taught, and it did not enter into her head to use religion as a last resource, when everything else had turned out a failure. She regarded it with respect, and believed that most people grew good when they grew old, and the service passed over her head with a vaguely pleasing effect of music and light.

She leaves the church as hopeless as she entered and the significance of the failure is apparent as soon as she comes outside the church. Lambert is waiting in the dark porch and steps forward to meet her. 'Francie started violently. "Oh, goodness gracious!" she cried, "you frightened my life out!" But for all that, she was glad to see Mr Lambert.'

Despite the title of the novel much of our interest is centred on Francie. For some time the authors were uncertain which of the two women was the central character. The first title, *The Welsh Aunt*, was chosen as a skittish successor to *An Irish Cousin*. Then came *Charlotte Mullen's Responsibility*, *A Moral Legacy*, *By an Irish Lake*, *A Dublin Aborigine*, *Out of the North Side*, *The Revealing of Charlotte*, *A Romance of Two Vulgar Women*. The three main characters are Francie, Charlotte and Lambert, united by their passion: Lambert's for Francie and Charlotte's for Lambert. Francie is the only one of the three to develop. Torn between Hawkins and Lambert she is made to realise that there are such things as good and evil, duty and irresponsibility. She learns to make her own judgment from an idea of what is right rather than what other people would like her to do, or what will make her happy. Charlotte and Lambert merely reveal new depths of crookedness.

Francie is beautiful, thoughtless and unintellectual. She is uneducated, naturally tasteless, and even her zest for life is a little vulgar, so lacking is it in discrimination. She has no talents beyond making a good sponge cake, and no ideas beyond marrying a good-looking wealthy man; and yet she does not bore us. Her zest for life does in fact give her a gaiety and brightness which shines like innocence compared with the deviousness of the other characters. Her naturalness which makes her always the same with no idea of compromising her instinctive responses for the sake of fashion, advantage or society, is a kind of sincerity. She is naturally modest: falling in love with a penniless, none too attractive, soldier she does not expect him to love her in return. In her eyes Christopher Dysart is so far above her that she cannot conceive of his falling in love with her. In her ignorance of how people should behave it never occurs to her that Lambert is acting strangely for a married man when he buys her presents. The mere fact of his being married means that she sees him only as a friend.

Francie's high spirits are always in evidence from the opening when she refuses to panic as the milk horse bolts with her in the van. 'In spite of an irresistible alarm as to the end of the adventure, Francie still retained sufficient presence of mind to put out her tongue at her baffled enemy. . . .' When Lambert warns her that Christopher Dysart is laughing at her for flirting with Hawkins she unhesitatingly responds, 'I don't care a jack-rat what he thought, or what you think either!' Francie is genuinely ignorant of social convention and has nothing but her natural kindness and delight in being happy to guide her through life. She is thoughtful for others, she appreciates Pamela Dysart's goodness, and she feels for Mrs Lambert in case she is lonely. There is no nastiness in her and she neither bears resentment nor expects other people to do so (Francie is quite lacking in imagination). After Charlotte has fought with her and sent her away Francie has no ill will for her:

Dislike, as has been said, was a sentiment Francie found great
difficulty in cultivating. She conducted a feud in the most
slipshod way, with intervals of illogical friendship, of which
anyone with proper self-respect would have been ashamed,
and she consequently accepted, without reservation, the fact
that Charlotte was making herself pleasant with a
pleasantness that a more suspicious person would have felt to
be unwholesome.

Francie is easily the dupe of Charlotte just as she is the victim of
Hawkins.

Her infatuation with Hawkins is pathetic. He is a careless and
self-indulgent young man who has no principles and always
gives in to the impulse of the moment. Whether he is engaged to
marry someone else, or whether Francie is married, makes no
difference to him. The affair means little to him until she is
married, and he never has any conception of how much he
means to Francie nor how much suffering he causes her. Her
love for him is quite unreasonable: he is penniless and he is not
even very attractive—the authors often speak of his red face and
lack of height: he is so short that when he shakes hands with
Charlotte he is seen to do 'his best to shake it at the height
presented by existing fashion'. It is the lack of reason which
makes the relationship serious: Francie cannot help herself and
when she has to turn down Christopher's proposal because of
her feelings for Hawkins we realise how much she is in love. She
is in the grip of a passion as strong as Charlotte's for Lambert,
and Lambert's for Francie. Unlike the traditional heroine
Francie does not gain by suffering. The purgatorial plunge into
the discomforts of Bray merely makes her long for Lismoyle.
When she marries Lambert it is no conscious resolution of
anything. She is in a spineless depression, and the only merit is
that she does not pretend it is anything else. 'She had never
pretended either to him or to herself that she was in love with
him; her engagement had been the inevitable result of poverty,
and aimlessness, and bitterness of soul.' The marriage makes her
no stronger and she is still very much in love with Hawkins, and
as incapable as ever of bearing resentment. 'She forgot her
resolutions; she forgot her pride; and before she reached home

that afternoon the spell of the new phase, that was the old, only intensified by forgiveness, was on her.'

It takes the revelation of Lambert's professional crookedness and his breakdown to awaken her to a sense of duty. The shock of seeing his collapse makes her see how right and wrong matter, 'how tremendous were sin and duty'. Her decision not to go off with Hawkins but to stay with her husband is not just her natural kindness, 'it had touched her slumbering moral sense as well'. The confrontation with Hawkins, ready to take her away, immediately after this awakening of conscience is almost too much for her; she does not weaken, but 'she was giddy with struggle'. Her death is amidst confusion; she is wrapped up in her own agony and she is as ignorant as ever of social convention, 'heedless of the etiquette that required that she and Hawkins should stop their horses till the funeral passed'. There is nothing mock heroic in the description of this judgment which she feels is being made as the funeral cortège stare at her and 'she felt as if she were enduring, in a dream, the eyes of an implacable tribunal'. The next moment she is lying on the road with her neck broken.

Charlotte, the main character, is the antithesis to Francie. Whereas Francie is beautiful and skips about in brightly coloured silks, Charlotte is ugly, squat and stout, stomping around in the thick dull clothes of the peasant women. Lambert is all the more aware of Francie's tiny waist and golden curls when Charlotte is next to her 'with her short arms akimbo, and a smile that was meant to be jovial accentuating the hard lines of her face'. She is twice Francie's age and she has always been painfully ugly. Their life styles are antithetical too; where Francie is blown about like a butterfly, Charlotte forges a determined path through life. She knows her own self and she knows other people. She is hard-headed and knows the ways of the world. Intent on buying what she will not be given, mainly Lambert, she uses all her cunning and determination to get the manor house and land partly to attract him. A merciless bully, she has such will power that everyone gives way to her. Mrs Lambert does what is for her the most difficult thing to do: she unlocks her husband's desk and reads his letters, to please Charlotte. The tailor and his wife are bullied and twisted into divulging family secrets. Charlotte gets into Lambert's study and steams open his business correspondence. She makes the tenant of the manor farmlands bankrupt so that Julia Duffy is bankrupt too; she hounds Julia Duffy into an asylum. When faced with the alternative of reading Lambert's letters or saving his wife's life by giving her the pill she needs, she lets the woman die. She hesitates about saving Francie's life when the horses are stampeding, 'Should she stumble and so not reach the gate in time? It was fascinatingly simple.' But society has no idea of this reality. She is so cunning that nobody sees what she is at, 'By sheer strength of will she could force her plan of action upon other people, as a conjurer forces a card, till they came to believe it was of their own choosing'. She appears as a good-natured, affable eccentric, who will take a drink, tell a story, and be relied upon to be amusing. She can talk on 'spiritualism, or books, or indeed any current topic, with point and agreeability'.

Her social inferiors know her bad temper, and Christopher begins to see reasons for his instinctive dislike of her. He is embarrased by her vulgarity when she tries to excuse Francie's lack of *savoir faire*, 'that poor girl, brought up from hand to mouth, and her little fortune that should have been spent on herself going, as I may say, to fill the stomachs of the Fitzpatricks' brood!' And by her want of reserve when she excuses Francie's behaviour, 'all my affection for the girl can't make me shut my eyes to what's unladylike or bad style, though I know it's not her fault'. He observes her insincerity as one moment she is seemingly flattened with grief at Mrs Lambert's death, and the next bartering shrewishly with the fishmonger. But he, like everyone else, is quite unaware of the depth of passion in her. 'There was an almost blatant simplicity about her, a humorous rough and readiness which, joined with her literary culture, proved business capacity, and dreaded temper, seemed to leave no room for any further aspect, least of all of a romantic kind.'

Charlotte has control over everything but her passion for Lambert. The picture of this ugly intelligent woman fated to bear the burden of unrequited love is given with a clarity which does not lack compassion. Jealousy is very much a part of her obsession. She is instinctively jealous of Francie. Even when the

old aunt is dying Charlotte cannot bear to hear her praise
Francie, ' "Good little thing!" she exclaimed, pushing the
brandy bottle noisily in among a crowd of glasses and medicine
bottles, "a strapping big woman of nineteen!" ' Once she
suspects Lambert's love for Francie she is jealous of Mrs
Lambert's complaisance and she *has* to destroy it, even though
doing so brings herself more suffering. She not only cannot
control her passion, but she loses control of herself when that
passion is most frustrated. When she believes Lambert is dead,
as his and Francie's bodies are dragged on to the boat, she
throws herself down on them with 'yell after yell of hysterical
lamentation'; everyone presumes her sorrow is for Francie. As
she tells Christopher about Lambert's professional deceit in
order to get her own back on Lambert for marrying Francie,
'She was losing hold of herself; her gestures were of the sort that
she usually reserved for her inferiors, and the corners of her
mouth bubbled like a snail. Christopher looked at her and
began to walk away.' She is beside herself with rage when she
cannot get Francie out of the way by marrying her off to
Christopher. At the height of her fury she is struck with Francie's
beauty, 'it brought with it a swarm of thoughts that buzzed and
stung in her soul like poisonous flies', and she comes near to
admitting the cause of her anger, 'I daresay . . . ye'll go
whimpering to Roddy Lambert, and asking him to make ye
Number Two, and to pay your debts and patch up your
character!' When Francie, without any real awareness retorts
that Charlotte may keep *him* to herself, only the timely
intervention of the cat stops Charlotte's fist from striking
Francie. It is a macabre touch emphasising the witch-like aspect
of Charlotte. The most awful outburst comes when she hears of
Lambert's marriage to Francie.

> 'Oh, my God Almighty'—she tried to laugh, but instead of
> laughter came tears as she saw herself helpless, and broken,
> and aimless for the rest of her life—'I won't break down—I
> won't break down—' she said, grinding her teeth together
> with the effort to repress her sobs. She staggered blindly to the
> sideboard, and, unlocking it, took out a bottle of brandy. She
> put the bottle to her mouth and took a long gulp from it, while
> the tears ran down her face.

She rips the letter to bits with her teeth, upturns furniture, and loses all reason, 'rage, and hatred, and thwarted passion took her in their fierce hands, and made her for the time a wild beast.' The grotesque episode is comic but it is also horrible, and utterly convincing.

The way in which Charlotte gets her revenge by breaking Lambert professionally and privately is an amazing study of the way in which evil is an integral part of ordinary life. She pushes Francie and Hawkins together again with almost good-natured joviality, pretending to Lambert that she is keeping an eye on his young wife while she actively breaks up his marriage. She praises Hawkins to Francie while she tells the young girl disagreeable facts about Lambert: 'He had been refused by such and such a girl; he had stuck so-and-so with a spavined horse; he had taken a drop too much at the hunt ball'. Whenever Hawkins comes (at Charlotte's invitation) to the Lamberts, 'Charlotte, that guardian of youth, that trusty and vigilant spy, sat in her own room writing interminable letters, or went on long and complicated shopping expeditions'. Charlotte behaves with real wickedness but the portrayal of it never steps outside the conventions of the realistic novel. There is nothing melodramatic about the prose style.

Lambert's obsession for Francie renders him as helpless as Francie and Charlotte though he is different from the women, lacking Francie's innocence and Charlotte's deviousness. He has loved her since she was a child; his marriage is one of convenience—he married his hypochondriac wife for her money. He has watched Francie grow up, seeing her when he can, and spending whatever money he can spare on presents and clothes for her. When he has spent his wife's money he steals from the Dysart estate to buy Francie things. He does not plot to get his own way, but he is an opportunist and without any sense of sin or guilt. He is class conscious, jealous of Christopher, proud of being superior to a solicitor's clerk. Envious of those drinking in the Kildare Street Club, and the St George's Yacht Club, he is miserably aware that the Royal Marine Hotel in Kingstown is his limit. He is an ambitious and a vulgar man, and even his passion for Francie is slightly comic in its excess. When he thinks she is drowning he is ready to die himself but he panics too much to be of any help; and when she has married him:

> He looked at her half wonderingly, she was so lovely in his eyes, and she was so incredibly his own; he felt a sudden insanity of tenderness for her that made his heart throb and his cheek redden, and would have ennobled him to the pitch of dying for her on the spot, had such an extravagance been demanded of him.

When his passion is thwarted however, he is as jealous as Charlotte. Their telling tales is paralleled—Lambert tries to turn Christopher off Francie by telling him some of her past; and so is the way in which they cannot do it without losing control. Both show Christopher aspects of themselves which they are usually careful to keep hidden. Lambert is as vulgar as Charlotte when he tells the disdainful Christopher, 'I can tell you I've known that girl since she was the length of my stick, and I never saw her that she wasn't up to some game or other; and she wasn't over particular about engagements or anything else!'

The relationship between Charlotte and Lambert is subtly explored. Throughout the novel she is acutely aware of his presence, his every look and gesture, and trying hard to restrain her natural desire to flirt with him. 'She turned her eyes towards him, and the provocative look in them came as instinctively and as straight as it ever did from Francie's, or as ever it has been projected from the curbed heart of woman.' He is well aware of her feelings for him, desperately in love with Francie and full of disgust for Charlotte. Both Charlotte and he are well aware of how much property means to each of them. Lambert knows only too well why the hard business woman, which Charlotte is, lends him money when there is little chance of any financial return. He knows the emotional reality which lies behind her phrase, 'a joint-stock business out of it' and he deliberately exploits it. The scene in which they plot to evict Julia Duffy is a marvellous portrayal of both of them, held in judgment by comedy which nevertheless lets the horribleness and the pathos of Charlotte show through. She speaks with 'a curious, guarded tenderness' and laughs nervously like a young girl as she tells him he will be able to keep as many horses as he likes at the manor so long as he leaves her the attics for her cats:

Lambert turned his head upon its cushion, and looked at her.

'I think I'll leave you a little more space than that Charlotte, if ever we stable our horses together.'

She glanced at him, as aware of the *double entendre*, and as stirred by it as he had intended her to be. Perhaps a little more than he had intended; at all events, he jerked himself into a sitting position, and, getting on to his feet, stretched himself with almost ostentatious ease.

'Where's Francie?' he asked, yawning.

'At home, dressmaking,' replied Miss Mullen. She was a little paler than usual. 'I think I'll go in now and have a cup of tea with Lucy,' she said, rising from the garden bench with something like an effort.

At the end of the book when Lambert and she face each other in the rat-ridden potato loft, both are reduced to wild beasts, spitting hatred and venom at each other. Both are victims of the grossest manifestations of love, and these have poisoned their lives. In this realistic novel there are no magical coincidences of Romantic Comedy to untie the knots of love. Charlotte has been doomed to misery from the start, love had come to her 'twisted to burlesque by the malign hand of fate'. Francie does achieve some insight but she is killed, and our last glimpse of her is the pathos of the hymn she remembers singing at the funeral of a Sunday School friend,

> Brief life is here our portion,
> Brief sorrow, short-lived care,
> The life that knows no ending,
> The tearless life is there.

Christopher too has developed, through learning first to love Francie and then to cope with unrequited love. He has moved from self-pity at the loss of an ideal to gratitude for an escape from it, and though he then falls into his customary self-denigration by seeing his ability to cope with suffering as an inadequacy at falling in love, he is still able to act with charity to Lambert—out of his love for Francie.

The Real Charlotte gives us a detailed picture of the Anglo-Irish community in Ireland at the end of the nineteenth century. It is a skilfully constructed novel, full of drama with great variety of scene, mood and character. But its ultimate value is in the way in which all these fuse to become a bright book of life, a serious book in which judgment is made through comedy. Like Jane Austen they focus on a small group of families who have to know each other and meet each other. Francie, like Emma, is often in a room with the man she wants to marry, the man who wants to marry her, and the man she is expected to marry. As with Jane Austen's novels there is depth of passion and emotional involvement that goes far beyond manners. But *The Real Charlotte* is closer to *Mansfield Park* than any other of Jane Austen's novels, and in the end it almost breaks the bounds of the comic convention. The tangled love affairs do not resolve themselves happily, and the authors make no attempt at tidying up the suffering. The fate of Francie, Charlotte and Lambert belongs more to tragedy than comedy.

But the comic vision is retained to the end, and the characters are seen with a steadiness which includes misery, guilt and the all but tragic. The characters here might indeed be 'attached to country pleasures' but none of them is to abide in affection and comfort. There is only the 'odious subjects' of guilt and misery at the end. But all is held in control by the masterly stroke of giving us Francie's death in the penultimate chapter, so that the last chapter works through the dramatic shared-secret device. We know that Francie is dead, Charlotte does not. Lambert is financially at his lowest; he has never needed Charlotte's money so much, and with Francie out of the way he would no doubt soon overcome his distaste for Charlotte, as he had when a youth and in need of money. She would pay his debts and he could have Gurthnamuckla and keep his horses. Charlotte is still a victim of her love for him. She is doing a workman's job in the filthy loft, but as soon as he is in sight she becomes like any other woman. 'It is a fact so improbable as to be worth noting, that before Lambert found his way up the ladder, Miss Mullen had unpinned her skirt and fastened up the end of a plait that had escaped from the massive coils at the back of her head.' She has plotted and manoeuvred with great cunning and now her end is—all unknown to her—in sight. But at the last she loses him, and through her own stupidity. She lets 'the gratification of her temper' have its way. She cannot resist turning the knife in the wound, and hurting him to the utmost, so she tells him it is she who has exposed his crimes to Christopher. Her passion for revenge overcomes everything else in the end. There is no need for narrative comment, the sharp irony says it all and lifts the novel above the pathos of Francie's death.

Chapter V

The Silver Fox—The Irish R.M. and His Experiences —Dan Russel the Fox

The Silver Fox was written for serialisation, and plot and characters are extremely simple. It is similar to Thomas Hardy's *Mayor of Casterbridge* in so far as it is a study of an old way of life which is being destroyed by modern civilisation and its new values.

> The ring of the trowel travelled far on the wind across the heather, a voice of civilisation, saying pertinent, unhesitating things to a country where all was loose, and limitless, and inexact. Up here, by the shores of Lough Turc, people had, from all ages, told the time by the sun, and half-an-hour either way made no difference to anyone; now—most wondrous of all impossibilities—the winter sunrise was daily heralded by the steely shriek of an engine whirling truck-loads of men to their work across the dark and dumb bog-lands.[1]

The book also attempts to assess the nature of the Anglo-Irish race, by comparing it with the English and the Irish races. The story unites the two themes: the English come bringing their more advanced techniques into the Irish way of life. The catalyst by which we know the racial reactions is a silver fox. The point of view is that of an omniscient narrator who is usually quite detached, but at times descends into scornful generalisations. The scales are always weighted against the English characters: 'With Mr Glasgow, as with most of his countrymen, smartness came next to cleanliness and considerably in advance of godliness.' This rather clumsy scorn was probably a reaction to a review of *The Real Charlotte*. Edith Somerville has said that *The Silver Fox* was inspired by T. P. O'Connor's remarks on the earlier novel, and she quotes his words, 'hard and pitiless censors, as well as sardonic, squalid, and merciless observers of Irish life', commenting: 'We felt this to be so uplifting that we lost no time in laying the foundations of a further "ferocious narrative".'[2] But in the same review O'Connor condemned them for caricaturing Irish people:

> Not a gleam of their kindness, tenderness, and loyalty; and it is only class prejudice which could induce such a picture of the Irish servant . . . It is not accident that, while every Irishman and Irishwoman in the story is fiercely exposed, the few English characters have nearly all the virtues . . . I regard it as one of the vulgarist traits in the character of the 'Shoneens', that, while they have so microscopic an eye for the faults of their own land and their own people, they can see nothing but virtue and excellence in any person with English blood.[3]

Wrong as his comments are—Hawkins and Miss Hope-Drummond are 'exposed' as much as any character—they must have rankled. In *The Silver Fox*, Lady Susan and the Glasgows are faulted much more than any of the others. Glasgow is more of a bounder than Hawkins, eager to have an affair with the virginal Slaney and then quick to forget all about her in the excitement of an affair with the married Lady Susan, 'He remembered only as a transient caprice the moment, unforgettable for her, that had given her life its first touch of passion'. With Mrs Glasgow the narrative poise is lost and she comes over as the stock loose woman of melodrama: 'Her hair was straw-coloured, and drooped in nauseous picturesqueness over her coal-black eyebrows; her face was fat and white, her dress was a highly-coloured effort at the extreme of the latest fashion but one; the general effect was elderly.'

Characters are of two kinds: minor ones who partake in the story, and major ones who are necessary for the themes as well. The minor ones are almost entirely comic and are given in neat sketches; they are static and judged as they are made. Three humorous sentences tell us all there is to know about Slaney's uncle. 'The Honourable Charles Herrick was an elderly and prosperous bachelor, whose blameless life was devoted to two pursuits, gardening and writing controversial letters to the Church papers. He was a small, dry gentleman, very clean, and not in the least deaf. Strangers always experienced a slight shock in finding that he was not a clergyman.' We laugh at his attempt to convert the pantry boy to Protestantism, and at his complaints about the Canon's papish practice of turning to the east for the Creed. Major Bunbury is to marry the heroine but he is given the same comic treatment. His solid masculinity is gently made fun of when he reads the newspaper as if he were serving his country, 'No woman can hope to read *The Times* as though it were a profession; it is a masculine gift, akin to that of dining'. And his capacity for romantic love is held in check by the comic tone. He looks at Slaney and the narrator comments, 'Major Bunbury felt that his special sister (who read Carlyle and played Scarlatti) would like to meet her. Although he hunted six days a week, he kept a soul somewhere, and his sister knew where it was.' The two major characters are women whose roles are to carry the themes of the two ways of life, and the two races: Lady Susan is English and modern, Slaney is Anglo-Irish and traditional. The Irish point of view is given by a third woman, Maria Quin. The barriers between them are not too simple: Lady Susan and Maria share an abandonment which Slaney's quietness and reserved manner spare her from. Lady Susan ignores everyone else in the hotel dining room by taking the best position at the fire and doing her hair in the looking glass; when she has eaten all she wants she flings her napkin at her husband's head, and snatches Major Bunbury's plate from him—regardless of the fact that he is still eating—and gives it to the cat. This sort of behaviour is as foreign to Slaney as is Maria Quin's when she ignores the roomful of people, and throws herself across the table in convulsions of grief when they come to nail down her father's coffin.

The contrast between the traditional values and the modern ones is made mainly through the characters of Slaney and Lady Susan. The English woman wears too much makeup, dyes her hair red, drinks too much, smokes too often, and laughs too loud. She is shrill and arrogant and pretends to be even more so. She poses as an emancipated woman and a frivolous one, hence all her talk about disliking poetry, and her professed ability to play cards for hours on end. At all costs she will be fashionable. Beside Lady Susan, Slaney is dowdy and dull. She cannot ice-skate or ride a bicycle; she plays the piano instead of strumming on a mandolin. Given the choice she will spend a free afternoon reading Swinburne's *Atalanta in Calydon*. She says her prayers every night. At the start of the story the one is trivial and superficial, the other solemn and idealistic; both are modified by events. Slaney develops from the 'guileless egotist' who is incapable of seeing through Glasgow, into the young woman who loves and marries the very ordinary Major Bunbury. Lady Susan learns to love and respect her husband. Lady Susan and the new railway both threaten to undermine the traditional values of the Irish community. Her casual affair with Glasgow, and the way in which the railway destroys the fairy hill are of a piece. Neither belong in the Irish country side: when she is flirting with Glasgow in the new railway station the simple description is telling: 'Behind her the empty window framed gaunt mountain peak, a lake that frittered a myriad sparkles from its wealth of restless silver, and the grey and faint purple of the naked wood beyond it. It seemed too great a background for her powdered cheek and her upward glances at her host.' When the crucial accident occurs on the railway the blow is struck simultaneously for Lady Susan and the railway. The truck crashes and her escape with Glasgow is stopped.

The analysis of racial characteristics is made primarily by the ways the characters react to the possibility of the supernatural, or at least to the possibility that a view of life which excludes the mysterious is severely limited. The Irish reaction to the rumour of the silver fox is explicit—they are terrified. In Irish folklore the silver fox is a witch or fairy, and his appearance at the time in which the railway is disturbing a fairy hill is doubly portentous. He is united with the prophecy of trouble if Cahirdeen hill is thrown into the bog of Tully. Two Irish men die haunted to death by the silver fox, and consumed with guilt for their part in touching the hill. The young man is simple, 'he was always innocent like, and when he was a child not a word out of him the longest year ever came only talkin' of God and the fairies, and the like o'that'. But the old man is not, and his reaction to the fox is thoroughly credible, his wife describes his agony in her own words which add to the credibility: he 'felt like a wind from the say coming bechuxt his skin and his blood afther he seeing the same fox'. The reaction of the whole Irish community is unanimous, 'Bether for him not to be intherfarin' with the likes o'that place'. When Maria Quin meets the fox she does not stop to wonder about its reality, instead she automatically falls on her knees and prays. The English response is quite different. Glasgow is a rational man and simply denies that there is anything outside the control of man. Lady Susan thinks the whole business about the fox 'Such rot!' The Anglo-Irish do not laugh at the fox story; Hugh, Lady Susan's husband, not only comes face to face with the animal but he sees Danny Quin's ghost reliving his death. Slaney respects the beliefs of the country people; she is as open to the psychic as Hugh but like Maria Quin she is still able to pray. One night she is bothered when saying her prayers by Lady Susan's carrying on with Glasgow while Hugh is away:

> She remained for a long time on her knees, with a blank, spent mind, soothed in some dull way by the suggestions of her attitude, till a slight sound on the terrace, under her open window, made her lift her head and listen.
>
> The sound came and went, and Slaney was roused to put aside the curtains and look down. There was nothing to be seen but the fog that had risen out of the sea and settled on the land, with frost and moonlight blended in its whiteness; all the world seemed arrested and tranced, all the air charged with its cold and mysterious presence.

The next moment the Quins' collie slips by on the trail of the fox.

The differences in attitude to the supernatural are made to relate to the whole moral consciousness of the characters. It is made to seem better to believe. Glasgow's failure as a man—so that he will think nothing of adultery for example—and his failure as a business man, both stem from his belief that reason is supreme. The Irishmen cannot be treated as rational facts so Glasgow's economic calculations are wrong and he is made bankrupt. Lady Susan's failure as Hugh's wife, and her complete lack of sympathy, are a part of the obtuseness which makes her blind to the druids' stones and so almost cause her death and Hugh's. The standing stones which tell the Irish and Anglo-Irish of a huge cleft in the rocks say nothing to the English. Maria Quin tells Lady Susan scornfully, 'While ye live ye'll mind yerself whin ye see thim. I thought everyone in the counthry knew this place. But sure what are you but a sthranger!' The authors' belief in the sensitivity of the Celtic people to the other world, compared with the opacity of the Saxon race, does lead them to oversimplification.

Where it is a question of contrasting the Irish and English nations the dice is rather heavily loaded by showing us the English race through the eyes of the romanticised Slaney. In the early chapters the ice-skating on the Thames and the champagne luncheon is contrasted with the Irish wake. In the dialogue the Irish are far superior, Lady Susan's strident soprano and shrill silliness have none of the vigour of the peasants. When Danny Quin is said to have 'sustained fatal injuries' the response is, ' "Arrah, what fatal injuries?" returned the old woman with scorn; "no, but to break his neck was what he done. Didn't he walk out over the brink o' the big sand-pit in Cashel the same as one that wouldn't have the sight, an' he a fine soople man no more than seventy years?" ' The judgment on this whiskey-sodden group is undermined because it is made by Glasgow, ' "What swine they are," he thought,' with whom we hate to agree. Whereas we *are* tempted into agreeing with the sensitive and refined Slaney that the English scream 'inanities to each other', and that their talk is 'either babyish or vulgar', and they themselves 'over-dressed and artificial'. When the Quin boy commits suicide Glasgow and Slaney are brought together and once again there is no doubt where our sympathies are directed:

> 'It would be simpler if you said at once that honest or sane people had better give up having any dealings with the Irish,' he returned hotly.
> 'Do you mean English people? They certainly have not been eminently successful so far.'

There is a more balanced picture of the two nations when Slaney is not involved. The scene for example between Lady Susan and Maria Quin, where the former is grieving for the death of her horse, and the Irish girl has absolutely no understanding of her sorrow:

> Maria Quin looked at Lady Susan with eyes that were as dry as glass. The Irish peasant regards the sorrow for a mere animal as a childishness that is almost sinful, a tempting of ill-fate in its parody of the grief rightly due only to what is described as 'a Christian'; and Maria's heart glowed with the unwept wrongs of her brother . . .
>
> 'Little ye cried yestherday whin ye seen my brother thrown out on the ground by the pool,' said Maria, with irrepressible savageness, 'you that's breakin' yer heart afther yer horse.'

The Anglo-Irish are seen to have the best characteristics of both races, but so far as education and civilisation are concerned, they are closer to the English. Slaney's marriage to Major Bunbury carries this point. It is inconceivable that she should marry an ordinary Irishman. From the Irish people's point of view they belong together too. When Maria Quin is angered by the hunt riding through their yard, while her brother's corpse is there she makes no distinction between the riders. She is 'maddened by their brutal self-engrossment, their cheery and inconsequent voices', and Hugh himself despite all his visionary capacities is the M.F.H.

There are too many themes in the story and the attempt to make Slaney develop from 'the guileless egoist' to a young woman 'with a new and strong understanding of herself' is too ambitious for the length of the tale. We are told that her knowledge of her happiness with Major Bunbury came 'with all the tenderness and strong romance that were hidden in her nature, with all the comprehension of herself that had grown out of bitter experience'. But we have to take it on trust, we do not see the self-knowledge nor the suffering. We do see a change in Lady Susan, the potentially passionate character. She learns to love her husband and to show solicitude and affection, and to recognise that there might after all be something in 'bad luck, and everything'.

The movement of the whole is different from any of their previous works in so far as it moves from the ill-fated gloom of desolate Co. Galway into the light and sweetness of a happy ending. There is harmony and peace at the end, at the polo-ground in Phoenix Park:

> The afternoon was more balmy sweet as the shadows lengthened and the coolness came; beyond the beautiful miles of grass and trees the western sky was gathering the warmth of sunset; opposite in the east, the brown smoke of Dublin stained the tranquil heaven, and above it a ghostly half-moon stood like a little white cloud in the depths of blue.

The Silver Fox was followed with *Some Experiences of an Irish R.M.* This collection of stories along with *Further Experiences of an Irish R.M.* and *In Mr Knox's Country* make up the collected edition, the volume *The Irish R.M. and His Experiences*, which I shall deal with here. All of the stories were first published in magazines, and were written specifically to amuse an English middle-class public, a group of people confident of their knowledge of correct behaviour and their right to set the tone of society. The Anglo-Irish society, which is the subject of many of the stories, shared some of the social attributes of the reading public's own society. But outside of these common social norms were the native Irish who did not belong to the polite society. The stories are written to amuse, and they are strictly within the form of comedy. They do at times verge on the grotesque, but there is no concern with the inward and passionate, no attempt to deal with profound feelings which go beyond manners. So that although they are dealing with nineteenth-century Irish society, the stories are quite different from the novels; and being simply comedy of manners, they are in their limited way more perfect forms of fiction than the novels. Romance is kept to a minimum and though the protagonist needs his post of Resident Magistrate and his house because he has just got engaged to be married, his relationship with his fiancée, Philippa, is never explored on an emotional level. Sally Knox and Flurry Knox run a rugged path before they are married and several of the stories deal with their difficulties, but the traditional parental opposition is merely a cause of sportive hoodwinking and one-upmanship on the part of Flurry. They wrote with their readers in mind and Edith's soldier brother's tastes were respected in the matter of romance. She writes to warn him of 'the fatal taint of love-making' in one story, and tells him to avoid 'Oh Love! Oh Fire!' altogether. 'If you only knew it, the Bad Mag people wanted whole slushes of affection, but we denied it to them, in order to gratify the tastes of horny little things like you. Now however we are going to loose a love episode at the public, so you had better sit tight and keep your September shilling in your pocket.' However the story is one of intrigue and outrageous incidents without a touch of the emotional or passionate.

The main social issues of the time are not entirely ignored; 'The Finger of Mrs Knox' is concerned with a small farmer who gets into the clutches of a gombeen man, and who comes to Mrs Knox, his one-time landlady, to help bail him out. Mrs Knox tells him sharply, 'the Government is your landlord now, and I wish you joy of each other!' But her bitterness is towards the government not her ex-tenants—'When those rascals in Parliament took our land from us, we thought we should have some peace, now we're both beggared and bothered!' and she helps Casey out. There is no mincing matters in the picture given of the Ireland of the middle-man:

> The hill-sides were set thick with tree stumps, like the crowded headstones of a cemetery, with coarse grass and briars filling the spaces between them. Here and there slender, orphaned ash sapling, spared because despised, stood among the havoc, and showed with its handful of yellow leaves what the autumn colours might once have been here. A starkly new, cemented public-house, with 'J. Goggin' on the name board, stood at the fork of the roads. Doubtless into it had flowed the blood-money of the wood; it represented the alternative offered to the community by Mr Goggin . . .
>
> Mrs Knox was staring through her spectacles at the devastated hill-side . . .
>
> 'Well, Goggin,' said Mrs Knox, waving towards the hill-side a tiny hand in a mouldy old black kid glove, 'you've done a great deal of work here! You've destroyed in six months what it took the Colonel and the Lord Almighty eighty years to make'.[4]

The outcome is happy for Casey; the issue depends on personal relationships and the poor gombeen man is no match for Mrs Knox's authority, wit and devastating nerve. The Irish Literary Revival is dealt with in the characters of the R.M.'s English wife and her step-brother, and it is dealt with satirically. She is mocked for thinking herself a pillar of the revival because she takes Irish lessons from the National schoolteacher. Maxwell Bruce, a collector of dialect and folklore, is laughed at for confusing the Gaelic of ancient Ireland with the speech of the peasants of his day, and for his romanticisation of those peasants. When he goes to a cottage he apostrophises the woman 'O worthy woman of the cows!' and follows it up with a lengthy blessing dating from the times of Cuchulain. When Flurry Knox leaves Ireland, between the first and second collection of stories, we are told that he has gone with the Irish Yeomanry to the Boer War, but really the stories are timeless, and not concerned to represent social fact.

The setting of the stories is that of the novels, the Big Houses of Anglo-Ireland in all their discomfort and shabbiness. But the houses are merely causes of laughter and no longer reflect the characters of the inhabitants. Shreelane, the Irish R.M.'s house, is eternally draughty, damp, full of rats and with smokey chimneys, and he can no more impose order and tidiness on it than he can impose them on the Irish people. After two years in residence rat holes are still being nailed up with lids of biscuit tins. Dirt and decay no longer signify moral slackness but the carefreeness and wildness of that charming country beyond the pale.

The form of the short story provides a sharp discipline; the overall idea of making the stories one person's reminiscences unites the stories, as well as giving us the comfortable feeling of knowing the narrator, and the community. The consistent point of view gives unity of tone and mood, and an overall harmony. As with most reminiscences, we know as much about the narrator as we do about the objects of his memories. The narrator is an admirable choice; he is by nature an observer and a critic of life, with an ironical detachment that assesses everyone unemotionally. He comments wryly on his elder son: 'Andrew was still in the condition of Being Good (a condition, nevertheless, by no means to be relied on, and quite distinct from Goodness)'. He is equally urbane and uninvolved when he talks about his wife: 'I have seen her cry when a police officer won a bicycle race at Skebawn; she has wept at hearing Sir Valentine Knox's health drunk with musical honours at a tenants' dinner. It is an amiable custom but, as she herself admits, it is unbecoming.' This objectivity, combined with a remarkable gift of fluency, wins the reader's confidence. We hardly doubt the narrator's judgments and usually admire his perception; his assessment of Flurry Knox at once becomes ours: 'In dealings with Flurry Knox the possibility that he might be speaking the truth could never safely be lost sight of. It was also well to remember that he generally knew what the truth was.' The narrator has few ideas and is far from being a modern intellectual; he is well read and well able to cap Mrs Knox's classical quotations. His lack of introspection and psychological subtleties makes the stories so refreshing. He is a man with little private existence that he wants to talk of, and when he does express some inward state it is always in an amusing manner. He declares his nervousness as he waits to make an after-dinner speech thus, 'through much and varied conversation I strove, like a nervous mother who cannot trust her offspring out of her sight, to keep before my mind's eye the opening sentences that I had composed in the train'.

Morally he embodies the ideal perfect gentleman of public school England; he is honest, upright and straight, his steady steps guided by an innate sense of duty and justice. Much of the comedy comes from the incongruous situations which he is found in, usually having been put there by the wild Anglo-Irish. He is found house-breaking, poaching and horse stealing; he is discovered by the police in a shebeen full of illicit poteen, sitting clutching an empty glass and wearing the best blue suit of a one-legged man. He is always innocent and usually it is Flurry Knox who has hood-winked him into these situations. His crimes are slight, but they are specifically aimed at a disruption of the very social law and order which it is his job to preserve. Many of the court sessions and incidents are based on things which actually happened, but they are never serious enough to make seeing them with a sense of the ridiculous, offensive. The disorder is usually kept within the limits of crime which we can see the funny side of, similar to the way in which the evil in *The Importance of Being Earnest* is limited to schoolboy greed and selfishness with the battles fought over muffins and cucumber sandwiches. So the setting and the narrator are ideally suited to comedy of manners. His ability to observe with ironical detachment this closely-knit polite society and the wild extravagances which exist just outside it and often intrude into it, is a felicitous point of view for such a genre.

The patterns of the stories are very much of a kind: after an easy start a situation is brought about (by the typical action of an established character or by the action of a new character) which leads to a series of events, each one inevitably leading on to the next and rising to a climax of disaster. The nature of the disasters varies of course, but usually we are taken by surprise and the unexpected is always made to seem inevitable. Typical is 'The House of Fahy', where the series of events is triggered off by Bernard Shute's hiring a yacht in Queenstown and insisting that the others accompany him on a cruise. The first disaster is that Maria, the incorrigibly greedy gundog, escapes from Shreelane and forces herself on the yacht. The narrator who detests the sea comments with the mock resignation of a Greek epic, 'Thus was Maria installed on board the *Eileen Oge*, and the element of fatality had already begun to work.' They are shipwrecked. The series of incidents that follows is a terrifying one; these eminently respectable, law-abiding citizens find themselves caught up in vandalism, destroying private property, and finally, an invaluable cockatoo, the priceless pet of the house which they invade, is killed by Maria. The narrator finds himself at dawn disturbing the flower bed of stocks as he digs a hole to bury the bird. They creep away from the scene of chaos as the owner awakes. As they near the yacht the narrator and Bernard Shute agree that at all costs the fate of the bird must be kept hidden from the ladies of their party, 'At this juncture Maria overtook us with the cockatoo in her mouth.'

The beginnings of the stories are calm and leisurely, there is such a reasonable quietness and almost inconsequential ramblings that the sudden speed with which things happen comes as a surprise. Each time we are deceived by the complacency of the narrator's voice. The endings are, by contrast, sharp, sudden, intensely to the point and rich with meaning. Two fine examples are 'The Man That Came to Buy Apples' and 'The Pug-Nosed Fox'. In the first of these tales there is the usual casual opening, it is a freezing winter's night, a shoot is planned at Aussolas the next day. The morning finds the narrator with Mrs Knox who asks if he would like Irish stew or curry for lunch. The man comes to buy apples and the series of outrages begins that ends with a crashing dénouement where all is unravelled in a chase, a fall and the discovery of Mrs Knox's dead rabbits. The finale is superb as to top it all the greedy Maria appears to go berserk:

> Twice she flung herself by the roadside and rolled, driving her snout into the ground like the coulter of a plough. Her eyes were starting from her head, her tail was tucked between her legs. She bit, and tore frantically with her claws at the solid ice of a puddle.
>
> 'She's mad! She's gone mad!' exclaimed Philippa, snatching up as a weapon something that looked like a frying-pan, but was, I believe, the step of the phaeton.
>
> Maria was by this time near enough for me to discern a canary-coloured substance masking her muzzle.
>
> 'Yes, she's quite mad,' I replied, possessed by a spirit of divination. 'She's been eating the rabbit curry!'

In 'The Pug-Nosed Fox' the ending similarly caps the crisis and reverberates back through the rest of the story. The opening is desultory and ambling, then events quicken, disasters lead to more disaster until at the climax the hounds are discovered eating a wedding breakfast while the family are at church. The narrator, now responsible for the pack, finds to his absolute horror that they are ensconced on the table crunching cold chicken, lapping up bowls of spilt cream, 'President, the patriarch of the pack, was apparently seated on the wedding-cake, while he demolished a cold salmon.' At this point the bride and bridegroom and guests arrive home. The story ends with a quotation of a paragraph from the local newspaper. There is no need for comment. The discomfort of wearing full hunting gear on a baking August day for a photograph of the hounds, the ensuing chase, the practical joke on the inebriated best man of sewing him up in his evening clothes and then stuffing him in a feather bed and sewing that up; the destruction of the magnificent feast by the hounds, are all as nothing. For the narrator the earlier catastrophes dimmed beside the enormity of the wickedness of the hounds, and for the retired coal merchant's family, the McRorys, that is forgiveable provided that the world knows that the Resident Magistrate, Master of Foxhounds, went to their wedding.

After the ceremony a reception was held at Temple Braney House, where a sumptuous collation had been provided by the hospitable Mr and Mrs McRory. The health of the Happy Pair having been drunk, that of the Bridesmaids was proposed, and Mr T. Flood, who had been prevented by a slight indisposition from filling the office of Best Man was happily sufficiently recovered to return thanks for them in his usual sprightly vein. Major Sinclair Yeates, R.M.,M.F.H., who, in honour of the festive occasion had donned sporting attire, proposed the health of the Bride's Mother in felicitous terms.

The language of the stories is ideal for the comedy of manners; it is full of life and gaiety and delightfully mannered though at the same time it has all the seeming spontaneity of good literature. The educated, ironical character of the narrator makes a wide range of styles possible; and his sense of humour and detachment makes a kind of mock literary style verging at times on the mock heroic plausible. He can laughingly use outrageous imagery, such as when he describes the transition from a road to a boreen as he cycles along, 'my bicycle was transformed from a swallow to an opinionated and semi-paralysed wheelbarrow'. He describes a smooth start to a hunt where everything is blissfully easy as 'we went, for the first twenty minutes or so, as on rubber tyres, through bland dairy farms wherein the sweet influence of the dairycow had induced gaps in every fence, and gates into every road.' Such conscious use of metaphor is all part of the fun. When he takes Flurry Knox by surprise, Flurry's dislike of being found out and determination not to give anything else away is captured in an amazing image: ' "Well, that might be, too," assented Flurry, regarding me with an eye that was like a stone wall with broken glass on the top.' Nature is important for the mood of the stories but the treatment of it is quite different from the novels; the language is condensed, the images sharp and vigorous. A winter landscape, 'the fields lay rigid in the constraining cold; the trees were as dead as the telegraph poles, and the whistle of the train came thin and ghostly, across four miles of silent country.' And the feel of a new day in early summer is there in an image that might almost be called metaphysical, 'It was a gleaming morning in mid-May, when everything was young and tense and thin and fit to run for its life, like a Derby horse.'

Words are used with care and precision; nothing is super-fluous, and the descriptions of characters are brief and perti-nent, with small touches of observation that tell so much. The superior, arrogant side of the narrator, and the tastelessness of the farmers' women are both evident in three well chosen adjectives: 'The farmers, from regions unknown to me, had abundantly risen to the occasion; so also had their wives and daughters; and fashionable ladies, with comfortable brogues and a vigorous taste in scent, closed us in on every side.' Descriptions of animals are controlled and sensible, completely lacking in the sentimentality and absurd humanising of pets of so many writers. Maria is there with all her greediness, her boldness, and her knowingness; sometimes in the simplest prose, 'When she laid her brown snout upon my knee, and rolled her blackguard amber eyes upon me, and smote me with her feathered paw, it was impossible to remember iniquities against her.' When imagery is used, even the personification is within the bounds of dogginess. Maria makes up to visitors until, flattered by her attention, they feed her titbits, 'and Maria, with a furtive eye upon her owners, would softly draw the guest's third piece of cake into the brown velvet bag that she called her mouth.'

The main tone of the stories is comic, ranging from the farce of shutting a pack of hounds up in the bedroom of a drunken man—so that he thinks he has gone mad and is seeing things—to comedy of manners. But there are many other moods within the comic vision. In 'The Waters of Strife' there is the sombre ending where a man, haunted by the ghost of a man he has killed, shoots himself; in 'Harrington' there is another ghost and the near death of the narrator's son; and in 'The Whiteboys' there is the pathos of an old man who gives away hounds which have been in his family for over a hundred years, because he has no heir worthy of them. These stories, particularly the last, with the moving touch of having the old man send out his battered old hunting horn as a luck-penny, strike other chords. Often the laughter is a little uneasy, and there is usually a great sense of relief at the end of a story, because it might so easily have ended otherwise. Events usually teeter on the edge of complete disaster and this gives a nervous tension to the stories. The marriage between Sally and Flurry is made by the skin of their teeth. The awful situation the narrator gets into over Trinket's colt is saved simply by Mrs Knox's unexpected sense of humour; the event looks to her so much like something out of *She Stoops to Conquer*, that she bursts into 'wild cackles of laughter' and forgives them, 'Upon my conscience, Tony, I'd give a guinea to have thought of it myself!' As it is, even when the final outcome of the stories is not disastrous there are plenty of awful things happening before the end. And many of the stories contain violence and ugliness. When the narrator asks if the new hounds have settled in, he is told, 'They weren't in the kennels three days before they had Rampant ate, and nothing only his paws left before me in the morning!' That day the hounds 'hunted with blood-thirsty intentions and entirely after their own devices. Their first achievement was to run the earth-stopper's dog, and having killed him, to eat him.' There are many moments of sheer disgust such as when the dead donkey is cut up into joints and spread out in the dining room table ready for breakfast; and the scene of the people at the wreck drinking themselves paralytic on the rum that is washed ashore. They gulp it down out of their hands, hats, boots and filthy rusty buckets. But even this is contained within the comic vision, although the judgment is made too, 'Near the public-house I stumbled over something that was soft and had a squeak in it; it was the piper, with his head and shoulders in an overturned rum barrel, and the bagpipes still under his arm.' One can sympathise with one of their contemporary reviewers who said, 'The realism of the pictures is now and then appalling . . . the total absence of "sweetness and light" cannot be made up for by the undeniably liberal allowance of vivacity and coarse humour.'

But most criticism of the stories has been the old cry of 'stage Irishman', that by showing us the Irish people through the eyes of an Ascendancy narrator the Irish nation is reduced to a race of Handy Andys. This criticism misunderstands both the nature of the comedy of manners and the range of the stories. Most of the humour deflects on to the narrator himself; he is usually at the mercy of the indomitable Flurry Knox, and the butt of Flurry's jokes. And he is by no means spared from judgment himself. In 'Sharper Than A Ferret's Tooth' he and his friends are the ones guilty of bad manners and of a failure of response on a personal level which is unforgiveable. The McRorys rescue them from their sinking boat and give them the very best of their hospitality—shelter, hot water, changes of clothes and food, and all the narrator and friends can do is sneer at their hosts. The changes of clothes are 'gorgeous garments' that are 'flung before us with a generous *abandon* worthy of Sir Walter Raleigh'. He mocks the newness and smartness of the clothes he puts on, 'I . . . found myself immaculately clothed in what is, I believe, known to tailors as "a Lounge Suit", though not for untold gold would I have lounged, or by any carelessness endangered the perfection of the creases of its dark grey trousers.' And Philippa is as bad, whispering to him that 'We had the choice of about eighty silk blouses.' They find the food as common as the clothes, 'a mountainous dish of trifle, in whose veins ran honey, instead of jam, and to whose enlivenment a bottle at least of whisky had been dedicated'. And, worst of all, he mocks the shyness of Mr McRory, 'He maintained an unbroken silence throughout the meal, but whistled jigs secretly through his teeth, a method of keeping up his courage of which I believe he was quite unconscious.' Our narrator determinedly refuses to talk to any of the family after lunch. Instead he sits in the hall, 'turning over the pages of a dreary comic paper, uncertain what to do, but determined on one point, that neither principalities nor powers should force me into the drawing room . . . At times I was aware of the silent and respectful surveillance of Mr McRory in the

inner hall, but I thought it best for us both to feign unconscious-
ness of his presence.' He is a snob and he is far from always at his
ease. Our laughter, in this story, contains sharp judgment of
him.

When we laugh at the other characters we are laughing at the
Anglo-Irish far more than at the other Irish. Flurry and his
family cover the whole social range of Irish Protestants. Lady
Knox, the pinnacle of the family, and of the community, resides
with her characterless husband, Sir Valentine, in splendid order
and draught-proof windows and surrounded by silent servants,
but she unfortunately has a short, square figure and a red face
which remind everyone of a coachman. The few English
characters present are also objects of mirth. The Honourable
Basil Leigh Kelway, the earnest young radical who comes
armed with notebook and pen to collect statistics on the Liquor
Question in Ireland, is made a proper hare of in the well-known
'Lisheen Races, Second-Hand'. While the English *nouveau riche*,
Mr William Tebbutts, murders the English language, under-
estimates Mrs Knox and is easily got rid of by Flurry.

Class is used as a means of placing characters, it is a part of
their make-up, but this does not mean that the class itself is being
laughed at, nor that the characters lack individuality. The short
story form necessitates sharp, brief character studies without the
leisurely psychology of the novel. Mrs Knox is typical of a class
but she is also strongly individual (though indeed her individuality is itself a strong trait of her class!). She is eccentric in
appearance and manner. Her purple velvet bonnet she is
reputed to have worn for fifty years, her layers of old shawls are
held on her with a beautiful and priceless diamond brooch. For
dinner she merely changes the shawls, and to go out she adds a
couple more shawls. When the hunt takes her by surprise one
morning as she is in the middle of reading prayers, she abandons
the worship, dons boots and a fur cape on top of her dressing
gown and follows the hunt. Her charm lies in her utter disregard
of the opinion of the world, and her complete absence of interest
in the material, economic value of things. The dining-room in
her castle is reputed to have been a stable for Cromwell's horse
and it looks as if it has not been cleaned since, pigeons flying in
and perching on the window frames. Meals are in harmony with

the rest of her life style: she is too busy quoting Virgil to notice if anyone has any cutlery; dish-wash soup is served in a solid silver tureen, a whole fresh salmon comes on a cracked and chipped kitchen dish, gut-rot sherry is poured into invaluable cut-glass. Her character and way of life cocks a snook at all middle-class values.

The prosperous Catholic middle classes are represented by two families, the retired coal merchants, the McRorys; and the Flynns who are wealthy farmers. The McRorys' values are the opposite of the Knoxes'; they care primarily about what people will think of them and about the material value of things. Their aim is to rise in society and to ingratiate themselves with the Ascendancy. Their manners ape the Anglo-Irish when they can; their friend Tomsy Flood remarks, 'They take the English *Times*, if you please, and they all dress for dinner—every night I tell ye! I call that rot y' know!' They are acquisitive and gay, their silk blouses and brocade and velvet skirts showing up gaudily beside the drab tweeds of the Ascendancy. They attend the Protestant church bazaars and buy their way with aplomb, and endear themselves by buying a whole row of seats for the local concert. They are social assets too; their many accomplishments—dancing, tennis, golf, shooting—make them extremely acceptable at social gatherings, and the younger generation of Anglo-Irish like the McRorys only too well. It is only the parents who find the McRory girls' eyelashes too long, and hair too curly; the boys too are handsome enough to overcome the disadvantage of not being in the *Irish Landed Gentry*. Mr Flynn is a District Councillor, strong farmer and cattle dealer. His daughters are so grand that reputation has it that they never leave the house except to go to Paris. Like the McRorys their innumerable articles of clothing are legendary; their morning attire is suggestive of a garden party or theatre, with necklaces, bracelets and elaborate hairstyles. Miss Lynie Flynn drinks her tea with an elegantly curved little finger. The daughters speak in almost unimpeachable English accents, and their conversation consists mainly of downgrading Ireland by comparing her with London or Paris. The father, Jeremiah, has not their airs and graces, and he comforts one of his daughters whose girlfriend is being unfriendly, by saying the woman is little loss, 'She's like a cow that gives a good pail o'milk and spoils all by putting her leg in it.'

The Irish tenants are not main characters; they form a background vigorous and colourful or sombre and dark, whichever the mood demands. The comedy of manners has sharply defined borders and much play is made of the blatant contrast between classes. In 'The Waters of Strife', the contrast makes us laugh at the narrator, who goes to a local football club's regatta on a lake, expecting to see familiar scenes of Oxford days—gay parasols and white clad youths elegantly skimming through the water. He finds 'The Sons of Liberty' in boats of every conceivable shape and size, while the club's brass band, 'stimulated by the presence of a barrel of porter on the box-seat, belches forth "The Boys of Wexford"'. But within the class the characters are still highly individualised, no matter how short their appearance. The sturdy servant of Mrs Knox is there only a moment but the appearance is memorable:

> A being stood in a dark corner under the gallery of the hall at Aussolas Castle; a being who had arrived noiselessly on bare feet, and now revealed its presence by hard breathing.
>
> 'Come in, Mary,' commanded old Mrs Knox without turning her head; 'make up the fire.'
>
> 'I will, ma'am,' murmured the being, advancing with an apologetic eye upon me, and an undulating gait suggestive of a succession of incipient curtsies.
>
> She was carrying an armful of logs, and, having stacked them on the fire in a heap calculated to set alight any chimney less roomy than the Severn Tunnel, she retired by way of the open hall door with the same deferential stealth with which she had entered.
>
> 'The hen-woman,' explained Mrs Knox casually, 'the only person in this place who knows a dry log from a wet one.'

The R.M.'s servants are strikingly individual throughout and entirely consistent. His cook, Mrs Cadogan, is a formidable person, 'travelling' the house in the Major's old boots, and stating outlandish and original opinions with such dogmatism that nobody dare question them. Philippa, the unfortunate victim of the *fou rire*, and quite unable to control her countenance, is forever having to leave the cook's presence suddenly. The relationships between the narrator, the cook and his wife give rise to some of the best domestic comedy. He is typically unaware of his wife's dress on the evening of a dinner party.

I was tying my tie when my wife's voice summoned me to her room in tones that presaged disaster. Philippa was standing erect, in a white and glittering garment. Her eyes shone, her cheeks glowed. It is not given to everyone to look their best when they are angry, but is undoubtedly becoming to Philippa.

'I ask you to look at my dress,' she said in a level voice.

'It looks very nice—' I said cautiously, knowing there was a trap somewhere. 'I know it don't I?'

'Know it!' replied Philippa witheringly, 'did you know that it had only one sleeve?'

She extended her arms; from one depended vague and transparent films of whiteness, the other was bare to the shoulder. I rather preferred it of the two.

'Well, I can't say I did,' I said helplessly, 'is that a new fashion?'

There was a spectral knock at the door, and Hannah, the housemaid, slid into the room, purple of face, abject of mien.

'It's what they're afther tellin' me, ma'am,' she panted. ''Twas took to sthrain the soup!'

'They took my sleeve to strain the soup!' repeated Philippa, in a crystal clarity of wrath.

'She said she got it in the press in the passage, ma'am, and she thought you were afther throwin' it,' murmured Hannah, with a glance that implored my support.

'Who are you speaking of?' demanded Philippa, looking quite six feet high.

The situation, already sufficiently acute, was here intensified by the massive entry of Mrs Cadogan, bearing in her hand a plate, on which was a mound of soaked brownish rag. She was blowing hard, the glare of the kitchen range at highest power lived in her face.

'There's your sleeve, ma'am!' she said, 'and if I could fall down dead this minute it'd be no more than a relief to me!

And as for Bridgie Brickley!' continued Mrs Cadogan, catching her wind with a gasp, 'I thravelled many genthry's kitchens, but thanks be to God, I never seen the like of her! Five weeks tomorrow she's in this house, and there isn't a day but I gave her a laceratin'! Sure the hair's droppin' out o' me head, and the skin rollin' off the soles o' me feet with the heart scald I get with her! The big, low, dirty buccaneer! And I declare to you, ma'am, and to the Major, that I have a pain switching out through me hips this minute that'd bring down a horse!'

'Oh God!' said Hannah, clapping her hands over her mouth.

My eye met Philippa's; some tremor of my inward agony declared itself, and found its fellow on her quivering lips. In the same instant, wheels rumbled in the avenue.

'Here are the Knoxes!' I exclaimed, escaping headlong from the room with my dignity as master of the house still intact.

In the stories characters are sharply delineated, dialogue and narrative are well blended, there is skilful use of suspense and all the situations are essential and tightly woven together. Many different moods are contained within the overall mode of comedy. The stories sparkle with fun, delighting in their own form, and no more ashamed of being stories than *The Importance of being Earnest* is of being a play.

Ulick Adare, the hero of *Dan Russel the Fox*, expresses the authors' opinion when he says, 'there's no such thing in literature as a Sporting Novel. The two things are incompatible.'[5] For them the division between their novels and their sporting stories was clear, and all the time they were writing the Irish R.M. stories, they were planning to write a novel which would be very different from the stories. *Dan Russel* was started in 1904, then put to one side for six years. When they returned to it they were thinking of it for serialisation. It was mainly Pinker's encouragement which kept them at it, and which kept it light and sporty. When it was finished there was difficulty placing it, and they feared that they might have made a business error as well as an artistic mistake. Pinker tried to persuade Edith

Somerville to illustrate it, but she refused, 'I detest an illustrated novel.' There seems to have been some confusion about this, because Violet Martin wrote to Lady Gregory saying that it was meant to have been a book of coloured pictures with stories appended, and that without the pictures it was a very light sporting story. She insisted that it was not a novel because a novel was a story 'that cannot be split up into isolated incidents', and this one had too obviously been written for serialisation. She even apologises when she returns proofs, 'It is, as a novel, a slight piece of work. We began it with a divided mind and an idea of short hunting sketches—but we hope it will read pleasantly.' Edith Somerville is equally lacking in confidence, and writes to a brother, 'We fear that everyone will be disappointed: the serious because it is sporting and the sporting because it is serious. I think about six people may like it'.

Violet Martin's wish, 'please goodness we need not write another hunting novel', was answered. And of all their work this is the one that is most concerned with the horse and the hound. It is so enthusiastic about hunting that it is almost a plea for the sport which took up so much of their time and energy. It is hunting from the point of view of avid enthusiasm. But, the enthusiasm is held in check by their literary talents, and the poise of the narrative does give detachment. Those who live merely for hunting are judged and in the judgment the book transcends the sporting story. The sub-title, 'An Episode in the Life of Miss Rowan' should not be forgotten. Miss Rowan, the protagonist, falls in love with John Michael, the personification of hunting, while Ulick Adare, the literary man, her social and mental equal, is cast to one side. The story of her relationships with these two men is quite different from anything in the sporting stories. The social background to the story is also done more seriously than anything in the tales.

Ulick Adare is hostile to hunting, which he sees as a waste of time, and to hunting people whom he sees as bores. He is Anglo-Irish but lives in London where his journalism earns him enough to keep his widowed mother and his Wicklow estate. Whereas his poetry is romantic and full of sentiment, he is ironic and detached, his friendships are intellectual. He enjoys Katharine's arguments and conversation, until she is rendered helpless by a

fall and he falls in love with her. She belongs to his world; she is a
writer too, and Ulick respects her literary judgments. After her
fall from a horse, her first words on gaining consciousness are
'How much the mental consciousness is in advance of the
physical!' When she is able to stand up she recalls a picture in
Punch and mutters, 'And there be t'owd mare, and she be
stearin' too, surely!'; two reactions which are quite lost on John
Michael, he just does not understand their language. When
Katharine meets Ulick unexpectedly in the middle of the Irish
countryside he seems like her saviour, 'She was suddenly aware
that she felt as might a marooned seaman, who, surrounded by
friendly natives, sees a man-o'-war's boat arrive at his coral
beach.' She admires Ulick's writing and his sensitive perceptions of life. She is an heiress, supremely confident and hyper-
critical, and yet through the lure of hunting she throws over all
her literary friends, all civilised company (Mrs Masterman can
hardly believe the uncouth community she enters, 'I have never
before been in any part of Ireland where there was not so much
as *one* white person,') and becomes as one with those who share
her passion for the chase. 'Those of Katharine's friends who were
wont to accuse her of excessive and wilful fastidiousness, would
have been entertained at beholding her, wind-ruffled, flushed
and voluble, riding along a bog-road with two buckeens of low
degree, deeply immersed in the affairs of a cultureless, not to say
barbarous community.'

   John Michael has the looks of a Spanish gypsy and not an idea
in his head beyond hunting. Mrs Masterman, who as her name
implies is not very susceptible to the charms of the other sex, can
only see him as 'that fox-hunting yokel; whose solitary means of
expression is to blow a horn!' But for Katharine he is 'like Saint
George on horseback . . . courage found its best expression in
horsemanship, and horsemanship was summed up in John
Michael'. When he is riding she actually purports to see his halo
and begins to string together words 'about Grace and Courage
and Speed'. He is unfortunately stupid and lacking in all
imagination. The differences between the two characters, and
the difference between John Michael as he actually is and John
Michael as he appears to Katharine are shown dramatically and
with humour. He is immensely shy, and at his mother's tea party

he perches on a piano stool so tense with nerves that Katharine feels 'if so much as a twig cracked he would melt into the upright piano, even as Daphne was merged in the laurel.' After she has made efforts at conversation he at last screws up courage to talk to her:

> 'I suppose you were never at Cahirmee?' said John Michael with an effort that wrung a creak from the music-stool.
> Katharine felt that she was witnessing the awakening of a social conscience. It was unfortunate that she was obliged to answer the question in the negative.
> 'Well, it's a chancey place to buy a colt.'

At this stage she can still see clearly, 'He's a nice gentle thing, . . . When I die I'm going to endow a hospital for the Shy, and there shall be a John Michael ward.' But as she falls deeper into the passion of hunting, her vision dims.

When the three main characters are together their relation- ships are expressed with comic contrasts. John Michael is hunting rabbits when he comes across Ulick reading his poetry to Katharine. She at once switches her enthusiasm from the poetry to the previous day's hunting, ending her rhapsody, 'One crowded hour of glorious life!' John Michael's reply, 'It was more than an hour, I made it an hour and seventeen minutes,' is all that Ulick could wish. When Katharine, to annoy Ulick, goes on to wish they were hunting on such a beautiful day, John Michael is as literal as before, 'I'm afraid there wouldn't be much of a scent.' To Katharine this naïvety and simple mindedness is attractive, 'She was in the mood to feel the charm of simplicity.' His limited consciousness and his one-track mind do give him a sincerity which Katharine is sophisticated enough to respect. What she fails to see is that his lack of complication, imagination and awareness of his own sexual attractiveness, is a kind of sub-normality. He is, as Captain Bolger says, 'A kind of a nun of a fellow' because he has no sense of people as being in any way different from his hounds. When he is at his most gentle he looks at Katharine, 'almost as kindly as if she were a hound'. When his mother tells him that Katharine would like to marry him he is most upset, 'angry, violently angry . . . to say a low, dirty thing like that about a lady'. He has no concept of marriage as being different from the mating of hounds, 'I'd hate to be married, I'd sooner sweep a kennel in America.'

The scenes of the misery of unrequited love are well done; all of Ulick's and Katharine's reading of love poetry is of no help to them. When he tells her of his love it is nauseating to her, deeply in love as she is with John Michael, 'it was not beautiful to her, nor eloquent, nor compelling; worst of all, it failed to enlist her sympathy. It was merely bewildering, and immensely distasteful.' She cannot help but cringe away from Ulick and deal 'helplessly and conventionally with the greatest miracle of all'. This scene is counterpointed with the one of Mrs Delanty confessing her love to John Michael. He knows that something is up, 'Suspicion, reasonless and deep, like that of a woodland animal, kept him silent', but he just does not know how to respond on a personal level. She begs him to stay in Ireland:

'You and me would run the whole show between us!'
Her cheeks were hot and her voice was changed and wavering.
'It'd be like old times when we were friends first!'
John Michael was aware of a pang approaching physical terror, and, by some sub-connection of ideas, saw before his eyes an ornate cigarette case, bestowed upon him four Christmases ago by Mrs Delanty, and never since revealed to human eye, an object at once abhorrent and alarming to him.
'Thank you,' he said hurriedly, 'I don't think that would do very well.'

When she seizes hold of him and bursts into tears asking him to stay for her sake, he is paralysed with tension and embarrassment. Whereas Katharine is alarmed at Ulick's suffering and deeply sorry for him, and does her best to tell him the truth as gently as she can, John Michael, in a similar situation, says nothing. When Mrs Delanty has gone he begins to stir the hounds' pudding dragging the shovel round and round and says, 'Oh, my goodness! That was awful!' In their different ways the characters here do feel much more than any of those in the Irish R.M. stories. There is none of the agony of the passion of the novels, and compared with *The Real Charlotte* the suffering is not deep, but Katharine, Ulick and John Michael do each get involved emotionally. The novel does prove Ulick wrong when he denies the existence of the sporting novel because, 'Sentiment, romance, character, even humour, they simply don't exist where sport is concerned.' Sentiment and romance there are in plenty, character and humour too.

The most striking minor characters are all women. Katharine's travelling companion and Ulick's cousin, a wealthy English matriarch whose husband is tucked away in India, strides through the book dominating all, and amused by Ulick and Katharine. The plight of an unmarried penniless woman is dramatically presented in the character of Miss Scanlan. She, the eldest of eighteen, acts as cook and maid to her married sister, grateful for being given a home; 'education, especially for females, was deemed a superfluity, and the family talent for marriage not being bestowed upon her, she had spent her life as unpaid nurserymaid, unpaid dressmaker, and unpaid sick nurse to her relations. Having no money she had no influence, standing or significance.' Mrs Delanty whose share of the family's talent for marriage was to run away at the age of seventeen with a ne'er do well, is a young and attractive widow. She has life under control now and is eminently capable and self-sufficient. She can save money by turning her hand to most things, and by economising stringently she can keep a horse and hunt. She is on the look-out for a second husband, and she never overlooks a chance of personal advancement. But her vitality and gift of expression lift her far above her English equivalent, 'Of course Gus is an old friend of mine, but I must say I never liked him very much.' It is the voice of Francie Fitzpatrick we hear in Aix-les-Bains (where Mrs Delanty is an elderly woman's companion) when she takes her first sip of white wine:

'"Oh, Heavenly Powers!" she gasped, and the South of Ireland lay bare, "that's awful! That's the ugly wine! For gracious' sake, is it poison?"' Despite all her common sense she can do nothing about her hopeless love for John Michael, and makes a last bid for him even though it means risking losing the wealthy Englishman who is eating out of her hand. In her passion for the simple and beautiful John Michael, she herself is lifted above her life of calculations and economies, 'in that insane moment of surrender and self-forgetfulness, the small, second-rate, egotistical soul of Mrs Delanty found wings, and spread them in a larger air.'

Mrs Fitz-Symons, like Mrs Delanty and her sister, helps to give us the solid social background; John Michael's mother, she is very unlike him, being fat, coarse and extremely voluble with the Irish countrywoman's gift of the gab. When Mrs Masterman makes the perennial complaint about Irish servants, Mrs Fitz-Symons responds, 'I have one this minute, a great, good-natured-slob of a girl, that'd sit up all night with you if you were ill, and if you were well, maybe she wouldn't get out of her bed at all!' She is perfectly content with her lot in life, adores her son, John Michael, and really does not care whether her new neighbours bother to know her or not, 'I'm too old to go calling on grand English ladies like them! They wouldn't be bothered with me!' She is an excellent hostess and when Captain Bolger calls unexpectedly she immediately makes him very welcome, and sits down to talk to him.

> Mrs Fitz-Symons picked up a half-knitted stocking, and seating herself at the other side of the fire, began to knit in a comfortable and conversational manner. The fact that she had on her housekeeping apron, and a tweed cap that had been discarded by her younger son, did not disturb her in the least.

As for humour, the last ingredient which Ulick fears is swallowed up by the master passion sport, there is no shortage of that. The dialect is as humorous as in any of their writings. Mrs Delanty's servant girl, who is forced to wait at table, offers an omelette when there is no plate to put it on, and says afterwards, 'When a thing'd go wrong that way, an' I goin' round the ladies and gentlemen, I'd busht out shweatin'!' The blacksmith describes how weak he felt after having the flu, 'afther leaving the bed, if it was no more than the frivolity of putting on me little gansey, I'd be in a passpiration with the dint of it.' There is the conversation Katharine overhears on the boat as it draws near Kingstown; the stewardess asks, 'Will I get you some nice hot water to wash your hands?' and receives the memorable reply,

'Ah, thank ye, no. I'll not mind. I'm going to relations.' And there is the pervading humour of the whole, which presents the characters to us with detachment and holds the entire story, including the hunting episodes, in comic judgment.

Chapter VI

Mount Music—An Enthusiast

Mount Music, the first novel Edith Somerville wrote after Violet Martin's death, was started in 1918 and finished in just over a year. She read it aloud to no one and she was most diffident about the novel. She wrote almost in panic to Pinker when it was ready for publication, 'I am absolutely uncertain as to the merits or demerits of this book—which seems idiotic, but I have lost my eye about it; and have alternate hot and cold fits.' She was aware that the lack of humour and hunting would disappoint those who liked their Irish R.M. stories and *Dan Russel the Fox*. She warns Pinker, 'I have a little hunting in the book, and I think there are amusing features, but it does not attempt to be an amusing book any more than *The Real Charlotte*'. While writing it she had often despaired, and only the conviction that Violet Martin was still able to write with her, made her persevere. She was also able to include some of Violet Martin's unpublished writing in it— sections of an earlier 1908 novel which they had abandoned.

By 1919 the days of prosperity for the Anglo-Irish were clearly over. The novel is set in the Ireland of the period 1894-1907; it takes up the story of the Ascendancy where *The Real Charlotte* left off. Edith Somerville was careful to link fiction with fact, and dates were chosen with care. The facts of the period centre on the Agrarian Revolution. Property, and thus power, passed from the Ascendancy families to the tenantry. By 1894 two decades of land acts had begun to take effect, and dual ownership was giving way to peasant proprietorship. The Local Government Act of 1898 led to the establishment of County Councils, Urban District Councils and Rural District Councils. The Wyndham Land Act of 1903 reduced the interest rate on loans and extended the time of repayment to sixty-eight-and-a-half years. Landlords had the choice of either selling and emigrating or trying to adapt to an entirely different way of life. They felt bitter, not only towards their prospering tenantry but towards the British government, which was betraying their interests. In the novel Edith Somerville says of the Protestant aunts that 'Wolfe Tone or Robert Emmet could hardly have abhorred the Government of England more heartily than did these three respectable law-abiding, unalterably-Unionist ladies . . .' The tenantry—though benefiting from land acts, relief work, the network of railways set up on the west coast, and improvements inaugurated by the Congested Districts Board of 1891—were more suspicious than grateful. Home Rule was their aim. Parnell's linking of the issue of agrarian unrest to Home Rule meant that the change in land ownership was not just a personal loss for the Ascendancy but was a beginning of the disintegration of the British Empire. From the loyalist point of view Home Rule was a negative separatism, and Irish nationalism was seen as a disguise for socialism. The land war was a class war and a threat to the Empire.

For the majority of people in Ireland it was a time not only of personal gain but of the rebirth of their country. Plunkett's Irish Agricultural Organisation Society (the I.A.O.S.), formed in 1895, was the only one which offered the opportunity for all Irishmen to work together for social and economic reform. Otherwise the cultural movements isolated the Anglo-Irish from the rest of the country. The Gaelic League was ostensibly non-political; but the tolerance of its leaders did not extend throughout its work, which was used as the basis for the nationalism which Anglo-Ireland feared:

> More than any other movement the Gaelic League provided the atmosphere for the development in Ireland of the new-look nationalism then powerfully operating in Europe. According to this new nationalism politically independent states should be raised up wherever there existed distinct cultural nations. The Gaelic League was demonstrating that Ireland was a cultural nation; therefore, went the argument, Ireland was entitled to become a nation-state.[1]

In *Mount Music* Christian is eager to learn Irish, but her father's ferocious denunciation of the Gaelic League stops her.

This is the setting of the novel. The House, like Howards End, and Inver, is a microcosm of the land; the struggle between Major Talbot-Lowry and the Catholic Doctor Mangan is representative of the class war which was raging throughout Ireland at the time. Edith Somerville wrote in the Advance Notice that the House was 'at once the background, and the chief character, in a record whose object is to give a picture, of reasonable sincerity, of a phase of Irish country life that, in the clash of classes and creeds and politics, is daily losing something of its ancient charm.'

The house, Mount Music, is large, solid and cluttered with a combination of priceless rarities and tasteless rubbish. Although basement, kitchen and backstairs are full of rats and cockroaches, it has been kept up and only the yard has deteriorated. It is a huge house, Elizabethan, with room for three massive yews planted in the days of Queen Elizabeth I, in the grass square of the stable yard. Repairs and a quality of gracious living have been made possible by the Major's marriage to an English heiress. In the late eighteen-eighties they were given all the homage gentry demanded, which the Talbot-Lowrys repaid by leading the way at dinner parties, opening bazaars, attending grand juries and boards of guardians, and acting as Master of Foxhounds. She is genteel and frail, he a hearty sportsman; both are types but very credible. Their downfall takes them by surprise although it has been clearly charted: in 1897 he continues to order crates of whiskey from Dublin although he cannot pay the local butcher; when rents are lowered by government edict he economises by dressing his huntsmen in brown breeches and 'foregoing the yearly renewal of their scarlet coats, and other like humiliations.' Real economies, like fortitude, are foreign to him. He quarrels with tenants, with friends who sell their lands to tenants, and with government officials over the 1903 Land Act, and he refuses to sell to the tenants. He can say, 'You might as well have a mill-stone round your neck as Irish property these times'[2] but still he clings to Ireland. He takes tenants to court for their unpaid rent and they retaliate by poaching on his land and burning down his beloved copse that he planted twenty-five years ago. Their hatred is such that they not only put wire up to stop the hunting but actually threaten his youngest daughter with a hay-knife when she rides over their land, injuring her horse so that it has to be shot. Talbot-Lowry mortgages the house and demesne in order to pay tradesmen. And he feels very badly treated by everyone, 'When I think of how I've been treated, and plenty more like me, loyal men who run straight and do their best, I declare to God I feel I don't know which I hate worst, the English Government, that pitches its friends overboard to save its own skin, or my own countrymen, that don't know the meaning of the word gratitude.' By 1907 he cannot afford to stay in the house, servants and workers are dismissed. His scream of rage is reminiscent of Dominick's against class mobility in *An Irish Cousin*:

> Nationalists . . . Don't talk to me of Nationalists! Common thieves! That's all they are! There's no Nationalism about *them!* Call it Socialism, if you like, or any other name for robbery! They'd look very blue if *we* took to shouting 'Ireland a Nation!' and expecting to come in at the finish! They mightn't be able to call us English invaders then! . . . Look at the old places that they're squeezing the old families out of! It's the Protestant farmers and the Religious Orders that are getting them, swarming into them like rats! Don't tell me that I and my family aren't a better asset to any country than a lot of fat lazy Monks and Nuns!

He never faces the fact that he will never live in Mount Music again; he retires to an English suburb, thinking that it is only a temporary letting of the house he has arranged with a wealthy Englishman. There is never any dignity in his stand against socialism; his main characteristic is pigheadedness, and the authors mockingly compare him with the maligned King Canute. He is an archetypal male chauvinist: he really believes he owns his wife and daughters and tenants, and that it is for their good to submit to him. The family's hasty departure is seen with a mixture of pathos and farce; for generations their ancestors have ruled there, but it is all as nothing now; they are 'too agitated by their coming journey to have a spare thought for sentiment; too much beset by the fear of what they might lose, their keys, their sandwiches, their dressing-boxes, to shed a tear for what they were losing, and had lost.'

The new owner of Mount Music, Dr Mangan, is sympathetically presented: a big, lumbering man with a warm deep voice, gentle hands, a love of music, and an adoration of his attractive wife and daughter. He is a good doctor, and a good man who gave up a fashionable and prosperous Dublin practice in order to help his doctoring father in his native village. He dies doing his duty by a patient, going out into a dreadful storm and battling through floods to sit by the bedside of a dying woman, merely saying as he goes, 'Well, bad manners to the woman! Such a day to choose.' His weakness is his desire that his fine family shall be the first in their society, or at least the Mangans must be equal with the Talbot-Lowrys. He makes his daughter hunt because it is a way of making her friendly with the young Anglo-Irish. His wife is sent to the Protestant church's sale of work, and instructed to spend lavishly, 'It was evident to the meanest capacity that Mrs Mangan had paid her footing in society.' He accumulates money and then befriends Talbot-Lowry, so that by 1903 he is the mortgagee for Mount Music and the demesne. He easily becomes the leading man in the small town of Cluhir. He introduces the first motor-car into the district. His sense of timing is precise: he drives the Talbot-Lowrys skilfully, matching professional knowledge with friendly advice so that the Major's heart and income give way together. He then, gently, hounds the Talbot-Lowrys out of the country, 'his professional advice had usefully reinforced his unofficial advocacy of the move'. He manoeuvres his children and their sweethearts and the local politics so that personal and public crises coincide, and the champagne is ready for both. It is he who plans the May moon picnic to bring his daughter and Larry together. He uses the election in order to get Larry away from his relations, especially from Christian, by persuading him to stand as Nationalist candidate. He tells the priest to support Larry's candidature, 'I'll undertake to say there won't be much talk of mixed marriages then!' And by using the social and political changes—which Talbot-Lowry does not want to know about—he rises in direct proportion to the descent of the Major. His determination is very much like Charlotte Mullen's; and like her he will stop at nothing: he breaks up the engagement between Larry and Christian by convincing her that her father will die of a heart attack if it continues; he bribes his own daughter, giving her £10 if she will flirt with Larry. He has similar force of will to Charlotte's, his wife and children obey him without question; and he actually makes Larry and Tishy decide to get married when they are both in love with other people. He persuades his honourable son that it is to Larry's advantage to sell his land below market price, when all he wants to do is set the Talbot-Lowrys' tenants against their landlords for not doing likewise. His scheming is as successful as Jason's in *Castle Rackrent*, and without much of a fight the aristocracy lets itself be taken over by the middle classes. The main plot of the novel is this story of social change, the exchange of land, power and prestige. The ways in which nationalism and religion are minor issues, subordinate to the acquisition of land and money, is the main theme of the book. In the class struggle love of one's country and one's religion are all very well if they advance one's social position. The society, like that in *The Real Charlotte*, is primarily materialistic, other values are debased and idealism of all kinds must give way to what is expedient.

A letter to Pinker shows Edith Somerville's concern about religious intolerance at that time, just before the publication of *Mount Music:*

> I am a little nervous as to its possible reception in Ireland. Miss Martin's idea is to 'open a window in Irish social life' and we have for long planned a book of the kind, to be written boldly, but I admit to feeling a little afraid as to whether I have not in some ways, opened the window a little too widely i.e. on religious matters, from a social point of view. *(I am sure I need not say that this is strictly between ourselves.)* No one of my friends has heard a single word of what I have written. You must not think that I have said, or described, anything very terrible or epoch-making. I have merely tried to explain the extraordinary way in which the rival religions permeate Irish social life. No matter how liberal the atmosphere in the last resort, it is religion that has the casting vote, so it seems to me.

Although the novel was criticised for dealing with a problem which was out of date, the problem is perennial; when there are different religions within a society they can always be used to drive a deeper wedge between people. Once priests had given their support to agrarian unrest, the Ascendancy's fear of political change did include a genuine fear that 'Home Rule means Rome rule'. At the Thomas Davis Centenary Dr Mahaffy refused to address the meeting because of its nationalist undertones, and then when he heard that 'a man called Pearse' was to speak he banned the meeting entirely. George Russell wrote to W.B.Yeats,

> If such principles are allowed to permeate Ireland, a Protestant would equally be forced to refuse a Catholic lecturer on mathematics, and Catholics must insist that no Protestant shall shock their religious susceptibilities by speaking to them on chemistry or physics.
>
> Where is the line to be drawn? Is culture to become sectarian or a matter of political partisanship? Are we to have national mathematics and imperial chemistry?[3]

When Somerville & Ross had tried to explore these stresses in Irish life in 1908 they had been very nervous, 'We are discussing the new book. *Very* difficult. If we could write anonymously it would be all right, but what with Religion, Politics and Personalities "How many are the dangers through which we have to go".' By 1919 so much had happened that the period up to 1907 was far enough away to seem less formidable.

The novel then tries to explore how sectarianism was undermining life in Ireland, partly so that English readers would have some idea of the role religion played in Irish society. Ireland was vulnerable because religious differences were supported by race and class. The theme is worked out through the lives of two cousins: Christian Talbot-Lowry, Ascendancy, Prostestant and Loyalist, and Larry Coppinger, Ascendancy, Catholic (due to an English upper-middle class Catholic mother) and Nationalist. They fall in love and are seen as ideally suited to each other, except for their different religions. When they do finally come together, it is meant to show that, like the cousins, Ireland could transcend sectarianism. For various reasons this does not work.

Much of the novel is well executed. The theme is casually enough introduced in a conversation between the two cousins. Larry has just returned from Oxford where, to his Irish relations' horror, he has caught Irish patriotism—a sort of natural reaction against the English at Oxford. He in fact knows very little about Ireland, having spent much of his childhood in India, and his schooldays in England, and, the time before going to Oxford, on the Continent.

> 'You know, Larry,' Christian said, half-absently twisting and arranging Dooley's little tan ears, in order to express, on Dooley's behalf, with them, various emotions, 'it seems to me that all these political revolutions that you are so anxious to start, for the good of Ireland, are like putting the cart before the horse.'
>
> 'What do you mean?' asked Larry, eyeing her with undisguised surprise.
>
> 'Well,' said Christian, slowly, gazing across the valley with eyes more than ever like the clearest brown stream, 'you've got to begin with the individual. After all, Ireland is made up of individuals, and each of them contributes in some way to the big result. It seems to me that the real Spirit of the Nation is—is—' . . . 'It's Religious Intolerance, I think! That seems to me the Spirit of the Nation—my side as bad as yours, and yours as bad as mine—'
>
> 'Oh, the parsons and the priests,' said Larry, airily, 'Oh, you wait, Christian! You don't know! You've been stuck down here in a hole. If you met Father Nugent—'
>
> 'But I don't mean them only,' said Christian, standing to her guns; 'I mean the individual—you and me! Just anybody —we're all the same. The Shan van Voght has got to free us from each other before she takes on England!'

And the religious intolerance is sharply and convincingly explored through a large number of characters. The society is made up of Protestants and Catholics; its political and social boundaries have been clearly defined. One sees how, if these boundaries begin to blur, religious differences can be emphasised to reinforce them. When the Anglo-Irish begin to lose their political power and social prestige, they cling to their religion to maintain their sense of apartness. Religious differences are emphasised partly out of fear and dislike of another religion and partly out of social snobbery. Larry is an uncomfortable amalgam, and the timbre of the others is shown by their reaction to him. Major Talbot-Lowry does his duty to his ward, stifling as best he can, his inbred distrust of Larry's religion; but when Larry's political opinions fall in line with his religion, the Major will have nothing to do with him, and refuses to let Christian marry him. Talbot-Lowry's sister, Frederica, who has to live with Larry until he becomes of age, also tries to be tolerant, but she, unlike her brother, is passionately involved with her own Church, so it is even more difficult for her. She unbends so far as to invite Larry's priest to lunch, but she draws the line at asking him to dinner, and she makes sure that she has a dentist appointment in Dublin when Larry invites Catholic friends to his house. She belongs to the school of Irish Low Church Protestantism. The conflict between the two opposing religions is dramatically captured in the portrait of Frederica; the comedy holding the two in balance. Her deep involvement with her Church includes a weakness for a man of God; no matter how ineffectual he is, if he is a Church of Ireland clergyman she will love him—a trait which the Church of Rome would thoroughly applaud. Her Church is the centre of her life:

> To Frederica the practice of her cult both inwardly in her heart, and outwardly in the work of St. Matthew's Parish, was the mainspring of her existence. It was also her pastime. She would analyse a sermon, as Dick Lowry would discuss a run, and with the same eager enjoyment. She assented with enthusiasm to the Doctrine of Eternal Damnation, and a gentler-hearted creature than she never lived. She would have gone to the stake for the Verbal Inspiration of the Bible; she was as convinced that the task of Creation was completed in a week, as she was that she paid the Coppinger's Court workmen for six days' work every Saturday evening.

Her religious beliefs are comparable in their sincerity and simplicity with those of the Roman Catholic poor; she thinks they are damned to eternity, and they think she is. Frederica's friends are treated with the same detached irony as the

Protestant ladies in *The Real Charlotte*. They can never forget the other Church, and are continually trite and competitive; when they plan their Sale of Work, '*we're* not going to raffle bottles of brandy—as they did at that R.C. Bazaar in Riverstown!' The authors never need to make direct comments, the comedy makes the judgment. After a charity concert in which people of both religious persuasions take part, they meet to talk it over. Their annoyance is due to the simple fact that Catholics were allowed to be there at all; but of course they cannot be explicit about that, so they complain that the Catholics were inferior in talent; that they dominated the evening; and that they took more than their fair share of the profits. Worst of all, 'God Save the King' was not played at the end, 'I really think that George, who is in the Navy, might have insisted upon it!' It in fact comforts them to feel that they have been hard done by, so great is 'the web of jealousies, hatreds, fears and stupidities'. Mrs St George speaks for them all when she says, 'I hope I'm not a bigot, but I thank God I'm not a Roman Catholic!' The rector's wife, whom one might have hoped for something better from, is one of the most prejudiced.She tells a story of how a friend of her husband, a clergyman too, bought an expensive house and spent much on repairs, decorations and fitted furniture, only to discover that there was a convent at the bottom of the garden! He sold up at once. 'Weren't his daughters' souls more to him than book-shelves?' But the Protestant servants are even more bigoted than their mistresses. As a measure of safety the Anglo-Irish of the nineteenth century employed servants of their own religion whenever they could. When Lady Isabel, who is English, employs Catholic servants, the butler, Evans, sees it as a confirmation of his 'deep-seated suspicions as to the laxity of the English Church'. He is shocked that the Talbot-Lowrys let their children play with their Catholic cousin, 'the children of this house consorting with a Papist!' and he holds to his hatred of Larry throughout the book.

Comment is made on the clergymen of both Churches by giving us several contrasting characters, none of whom are bigoted, but neither are they specially interested in religion. The Reverend Cotton is a pathetic little man whose personality is quite obliterated by his wife; he spends most of his time withdrawn into a self-protective, semi-hypnotic trance. The Reverend Charles Fetherston was ordained in the days when the ministry was more a pastime for gentlemen with a concern for people than a career. He is a favourite among the poor Catholics because he tries to heal all sorrow with money, and among the wealthy Protestants because he is a good shot. The priests are drawn with the same critical detachment. Father David Hogan is a popular hunting man, stout and jolly, with a good eye for a horse. Father Greer is a cunning, foxy man who is against any fraternising with Protestants; he fancies his own wit and calls the Church of Ireland, 'a fortuitous concourse of atheistic atoms'; Larry's playing hymns on the piano for Protestants in a hotel in Switzerland is 'a melancholy instance of evil communications corrupting good manners'. The facetiousness of his wit and his unconscious malapropism, 'insinuendoes' put him in place. Father Sweeny is very different from this lean, dry man and he is satirised in a Chaucerian manner. He is a man of 'bovine countenance', who 'in voice, in appearance, and in manner, provoked, uncontrollably, a comparison with a heavy and truculent black bull'. When he is sick, 'His large face, with its broad cheeks and heavy double-chins, that was usually of a sanguine and all pervasive beefy-red, now hung in pallid purple folds'. He is ready to support Larry's candidature, even though he knows that Larry is a bad Catholic and does not go to Mass, in return for land on which to build a new chapel and money with which to decorate the building.

Persons of either religion who are not sectarian (except for Christian and Larry) are not really religious and merely use tolerance for material gains. Judith Talbot-Lowry wants her sister to marry the Catholic Larry, because he is wealthy, and his being a Catholic might be useful—she knows the priests will not support the boycott of Mount Music if Larry is the son-in-law of the house. Money and social position come first with her, and she gets as near as she can to telling Christian not to worry about anything else, 'I know it's a bore about his religion, and his politics are *more* than shaky . . .' But when Larry deserts her sister and gets engaged to the Catholic girl, Judith is as friendly as ever because her husband needs Larry's subscription to keep the hunt going. The Mangans condone mixed marriages so long

as they mean social advancement: their son Barty can marry a
Protestant girl so long as she is a Talbot-Lowry; but they break
up the match between Larry and Christian in order to get Larry
for their own daughter. The Mangans are no more vulgar than
the Protestant ladies; indeed their warmth of family feeling
shows up well beside the Talbot-Lowrys' polite coolness; and
their genuine love of music and actual practice of it, forming a
quartet and playing each evening at home, makes Mount Music
look like Shaw's Horseback Hall. The authors do create this
convincing small town community without bias towards any
special group in it.

The complications of the society are shown through the
character of Larry; his bewilderment and gradual realisation of
the situation reveals it to us. Amongst his Irish relations and
their friends he begins to feel an outsider. At the Sale of Work he
overhears someone say, 'Only an R.C. by accident', and he
becomes aware of sudden silences, quick changes of conversation. 'It was a matter of atmosphere; quite intangible and quite
perceptible'. It begins to be a relief for him to be with the
Mangans where this does not happen. The Mangans' son Barty
is a more interesting boy than the Talbot-Lowrys, and Larry
enjoys the debating society he introduces him to, and joins the
'Sons of Emmet'. With a few pushes from Dr Mangan he is soon
nationalist candidate. When Christian breaks off her engagement with Larry, for the sake of her father's health, he responds
with the stock phrases, by now having become fully involved
with the mass of complications himself:

> What about leaving father and mother and sticking to your
> husband, he would like to know! These Protestants who
> talked such a lot about reading the Bible! It was quite true
> what old Mangan had said: 'When all comes to all, a man
> must stick to his own Church!' All these others, these St.
> Georges, and Westropps, and old Ardmore, and the rest of
> them, had only been waiting to jump on him as soon as he put
> a foot out of the rut they all walked in. They had waited for
> the chance to make him a pariah. Now they had it. All right!

The story too is a good one and holds our interest most of the
time, only really faltering at the end when things are sorted out

too neatly without the feeling of inevitability. Tishy's elopement with a medical student on the morning of her marriage to Larry is just too easy. It leaves Larry free to marry Christian, and so breaks up a marriage between two Irish people of the same religion but different classes, and unites two Irish people of the same class but of different religions. Thus sectarianism is overcome, but, also, the class war is halted! Dr Mangan's death is perfectly timed to dove-tail in with this, for his widow will never want to live in Mount Music; Barty is too scrupulous; and Tishy will enjoy Dublin with her medical student.

The real weakness in the novel is that the authors lose their mocking perspective when it comes to the heroine, Christian. This is a similar failure to that of *The Silver Fox*, once they start to romanticise a main character the tone falters and their usual sharp observations are blurred. The reason for this here is perhaps mainly that Edith Somerville tried to incorporate many of Violet Martin's own characteristics into the portrait. Christian's spiritual aloofness is hers, also her role as confidante to her elder sister, her gift of mimicking the Irish accent, her sharp intelligence, her swiftness of reaction. Like Violet Martin she sees the situation in a flash and acts with the swiftness of lightning. They also share 'the gift of being able instantly to concentrate every force of mind and body upon a desired point—a rare gift and a precious one.' As a child and adolescent she is acceptable. Her spirituality is balanced by her adoration of the hounds and her tom-boy behaviour. At the age of four her extempore prayer, 'make me to have a good, fat, lively conscience, and even if God curse me, help me not to mind a bit!' is all right. At the age of six the Book of Esther enthralls her; a few years later she is spellbound by the glory of the images in the Book of Revelation; she sits in the schoolroom waiting for the pale horse to crash through the woods outside. Her adolescent detachment from the flirtings of the others, and her withdrawal from the world of dances and triviality is convincing enough. Her family are absorbed 'in the conjugation of three primary words—verbs, to be, to do, to have, in relation, exclusively, to themselves, and that merely from the skin outwards. Soul processes and development were unknown to them. 'Whereas she, outgrowing the voices and music which she heard in her childhood, grows in self-knowledge. She has 'a subtlety of mind, a clarity, a sort of pondering, intellectual self-consciousness (that had no kinship with that other form of self-consciousness that is only inverted self-conceit)'. She is open to the spirit world, and she sees Dr Mangan's spirit near his corpse and sees his 'newly learnt impulses of self-reproach and penitence'.

The difficulties of showing this kind of spirituality is side-stepped rather than overcome by giving us two characters who have no part in the story other than to reflect spiritual sensitivity on to Christian. The ways in which they talk to her are supposed to show us the maturity of soul she possesses, and how she transcends the dogmas and doctrines of the Protestants and the Catholics with a true Christianity. The two characters are simple country folk. The man, Peter Callaghan, is a gentle, remote person. Christian asks him about the young silent girl who is nearby.

> 'She's my daughter,' said Peter Callaghan in his quiet voice. 'She wouldn't know it was to her you spoke. She's the dark creature. Blinded she is. She's not long that way.'
> 'How did it happen?' said Christian, in a low voice.
> 'You could not say,' said Peter Callaghan; his dreamy eyes roved again over the broad river; 'God left a hand on her,' he said.

The woman, Mrs James Barry, tells Christian that her husband was in hospital for a fortnight:

> 'He had a bunch, like, under his chin, and they were to cut it.' She paused, and the wooden bump of the cradle filled the pause.
> 'When they had it cut, he rose up on the table, and all his blood went from him; only one little tint, I suppose, stopped in him. After a while, the nurse seen the life creeping back in him. "We have him yet!" says she to the Docthor.' "I thought he was gone from us!" says the Docthor.' The voice ceased again. The speaker slashed the frock in her hand at an over-bold hen, who had skipped on to the table beside her and was pecking hard and sharp at some food on a plate.
> 'They sent him home then. We thought he was cured

entirely. He pulled out the summer, but he had that langersome way with him through all.'

She was silent a moment, then she looked at Christian, with grief, crowned and omnipotent, on her tragic brow.

'As long as he was alive, I had courage in spite of all, but when I thinks now of them days, and the courage I had, it goes through me!' Her red-brown eyes stared through the open door at the path twisting across the field to the high road.

'Ye'll never see him on that road again, and when I looks up it me heart gets dark. Sure, now he's gone, I thinks often if he'd be lyin' par'lysed above in the bed, I'd be runnin' about happy!'

When Christian went home, Mrs Barry walked with her to the little green bridge, and stood there until her visitor reached the bend of the river where the path passed from her sight.

These two lonely figures are as isolated from their world, or from the world beyond their fields, as Christian is from hers. They are isolated not only by miles but by their attitude to life; they, in addition to Christian, are meant to be the only people with any real Christian values in spite of all the talk about religion. Both of them are attempts at exemplifying an acceptance of life, not without sorrow but without jealousy, resentment and self-pity. But they too are sentimentalised.

And in showing Christian's relationship with Larry, on which is pivoted the whole theme of the book, the authors fail utterly. The relationship is used to develop the thesis: in the coming together of these two one sees how the two Churches in Ireland might meet and unite, their common ground a mystical apprehension of reality which transcends all doctrine. Unless this is achieved the only workable alternative is 'a common atheism'.

Larry and Christian are in love with each other. When he paints her portrait we see the quality of their love: the force of his emotion enables him to transcend his customary skill and he paints his one and only good canvas. The painting shows too her response to him:

Christian's face was in shade, the brown darkness of her

loosened hair framed it and blended with the green darkness of the yew hedge. Faint reflected lights from her white dress, touches of sunlight that came through the leaves of the surrounding trees gave the shadowed face life. In the clear stillness of the eyes, something had been caught of the wonder that was latent in Christian's look, the absorption in things far away, seen inwardly, that in childhood had set her in a place apart. . . .

But Larry is not worth it. We get a picture of an Ascendancy dilettante, irresponsible, romantic, easily caught up in enthusiasm, not capable of much thought about anything. He has very little self-knowledge, little interest in religion and none of Christian's spirituality or mysticism.

'Larry was undevout, careless, thinking little of spiritual things, so little that he had scarcely troubled himself either to question or to accept what he had been taught . . .' Yet everyone loves him, with the exception of the Protestant butler. His beautiful looks and charming manner are presented winsomely enough. He is a conventional hero in his gaiety and charm and much more credible as such than Dorothea's Ladislaw in *Middlemarch*. Unlike Christopher Dysart he is a success with women, and lacking Christopher's self-knowledge he is constantly swept up in his latest enthusiasm. Once 'immersed' in painting in Paris he loses all interest in his Irish estate and tenants. After four godless years in art studios he is astonished to see it matter whether one is a Protestant or a Catholic. He is clay in the hands of Dr Mangan, who can manoeuvre him in all ways, and as susceptible to Tishy after he has fallen in love with Christian as he was before. He has no understanding of Christian's renunciation, no concept of what she is doing, and merely sees that he has been thrown over. When his marriage puts him in a blue funk he cannot do anything about it, and one feels that Tishy is quite right to make off with her red-haired lover—Larry was marrying her out of a spineless inability to stand up to her father and out of his own self-pity. It is a credible enough picture, but it is not easy to accept that this is the man who deserves Christian, and it is impossible to see him as capable of carrying the kind of transcendence of the spirit of the nation which the theme demands. Their whole relationship is sadly sentimentalised. They declare their love at a Druid Stone beside the *Tober an Sidhe*, the fairies' well, on the hill *Cnochán an Ceoil Sidhe*, the Hill of Fairy Music, that gave its name to the house. That is, they leave behind modern Ireland with its religious intolerance and find the good fairy influences of ancient Ireland. Here they kneel and plight their troth: 'While water stands in Tubber an shee, My heart in your hands, your heart in me.' They enact the sacrament by drinking the fairy water from each other's cupped hands. Although none of this action is out of character it strains the conventions of the realistic novel, and the writing encroaches on the artificiality of *fin de siécle* prose. Two passages must be quoted at length.

Christian and Larry passed through the shadowy grove, walking side by side along the narrow track, their footsteps made noiseless by its thick covering of pine needles. It was dark in the wood; the fir trees towered in the gloom above them; here and there in the deep of the branches there was the stir of a wing, as a pigeon settled to its nest; from beyond the wood came a brief, shrill bicker of starlings; all things beside these were mute, and in the silent dusk, spirit was sensitive to spirit, and the air was tense with the unspoken word.

The sun was low in the west when they came out on to the open hillside, and went on up the path, through the heather, that led to the Druid stone beside the Tober an Sidhe, the fairies' well. The mist, golden and green, that comes with an autumn sunset, half hid, half transfigured the wide distances of the valley of the Broadwater; the darkness of the woods, blended from this aspect into one, of Mount Music and Coppinger's Court, was softened by its veils; the far hills were transparent, as if the light had fused them to clearest brown, and topaz, and opal glass. The hill side, above and beneath them, glowed and smouldered with the ruby-purple of the heather.

Christian and Larry stood in the path beside the ancient stone and looked out over the valley; the vastness and the glory of the great prospect whelmed them like a flood, the

sense of imminence that was over them strung their nerves to
vibrating and held them silent.

'My God!' sighed Larry, at last, trembling, turning to her
who had never failed to understand him. 'Christian! It's too
beautiful—the world is too big—I can't bear it alone—' He
caught her arm. 'You've got to help me. Oh Christian!—'

Christian turned her face from him.

'I believe I could,' she said in a very low voice.

Even as she spoke, the truth broke out of her soul and ran
through her, running from her soul to his, like the flame of oil
spilled upon clear water. A voice cried a warning in her heart.
'Too late!' she answered it with triumph.

'Darling!' said Larry, holding her close.

The sunset

> 'bloomed and withered on the hill
> Like any hill-flower';

but long those two stood by the Druid stone, knowing,
perhaps the best moment that life could give them, facing the
dying radiance with hearts that were full of sunrise.

This is the most self-indulgent prose they ever wrote. It is a pity
Edith Somerville read the novel aloud to no one, for it is hard to
imagine she would have been able to read it with a straight face.
All the objectivity, all the detachment and sense of humour is
gone. She is writing purely for effect without any other interest
in what she is saying. The second awful passage is linked to this
with a chapter of down-to-earth plottings of priest and doctor.
At once the style is crisp and sensible, a balanced mixture of
satire and realism. The dialogue is as right as ever, and then we
are back with the two who are meant to transcend 'the Spirit of
the Nation':

In silence they had gone through the dark wood, and almost
in silence had made their mutual farewells in the fragrant
shadow of the pines.

When the soul is tuned to its highest it cannot find an
interpreter. The lips can utter only broken sounds, pathetic-
ally inadequate to express emotions that may, in some future
sphere, make themselves known in terms other than are
permitted to us. There is an inner radiance that is beyond

thought, that might conceivably utter itself in music or in colour, but can no more be translated into words than can the radiance of the mid-day sun be more than indicated by earthly painters with earthly pigments.

So it was Larry and Christian . . .

I do not believe it! The narrator's confession of inability at conveying mystical experience does nothing to mitigate the failure. The love between these two young people is never made convincing. Once Christian is turned into a symbol of the love which will conquer the spirit of the nation, she withers to a Pre-Raphaelite damosel clutching her basket of Christmas roses.

The ending is not inevitable and it does not ring true. They attempt to pull things together with an apocalyptic flood, Mangan is drowned, Tishy is evacuated beyond the promised land, and Mount Music is left to the good characters. The flood is melodramatic and the turgid language is merely rhetorical, with clumsy involved sentences:

> Trembling people in little, low-lying cottages, with thatched roofs held in place with ladders, and ropes, and stones, with doors and windows barricaded against the wind. But of what avail are barricades against the creeping white lip of water, crawling in under the doors over the earthen floors, soaking in through mud-built walls, coming against them at first as a thief in the night, falling upon them later as a strong man armed?
>
> From the lower side-streets of Cluhir the people fled. . . . Ghastly stories were told of drowned cattle that were swept against the closed doors, and came pushing and banging at the windows, carried there by their conqueror as it were with mockery, to entreat for the succour that was too late.

There is an attempt to suggest that there is a sunrise in the hearts of Larry and Christian. Even Mangan is made to be repentant. The overall balanced detachment of the narration is never rediscovered. The complete lack of discipline and restraint reduces the novel to the banal.

An Enthusiast was written between May 1920 and March 1921.

Just as *Mount Music* was an attempt to be fair about the part religion played in Irish society, this tries to do the same for politics. Edith Somerville wants to give English readers a balanced picture of what is going on. And as with the last novel she fears she will succeed in offending everyone. In the Preface she writes, 'There is something arrogant, if not offensive, in an attitude of Impartiality, and to be strictly impartial is to be equally disliked by all sides. In trying to keep on even keel in very strong seas I have risked this disaster.' Its subject matter is events in Ireland in 1920, bridging the time between the end of one era and, with the Treaty, the start of another. Politically it takes up where *Mount Music* ends: the Catholic farmers own much of the land, Home Rule is established, and political power is in the grip of the Catholic middle class. Many of the Anglo-Irish, without land and with houses they can no longer afford to live in, have either emigrated or moved into smaller houses. The First World War has ended, and, in the 1918 General Election, Sinn Fein had a majority and formed Dail Eireann. The English government, in an attempt to suppress the traitorous parliament, had sent over troops to Ireland. The reign of the Black and Tans was under way. Edith Somerville turned the daily events of her life into fiction. During the time she was writing it she went to stay at Lismore for a rest and the MS. includes, for example, copies of telegrams she sent to Drishane to arrange how to get home again when motor permits were only issued for twenty miles and a fresh car was necessary every twenty miles. So she plans to be collected by pony and cart taking five days each way—'Send oats rugs Burberry. Luggage trains impossible'—and stopping overnight with friends. The novel was based on immediate facts: her local court house had been burned out, the police barracks were destroyed and yet life went on as if nothing was happening; fairs, markets, agricultural shows were still held. The Sinn Fein made nightly raids for guns, or failing these—for most of them were confiscated by the police—war souvenirs, such as spears made of human shin-bones, Malay daggers, Crimean shakos, as well as money, cattle and food. The poor were pestered by the police and the Black and Tans by day and bullied by the Sinn Fein by night. The forces of law tried to frighten the people into betraying the rebels; but if they did they would be shot the next night by the Sinn Feiners:

> It's hard to blame them, and they having no protection good or bad! . . . And then, by night, those fifteen boys will come down to the house and will turn the poor man and the wife out of the bed itself, and get into it themselves by turn, to warm themselves! And they'll eat all those unfortunate creatures will have in the house for themselves![4]

This happened nightly to the folk in and around Castletownshend.

Into this setting she placed a small Anglo-Irish community, the members of the Rural District Council, a priest and a rebel. One sees their relationships with each other during the Troubles and the possibilities which were open to the Anglo-Irish in Ireland during this crucial time. The old way of life is represented by Colonel Palliser. Even though the novel opens with his funeral she is careful to make him possible, to anchor him in history; thus in MS. she sketches Colonel Palliser's life:

Born 1839
Crimea 1853-56 aged 17
Married 1893 aged 54
Dan born 1894
Colonel dies 1920 aged 81

In the first chapter his corpse is laid to rest for ever. His last act had been to reinforce the doors and windows of Monalour House against the rebellious natives. His funeral is similar to that of Edith Somerville's father in 1898: the Union Jack 'of victory' covers his coffin, his sword and shako of the Crimea lie on the flag, the tenants carry the coffin to the graveside and the whole countryside turn out. The Pallisers are old Protestant stock who have been in Ireland since Elizabethan times. Their land is now gone, and with it their social power; when the old colonel dies they are finally broken by death duties. The house is let to Lord Ducarrig, a colonial Anglo-Irishman who made his money and his title in rubber during his Governorships in the East. He is the archetypal bullying imperialist. His young wife hates him, and he despises her because she has not given him a

son. He has governed natives abroad and intends to do the same
at home. He is both merciless and bloodthirsty: he is attracted to
the idea of civil war and can see no difference between chasing
rebels and hunting grouse. He is egotistical enough to go and
shoot in the mountains when he knows they are full of Sinn
Féiners on the run, and thoughtless enough to send a telegram to
his wife telling her he is arriving with 'three guns' when the
police have taken away all guns and the raiders will do anything
to get them. His only other interest is sex and his wish that his
wife, twenty-five years younger, might die and leave him free to
marry again. Edith Somerville depicted few characters as
unattractive as this pink-pig-eyed, red-puffy-faced, bald-
headed fat loyalist from the North. The Palliser men are
ineffectual and amusing as exemplified by Dan's elegant uncle,
Admiral Caulfield, in his impeccable garden, where he weeds
in a long blue apron and white kid gloves and where the pebbles
look as if they were dusted each morning. The Ascendancy
women in this novel are the most unattractive of any in the
novels of Somerville & Ross: they are cruel to their men, ready
to fight, spiteful and a little too outspoken. Katie de Vere says
nobody has a right to call himself a gardener unless 'he's
prepared—when he's pricking seedlings for example—to hold a
slug in his mouth until he has a spare moment when he can
squash it.' The Colonel's widow is intractable, domineering and
thoroughly convinced of the superiority of her set to the Irish no
matter who holds power or wealth. She is altogether a nasty
lady, and only too real:

> 'The same thing runs through everything and every class' she
> asserted, having given that cautious circular glance, to make
> certain of the absence of the servants, that is, in Ireland,
> almost automatic, '*Un*reliability!' She planked her large
> hand, with its gouty knuckles and finger-joints, flat on the
> table, as if she were laying the foundation-stone of a public
> building. 'You *can't* trust them! Idle, unconscientious and
> dirty! They don't *know* what cleanliness is! I have never yet
> met with an Irish servant who *suffered* from dirt, as a good
> English servant does—'

The Catholic middle class is depicted with a similar clarity.

Mr Coyne, the Baby Bullet, is representative of the new order: he is a strong farmer, the owner of a large general store, vice president of the Agricultural Society, a coal merchant and a leading member of the Rural District Council. His success is due to his penchant for intrigue: because the Council is democratic and everything is decided by vote, he buys the votes beforehand. He bribes with aplomb, his tenders are accepted and his businesses flourish. Quarrels are no longer simply about land, with the gombeen men money comes into them too. Coyne calls himself a man of principle and illustrates his principles:

> 'There was a woman came to me a while ago,' resumed the Baby, 'asking me would I get her a job—washing-a-day-a-week at the Union, I think it was. I said to her, "My good woman," I says, "I might consider it, but I must have something for it." "Sir," says she, "I'm a poor woman, what could I give ye?" "Mary Bryan," says I (that was her name), "Mary," says I, "if it was only half a crown, I should have it. For the *principle* of the thing, Mary," says I.'

He is as morally corrupt as Lord Ducarrig and as physically repulsive. He hates Dan so much that he stoops to writing Ducarrig a filthy anonymous letter. The lack of standards in public conduct is more of a hindrance to Dan than the farmers' conservatism and dislike of new methods. He can do nothing with the corruption they take for granted.

The picture of the middle classes is balanced by the character of Jimmy Ryan, another strong farmer and District Council member. He is friendly and kind, and he likes people for themselves, not for what they can do for him. His weakness is his frivolity. At the meeting at which the Clerk of the Union is elected, the weaker man is appointed because his father could afford to spend over £200 in bribing for votes. The meeting degenerates into a bad farce of backchat and personal insults. A bout of fisticuffs is averted:

> The opponent then replied with the statement that it was easy seen that Mr Coyne had his share of drink taken, to give him courage, for he had a face on him as red as of the Earl of Hell's waistcoat; not content with this trope, he went on to say that

it was known to all that Mr Coyne's old mother had gone pucking at every back door in the country, with a bag on her back, and himself in it, begging spuds.

Mr Coyne's indignation rendered him, for an instant, inarticulate, but he lost but little time before replying with suitable spirit:

'Ye little weazel, ye!' he exclaimed, 'Ye dirty little weazel!'

The meeting is based on the *Cork County Eagle and Muster Advertiser's* 10, September, 1910 report of a meeting of the Skibbereen Rural District Council:

(After Uproar and near fisticuffs between Mr Healey and Mr McCarthy.)

Mr Healy—'I would very soon make you conduct yourself if I thought it worth my while, but you are not worth it.'

Mr D. McCarthy—'Sit down you little weasel.'

Mr Sheehan—'This is too bad' (Uproar) Here another squabble ensued, and several members interfered to prevent the gentlemen from 'getting at' each other. The Chairman repeatedly called for order but as his ruling was not obeyed he left the chair and endeavoured to pull away Mr D. McCarthy.

Ryan responds by roaring with laughter, 'Well, but aren't they great play-boys? . . . They were in grand forr'm altogether!' And though we laugh we judge Ryan's reaction as frivolous; it is not enough for men like him to refrain from putting their own personal profit first, they have to take public responsibility even more seriously if Ireland is to govern herself. The rebel is the only one beside Dan to have this kind of responsibility; he tells how an entire District Council has become inactive because half of the board members are in prison, and how amusing the remaining members find it when the clerk too is arrested.

Edith Somerville explores the state of Irish society at this crucial time through Dan Palliser's attempt to come to terms with it. He is of the school of Christopher Dysart and represents the best of the young generation of Anglo-Irish. He has returned from World War I with an M.C., a limp and a hatred of violence. He has chosen to study agriculture rather than completing his degree in Cambridge. His elders wish him to let the Big House and farm and live off the proceeds in a London flat; Dan moves into the smaller house on the estate and farms it himself. He loves his country and will not leave, 'His romance, his passion was Ireland'. He reasons that his country is mainly agricultural, and that to improve the farming is the best he can do for the country. And he believes that because change must start with the individual it is the local effort which counts, no matter how small that effort. He sets an example of improvements by buying a tractor and ploughing the park land; his workmen are entirely hostile to every new venture and to Dan's working with them. He joins societies advocating co-operative farming schemes, and he rides out daily to distribute pamphlets and talk about new techniques, co-operative farming, creameries, milk yields and the merits of Friesian cows. He manages to start a Milk Recording Society, a Creamery and a Co-operative Store. He really does put his country first and is never looking for personal returns. He has no political affiliations, just this passionate concern for the country. And he romanticises Ireland:

> There's no big lot of Irishmen are bad fellows, but there are blackguards everywhere, and they're the ones you hear most about . . . Look at this country! The police gone, our arms taken from us, either by raiders or by the Government—it comes to the same thing! Our houses absolutely defenceless— a baby could get into any house in the country if he wanted to, at any hour of the day or night—and what happens? My mother, and the rest of them, who want to 'drench the country with blood,' go to bed, and sleep as peacefully as if they were in London—and with far less chance of being burgled! . . . Even these murders of policemen and soldiers— God knows I don't defend them! Call them as brutal and cowardly and senseless as you like, I'll go all the way with you, but at least you must admit they're not personal, not done for private interests, or money.

He is most grateful to Ryan when he gets him elected to the Rural District Council Board, seeing it as an opportunity to meet the strong farmers and interest them in scientific farming methods.

The Rural District Council teach Dan a lot about his country. He discovers that most of them do take part for what they personally can get out of it. And to his amazement he sees that the standards of honesty they maintain in private life do not extend to their civic duties. Sensible, clever and hardworking farmers become corrupt as administrators of local government. Dan slowly realises they have two distinct standards of morality, and that he just does not see things their way. He knows 'himself to be unversed in the idiom of his new colleagues'. The corruption depresses him, 'How, with such materials as these, was he, or anyone else, to build Jerusalem in Ireland's green and pleasant land?' And he is forced to see that the farmers have no interest in his improvements; they want immediate returns and ready money. The co-op store takes money from private traders, especially the Baby Bullet's general store, so the tradesmen boycott Dan. When Dan tries to lend co-operative machinery to members of the Farmer's Society at harvest time, the Baby tells Dan he is misusing his money and position by taking away the living of his poorer neighbours—the Baby hires his own threshing machine out at exorbitant rates. Dan's own men are increasingly suspicious when he works with them at the harvest, and Dan is forced to see that he is not accepted by anyone. Nobody believes that politics can be transcended. In the scene where he invites everyone to a party to view his new tractor he is made to realise that he is an outsider. Conversations fade to a whisper as he draws near, or they suddenly become very loud discussions about the weather. Like Larry at the Protestant Sale of Work he senses the strain and tension. He can get no one to talk to him about what is worrying them all, and he sees he will never be trusted, 'He and his like were kept outside'. When the local rebel is captured, for all Dan's efforts to steer clear of politics everyone thinks he is the informer. Eventually he resigns from the Farmers' Society in disgust at their pretended patriotism. He tells them what he thinks of them before he goes:

And no more are you Sinn Feiners! I'd respect you if you were! I'd know where you were! But you're sitting on the top of the fence, afraid to move for fear you'd tumble down the wrong side! You're too afraid of your own boys to hide their breeches from them and keep them home o'nights! You're afraid of each other! Shall I tell you what a poor woman, whose son was a policeman and was shot from behind a fence like a mad dog, said to me? I said to her, like a fool, that this dirty work wouldn't go on: I told her, like a fool, that you farmers were decent men, and that you'd put a stop to it! She said to me, 'The farmers! they're afraid! They'd be afraid of a rabbit in their own field!'

Dan's own disappointment in them makes him harsh on them as he scorns them for letting Ireland be destroyed by gunmen, 'you're afraid to say what every one of you thinks of these blackguards, these strangers and Bolshevists . . . who are teaching, yes! and forcing your innocent boys to burn and rob and murder and bring ruin on Ireland and on her industries and her people!'

His disillusionment with the Irish farmers leaves him in a lonely position, because his interest in modern Ireland and his efforts at working with the farmers have antagonised his own class. They see the farmers as competitors and because they cannot see how they personally can gain from co-operatives they have already cast Dan off. Like the farmers they cannot believe that someone can be politically neutral so they think Dan's attempts to befriend the farmers show his political allegiance. They distrust him as much as the others. No one will believe in his disinterested love of his country, and as the novel progresses Dan becomes increasingly alone. When he refuses to give the Sinn Fein raiders the money they demand, they dub him a Unionist and steal his cattle. Dan learns the hard way that political neutrality is impossible in practice, and that at the very least he is 'Mr Facing-both-ways'.

But Dan is a romantic and he makes his conscious pledge to dedicate his life to his country after all this disillusionment. When he sees the grief of the rebel's family it symbolises for him all the suffering which Ireland has suffered in the past, was suffering in the present, and would suffer in the future. The emotion with which he reacts to the tenants' coming to bury his father, 'They haven't given us up yet! They know our hearts are Irish, even though our name isn't! In spite of Sinn Fein, they haven't given up the Old Stock!' is rekindled by seeing the people's distress. He can still romanticise the peasants, 'His manner caught from theirs something of its ease and pleasantness, of the social self-possession that is almost Latin in the feeling it imparts of an ancient civilisation, a traditional culture.' He sees in them the love that he has himself, the patriotism which is not economic or materialistic but, 'a spark of that divine folly that makes sometimes for madness, sometimes for misery, yet is sometimes a beacon telling of the high places of human nature'.

Edith Somerville's efforts to be fair to all sides give us the rebel and the priest. Eugene Cashel and Father Hugh match Dan in sincerity and patriotism. They too can serve, and have pledged their lives to their country. The rebel is an intelligent and literate man, a lover of English poetry, and a native Irish speaker. He abhors senseless murder, such as the unnecessary slaughter of a village policeman, and the police allow him to keep a gun, believing that the wilder, ruthless rebels listen to Eugene. Father Hugh brings Dan and Eugene together, and, as he expects, Dan feels a kinship with Eugene even though he dislikes his methods. The priest hopes that his country's destiny is to become the Land of Saints once more, the Sanctuary of the Holy Church. Unlike the rebel he does not know what to do at the moment. He and Dan, despite their differences of race, class and religion, find that 'their souls spoke the same language'. They do find comfort in each other's company, sharing their dreams and visions. As Dan's despair increases so does the priest's—he finds it impossible to go preaching peace to people who must defend themselves or die. But the sufferings of rebel and priest are familiar crosses; Dan can only vow, 'What I can do, I will do, so help me God!'

When Dan dies, the shot that kills him is fired by the imperialist, Lord Ducarrig. Dan is a ridiculous figure running across the tennis court clutching his father's Crimean sword. He is shot in error, by a man who cares nothing for Ireland nor for Dan's house which is being raided. The Ulster Unionists do appear far blacker than the Sinn Feiners; the old men come to life at the thought of murder and shoot the rebels gleefully, 'Bagged a brace, I think! I saw two fellows being dragged over into covert'; and 'I can see two chaps on the move—going your way! Mark cock!' They revel in the killings:

> 'They're off! They've bolted for their lives!' he shouted.
> 'We've beat them! A fellow came running up to reinforce them, a thundering big fellow, he was too, but Ducarrig got him!'
> 'Has he killed him?'
> 'Ra—ther!' said MacNeill exultingly. 'He never even kicked!'

The novel is the one which is closest to the author's own troubles as she wrote it. The changes which Dan undergoes, his hopes, disillusionments, and seemingly fatuous dedication (for his death is a farce and useless) are very near to the author. His practical efforts to do good to his country by the breeding of Friesians and farming were things she was trying; his feeling of loyalty to the British Empire was hers too. Although she is careful to state in the Preface that none of the characters express her views, 'each speaks for him or herself and not for me' Dan's situation and problems were very close to her heart. There is none of the distancing of time of the other novels, and this makes the comedy more savage, the pictures of the Anglo-Irish the most bitter of any of the books. It is her equivalent in mood to the 1919, 1920 poems about civil war of W.B. Yeats, and like him she is hard on all her countrymen. A few of the best, Father Hugh, Eugene Cashel, Dan Palliser, still remained but they seemed to have remarkable little effect on the whole. As she wrote for the Hudson Bibliography, 'if sadness is its final note, this does not make the tale less true'.

In many ways the novel is superior to *Mount Music*; it is tighter and more disciplined. There is the usual colourful dialect: Dan's nurse says when he was a small boy illness always 'hit him hot and heavy! If it was only a little thorn in his finger itself, it'd turn into a pig's foot on him!' And a countryman remarks, 'I rose when it was making day, and says I to myself "There's rain in it," but I'm thinking now that it will stagger on till th'evening.' But there is far less of it than usual; the strong farmers are not so close to the Irish language as they used to be. Dan, as the main character, sets much of the tone of the book, and he is quite without a sense of humour. In his relationships with the strong farmers there is a similarity with the Irish R.M. and the community around him; there is the same difference in standards of honesty and morality. Dan is as incapable of doing anything underhand as the R.M., but when he is put in a false position by his well-meaning groom who illicitly practises Dan's horse over the show jumps, it is no longer amusing. In this new, serious Ireland such a trick is judged and punished. The author was only too well aware of the solemnity of the book. When it was near completion she wrote gloomily, 'It gets sadder every day! I can't help it . . . I'm afraid the people who talk so much of our rollickingness will be rather sick. But *how* could a book about Ireland in 1920 rollick?' It is bleak, but this is preferable to the wishful thinking which mars the ending of *Mount Music*.

Somerville & Ross face facts and succeed in doing more than rage at what is happening to their beloved country. The writing of fiction carried on with a professional devotion to language, kept Edith Somerville sane in the midst of anarchy.

Chapter VII

The Big House of Inver—French Leave—
Sarah's Youth

The preliminary notes for *The Big House of Inver* were made soon after the local people had asked Colonel Cameron Somerville, President of the local branch of the Farmers' Union to stand as a candidate for the West Cork council election. By the time Edith Somerville was writing the novel the troubles of the last few years had settled down. The early notes show that to begin with she was writing about actual people she knew, taking them as types with which to humanise Violet Martin's description of Tyrone house and the St George family. She composed family trees in detail for the characters and drew them up against the reigns of the crown heads of Great Britain from 1702 onwards . . . She goes into more detail as she comes to the time she is centring on. She worked out the action of the novel checking it against a calendar: the first ride of Peggy and Kit is in May; Peggy and Kit go to the Big House together in June; the race-meeting is in July; Burgrave arrives in August; Kit and Peggy ride on the sands for a second time and meet Maggie there in September. The events of the last week of the action are done with more detail:

The Last Week. Time Table.

Tuesday: Peggy and Maggie. Ring sent back to Kit. Burgrave's letter comes.
Wednesday: Kit tells news to Shibby. Writes to Peggy. Goes to Cahirbwee.
Thursday: Burgrave arrives afternoon. Peggy gets Kit's letter. The horse fair. Mollie and Shibby talk. Telegram comes.

Friday: Sir Harold sees Big House. Shibby and Nessie away.
   Mrs Weldon talks to Peggy.
Saturday: Deed of sale signed. Shibby returns meets Peggy.
Sunday: Shibby goes to chapel and to Cloon, meets Maggie.
Monday: Peggy and Burgrave and Jimmy Connor.
Tuesday: Shibby goes to see Kit—All is over—

After great difficulty with the first chapter, in which she has to condense the history of the Prendevilles she wrote regularly and smoothly, reading aloud to her sister chapter by chapter as she wrote. She was never able to spend more than two hours a day at writing, but this was enough to finish the novel, including the clean-copying, by June, 1925. 'Got up early and finished copying *The Big House of Inver* with the word "finis" the ink in my pen ran out and the church bell began to ring'.

Although the story is a sombre one the whole book is quite different from *Mount Music* and *An Enthusiast*. There is no shortage of dialect* and the narrator's touch is sure and confident. The male characters are as lively as any, and there is great variety amongst them. The sound, good hearted doctor who has been sensitive enough to fall in love with Shibby, has his own voice, such as when he says of Old John's great age, 'Ah isn't that a terrible age for any man to be! Ah, the old man is worn out! It's only the force of habit keeps him going. He's been at it now for so long it's chronic with him.'[1] Old John himself is a marvellous creation; he is as richly rustic as any of Hardy's characters and has a much better gift of talk: he never gets over having a French convent educated granddaughter, 'I declare to ye she's that cultured ye'd say she was born in a droign-room! Upon me soul ye would. And to hear her play the p'yanna—Oh, t'would delight a Turk! And as for French!—Honest to God! she talks it as nice and as easy as meself talks the English!' He is a grossly fat old man, and completely different from his common son, a solicitor, and his granddaughter Peggy, who will marry a titled person. When the three of them first meet it is a comic occasion. Burgrave comes to woo Peggy and knocks down Old John who stands in the gateway; Burgrave thinks he is a pauper inmate, out for the day, and expects him to get out of his way. He

---

*Cf. chapter one.

tells Peggy he's knocked over, 'a fat old fool who stood in the way'. It is broad comedy as Peggy reacts by screaming, 'Good heavens! Grand-dad!' Old John's son, Young Johnny, is a snob, a social climber and altogether quite nauseating, compared with his delightful old father. But he can't help but slip into the voice of his background when he is not putting on graces. His efforts at refinement when he struggles through a lunch with Burgrave are grating, but he redeems himself when he describes it to his wife afterwards, saying of Burgrave, 'He was something livelier after he had a tooth driven into a bit of beef.'

The comedy in the book is good-natured and cheery; the many scenes of small town life, horse fairs, horse races, add colour and brightness to the overall mood. And the narrator does not identify too closely with any of the characters, nor romanticise them; we have a well rounded and nicely judged picture of all of them. Even Kit, the hero, can not only be seen as a rotter but he can be laughed at too, so confident is the tone. He has a bad fall from a horse he is trying out at a fair; he opens his eyes slowly and calls to a notorious crook:

> 'Con', he said, feebly, 'here, whisper—'
> Brendan bent down.
> 'Buy that mare for me!'
> 'I will so,' said Brendan. 'She's a sweet mare.'

Two other titles were considered for the novel, *A Victim of the Past*, and *Restoration*. The focus is on the year 1912 and the attempts to restore the Prendeville family to the Big House. The story spans the history of the family from 1739; by 1912 the land belongs to the tenantry, the demesne to the agent, and the family have lived in the old Norman tower for the last two generations. Although empty and neglected the Big House still dominates the landscape for miles around; Burgrave comes on it suddenly from the demesne where it has been invisible:

> Burgrave seated himself on one of the big stone blocks that were the stops for the gates, and regarded the house with interest.
> 'Jove, it *is* a fine house!' he said, with surprise. 'That's a fine portico!—well proportioned—and that stone balustrade

along the top—jolly good I call it! How many rooms are there, Weldon?'

'Twenty, I believe, on each floor, Sir Har'ld, more or less— I declare it's so long since I was in it, I'm not rightly—' . . .

Burgrave sat and smoked and contemplated the house with growing admiration.

'It's just the stamp I like,' he thought, 'who'd have expected to find a house like this in this God-forsaken place?'

The iron gates are bent and covered with rust; the avenue is overgrown. Inside the green marble slabs are clammy, the stale air is cold, but the amazing proportions of the rooms, the ornate ceilings, brass-mounted fireplaces, white stone staircase, and pillared hall are as classically splendid as ever. Inver is based on the Martins' home, Ross. The original house, Tyrone, which Violet Martin had seen and wanted to write about, Edith Somerville did not know. She merely had Violet Martin's description to go on, 'a bigger and much grander edition of Ross. A great square cut-stone house of three stories, with an area—perfectly empty—and such ceilings, architraves, teak doors, and chimney pieces as one sees in old houses in Dublin.' In the book Inver is 'a big, solemn square house of three stories, built of cut-stone, grandly facing west . . . A wide and deep area went round three sides of the house' which could well be a description of Ross. As is the flight of limestone steps leading to the hall door, and 'the back was guarded by the high walls of the stable yard . . .' Ross and Inver are both well fortified against intruders. Inver is the archetypal Big House, with its marriage stones, crests and family portraits. It is the abode of the family, made sacred by time and given scriptural authority, 'Look unto the rock whence ye were hewn, the hole of the pit whence ye were digged', and 'Children's children are the crown of old men; and the glory of children are their fathers'. Somerville & Ross would have us add, 'the sins of the fathers shall be inherited unto the fourth generation.' and would have us consider questions of pride and guilt. This is a story of a glorious race going to the dogs:

> And maybe the great-grandson of that house,
> For all its bronze and marble, 's but a mouse.[2]

What remains of the mahogany furniture of Inver is in the tower, so too are the remainder of the family, Captain Jasper Prendeville and his children, the illegitimate Shibby, and the legitimate Kit and Nessie. The Captain is senile and sits all day crouched over a small turf fire with a dirty horse-blanket wrapped round him. He smokes sailors' shag; he slops his tea into the blanket; food clings to his beard and his dogs steal his cake from his shaking hands. He is a similar mixture of seediness and gentility to Julia Duffy or old Henn in O'Faolain's 'Midsummer Night Madness'. His voice retains the accent of good breeding, his manners are still gracious with an old-fashioned formality, but most of the time he is incapable of carrying on a conversation, and sits in a mindless stupor. When he goes to visit his Big House he puts on a blue, knitted nightcap a long, orange frieze coat, and a thick, brown muffler; he looks ridiculous in the house, but his voice and manner belong to the house's style more than Burgrave's do. His favourite story is how he broke his wrist at a dance in Calcutta and brought the Colonel's wife a cropper at the same time, it ends, 'They used to say of me in the Regiment that "no one ever saw Jas blind, but if you boiled his bones, a fellow would get drunk on the broth!"' The family now is quite uncultured; they are like the Ascendancy Lennox Robinson writes about in his play *The Big House*:

> With no culture. Ignorant. Don't know whether the portraits that hang in their dining rooms are eighteenth-century masterpieces or photogravures, don't know if the silver they use everyday is old Irish or modern Brummagem. Don't know the history of their own family, don't know Irish history. Have nothing but a few religious prejudices and very good health. Can't even grow decent flowers . . . And the Irish gentleman! Ignorant. Asleep . . . They're divorced from all reality.

Kit, like his father, is a combination of the splendid and the shabby. He has been educated in the local National School and has picked up a 'commonness of mind and manner that Jas, sunken and debased though he was, had somehow escaped' from the Commercial College in the nearby town. He fails the preliminary exams for the Veterinary Surgeons' College, and is sent home from a racing stable because he tries to elope with the schoolgirl daughter of the owner. Since then he has stayed at Inver training horses and being spoiled by his two sisters. His morality is as debased as his manners; he has none of the uprightness of Willy, Christopher, or Dan; when he has an affair with the village girl and gets her pregnant he blames her. He actually cheats to win a horse race, and when Shibby bravely tackles him about it, he reacts by 'shouting down Shibby's interrupting questions, continuing to distribute the responsibility, impartially on all concerned, with the single exception of himself.' When he is engaged to the girl he is supposed to love (not the village girl) he boasts that she is his to do what he likes with. When she, broken-hearted, breaks off the engagement he simply forgets all about her in the excitement of a horse fair. Kit can forget anything, none of his failures or disgraces mean anything at all to him. As for respect for his father, this is the description of the way he looks at the old man, 'A vigorous young dog will sometimes thus survey an elder, lying somnolent and sick in the sun; with a sort of curiosity; not exactly with contempt. One could only say positively that there was no pity in it.' He is quite oblivious of his sisters and has no idea that he is making Shibby suffer. Tradition means nothing to him, and he is blind to the beauty of the house he is heir to. When Peggy Weldon sees the cross on the sands which marks the spot where Kit's ancestor, Beauty Kit, was killed, she thinks, 'how distinguished it would be to say that one's grandfather had been killed in a duel!' But Kit is 'oblivious to the privilege that was his'. Beside the the agent's daughter he is 'an illiterate country boy', and yet she loves him and wants to marry him.

Peggy's falling in love with Kit, against her better judgment, against all the discrimination which she has learnt in her fashionable French convent, adds to our understanding of his character. He has style. He has inherited all the beauty, grace and elegance of his fore-fathers. When he is first introduced to us we see a young god, a bright creature, a golden-haired, lithe youth riding a red-gold blood filly as if he were made to ride her. The words which he is said to conjure up. 'Truly the light is sweet, and a pleasant thing it is for the eyes to behold the sun', are used without a trace of irony. When Peggy thinks he looks, 'like some bright creature from another sky', we are not judging her as we do Katharine's romantising of John Michael; we accept that this is an integral part of Kit Prendeville. He is the image of his grandfather, so that when Peggy sees the eighteenth-century portrait of Beauty Kit, she thinks it is her Kit, 'When was he painted like that?' The pathos is that such glorious beauty is bound to such weakness and slackness. The words of the prophet are right: the echo of Beauty Kit is vibrant and Kit's beauty is even more ineffective, spineless and doomed. The author maintains a nice balance with him: at the horse race he does cheat but this is mitigated by the fact that the handicap-ping weight was unfairly heavy, and by the way in which he wins. The narrator's sympathies are with him, despite the fraud, as he wins after a bad fall, riding bare-back carrying his saddle on his arm, and the grace of his way with a horse—the mare giving the impossible for 'the rider she loved'—is irresistible. It is a hero's victory. When he finally falls in love with Peggy this is equally sympathetically presented: they are surrendering them-selves to the beauty they see in each other. And it is symbolically beneath a red harvest moon, 'It moved up the green sky, incredibly huge and red, and a long beam of warm gold came trembling down the sea, and was echoed in touches of light in the dark little lake at Peggy's feet . . .' But it is not enough.

Next in social importance to the Prendevilles are the Weldons, who live in a house built out of the stones of the original Prendeville house in the demesne. They are middle-class Protestants who have risen by effort and education until they have overtaken the Ascendancy family. But though they have benefited by the Prendevilles' slackness they have not caused their downfall. Old John is in the tradition of Thady's son and Dr Mangan, and he was 'a young man of unusual perspicacity . . . and a crafty brain' and a grabber, but like Dr Mangan he is seen sympathetically. He is a lovable old rogue of ninety-four, a fat bronchial old man who looks like a pauper and rides on an ass-butt. He is still bound by feudal ideas, and the one thing he wants from life is to see his grandchild married to one of the old family. When he learns of Peggy's engagement to Kit he says, 'My God! When I thinks of the Old Madam, that was Miss Moore of Gurtha, and no better in Ireland! And me

father, Mick, that was her servant! By gosh, it's like a merracle
to me that I should live to hear the like!' His feudalism excuses
Kit's behaviour entirely when he learns that Kit his granddaughter's fiancé, has got a village girl pregnant. 'Kind father
for him! What's bred in the bone will come out in the meat! And
why shouldn't he plaze himself when he's young!'

But his son and his son's wife, an English governess, consider
themselves superior to the Prendevilles. Their daughter must
complete their climb by marrying a man with a title and fifteen
thousand a year. The daughter has received the education
which her friends, Kit and Nessie, lack: an English school, a
Paris convent, expensive holidays, and the removal of an Irish
accent. Peggy has inherited her grandmother's good looks and
has her own quick temper and high spirit. She thinks well of
herself and is proud, seeing Kit as a country boy with a brogue;
and yet she cannot help herself from choosing him as a husband
rather than the cultivated wealthy Sir Harold. Kit's beauty, his
blue eyes and gentle West-of-Ireland voice are irresistible. She is
not materialistic (or she would have chosen Sir Harold) and she
does not think of herself as rising in the world by marrying a
Prendeville. Nor is she ashamed of her family's acquiring the
demesne—she merely wishes they had the house too: '*We*'ve got
the right of competence! The Prendevilles couldn't hold what
they had. . . .' Only when her grandfather leaves her the
demesne does the desire for owning land awaken in her, 'that
deep passion of possession, the desire for the tangible, living
land' which she did not learn in the smart schools. Because of
Kit's dissipation and deceit Peggy does not marry him and the
man she does marry is held in higher esteem than the
Prendevilles only by her family. The *nouveau riche* Sir Harold
Charles Burgrave, Bart, of Loxley Hall in the County of
Durham is seen for what he is by Peggy. He is a very
commonplace young man, physically unattractive, bad tem-
pered when he is bored and as ready to snatch a kiss as Kit is to
relieve his boredom. Common, stupid, conceited, dull-witted
compared with Peggy, but not a bad fellow. But he is mocked
rather than scorned when he buys his way into the small Irish
home with two dozen bottles of port, a huge down cushion, and
a box of chocolates in the shape and size of a cartwheel. So did

his father buy their coat of arms and crest from the College of Heralds.

The Prendevilles and Weldons live outside the village of Cloon. In Cloon the people are small shopkeepers and most of the shops are shebeens, a huddle of dirty little shops and cottages owned mainly by the Prendevilles or the Weldons. Cloon is like a rabbit-warren, of which the doctor says: 'The people in this village have been marrying and inter-marrying in a ruinous circle since the days of Adam! . . . and those that aren't mad are bad, and mostly they're both!' The ancient graveyard reflects this claustrophobic intermingling. New coffins are laid in the old graves and the old loose bones are shuffled back in on top. Generation after generation are thrust back into the same soil.

The mood of the place is captured in the descriptions of the scenery. It is at its most attractive in the stillness of an evening:

> It was a misty evening, very still and warm. The river glided past, dead smooth, the reflections of the Inver trees so deep in it that one would say they had stained the water with their heavy green and were pictured there for ever. Occasionally a fish broke the surface glassy into rings that shook the quiet of the painted trees for a moment; a heron stood in a reedy patch above the bridge, sunk in moody meditation. Lower down, by the village, at the mouth of the river, some seagulls swooped in dreamy, lovely curves above the anchored fishing boats.

During the day the stillness becomes a heaviness, a stagnation, sunshine bringing torpidity; light is absorbed. There is a continuous dull hum of insects. When the inhabitants manage to break the stupor they do so by the confused excitement of fair days or races. The sixty pubs of the nearby small town of Clytagh are all packed:

> The sunny, dusty air vibrated with noises of all kinds. Up through the steady din of talk flickered the shrill cries of little boys selling the local paper and cards of the races; horses whinnied to each other; donkeys, immured with their carts in entries to back yards, uttered their souls in those strange and

hideous sounds. . . . The town crier bell-ringer forced his way backwards and forwards, ringing his bell, and howling.

When nature changes, the stillness erupts into a savage violence bent on destruction. Gales tear through the village; the river overflows and joins with rain and gutter water to flood the main street and the houses.

The relationship between the Prendevilles and the villagers is different from that of the Ascendancy and the Irish in the other novels of Somerville & Ross. The Prendevilles are completely isolated from other Anglo-Irish people but not from the villagers. It is the story of a different kind of community from that of *The Real Charlotte, The Silver Fox, Mount Music* or *An Enthusiast*. It is much closer to the isolation of Durrus in *An Irish Cousin,* with its hints of ghosts and debauchery, where the isolation of both master and servants from the world at large encourages corruption to fester.

The motto of the Norman ancesters, 'Je prends', remained appropriate to succeeding generations. The present house was built in 1712 by Beauty Kit, whose generation saw the height of the family's power and graciousness. He was High Sherriff of the County, and with his wife, Lady Isabella, was the favourite of the Viceregal Court. A party of Italian craftsmen from Dublin were imported to beautify his house. Beauty Kit, gloriously attractive and as depraved, died at the age of twenty-eight; Lady Isabella then shut herself and her children up in the elegant house and refused to know anybody. Her pride in consciously isolating the family began a chain of events which in 1912 was still being worked out.

The immediate consequence was that her only son married the daughter of one of the gamekeepers and her two daughters ran off with two of her grooms:

> The glories and greatness of Inver therewith suffered downfall. Five successive generations of mainly half-bred and wholly profligate Prendevilles rioted out their short lives in the Big House, living with country women, fighting, drinking, gambling.

> The legitimacy of the succession was secured by means and stratagems that need not be recorded. Somehow out of the

mire an heir would be evolved and acclaimed, and the process of drinking and dicing away the lands of Inver would be carried on with all the hereditary zest proper to a lawful inheritor.

Jas's was a 'determined self-isolation' because of his heavy drinking, which made him unfit even for the social life of the thirsty gentry of the West of Ireland. Lethargy, a love of the sea and his drinking, kept him at Inver, moving from bed to bar, tended by Shibby, his illegitimate daughter by the girl in the pub he favoured. During the Land League days and the Plan of Campaign he borrowed money from Old John Weldon to make up for the failure in rents. In 1887, aged sixty-three, he rents Weldon the demesne and marries a daughter of the housekeeper in the Country Club. 'She got a snack for the gentry, helping the mother that way in the bar of the Club.' Kit was born of this marriage, and the girl then died giving birth to Nessie. In 1903, 'under the act', Weldon buys the demesne; 'these broad and beautiful acres' go to the 'grabbers'. Hence the relationship between the family and the village: it was the isolation of the remote district from the rest of the world which made possible this kind of outcome from Lady Isabella's pride. Half of the inhabitants of the village are illegitimate Prendervilles, 'Pindys'. Kit is acting like many of his fore-fathers when he dismisses his pregnant girl friend with, 'There's the full o' th' asylum in this village always.'

The story is not as simply chronological as the other stories; time past is continually present, 1739 and 1912 coalesce. Simple techniques such as the repetition of names—the same Christian names *would* be kept within the family—enforce the feeling that what is happening in the twentieth century is a direct result of what has happened in the past. The names of Kit and Shibby are distorted echoes of Beauty Kit and Lady Isabella. Kit's pregnant girl is called Maggie and Jas on hearing the name thinks it is his Maggie, Shibby's mother, they are referring to. There is terrible irony for Shibby when she curses Maggie because Kit is going about with her, 'That the Almighty God may strike Maggie Connor dead!' and then has to listen to Jas (who overhears) say of her mother, 'Is poor Maggie dead! I thought she died long ago!—She was a very pretty girl. I'm dam' sorry to hear it—'. Perpetuity of place and the sense of tradition given by objects like the cross on the sands, the crests and marriage stones, help to keep the past in mind. But ghosts more than anything else make one feel that the past is not shut off from the present. They are not as dominant a motif as they are in Yeats's *Purgatory*—where the theme is similar to this novel—but the Big House is haunted by the woman who brought about the degradation of the Prendevilles. She is tied to the house in which she lived her arrogant isolation, partly out of guilt and partly to revenge her family for acting the way they did. When Jas sees her he thinks he has seen Shibby; but Shibby knows very well who it is. She is always seeing clouds drift across looking-glasses and grey shadows in the depths of rooms, and hearing doors bang. When Shibby sings a song which expresses 'the regrets, the contritions, the longings' of the past generations, Lady Isabella returns; and she comes to spur Shibby on in her loathing of Maggie, 'darkening counsel, deepening hatred'. There is a suggestion that the spirits of the people are caught up in their portraits. The one of Beauty Kit acts as an icon for Shibby; she draws inspiration from it and the strength to go on. The one of Lady Isabella she always feels is mocking her, challenging her to restore order. When Shibby hears that Kit has got Maggie pregnant she looks at the disdainful face of Lady Isabella, 'and upon her spirit a shadow fell. A hopelessness. Who could struggle against this force, this inevitable drag of the tide of blood on to the rocks!' When Kit tells her that Peggy has ended their engagement and returned the beautiful diamond and ruby ring that was his grandmother's, it seems to Shibby that the portrait looks satisfied. She screams at Lady Isabella, 'it was you begun it! You that drove your own children to ruin and destruction! God curse you that brought this on my innocent child! Look at your ring that I gave him! God in Heaven! Wasn't I the fool to think that anything belonging to ye wouldn't bring him bad luck!' When she refuses to give in and begins once more to make plans which she hopes will still put Kit in the Big House, 'the portraits looked as if they also listened. The blue-velveted boy seemed to smile more gaily, and his greyhound seemed more alert; but no one, however sympathetic and imaginative, not even Nessie, could have persuaded themselves to fancy that there was any softening of the proud downward curve of Lady Isabella's perfect lips.' Kit and Shibby are the people in the portraits except for the difference in clothes and possessions. Kit wears faded blue serge and has a scruffy yellow mongrel cowering at his heels, where Beauty Kit is dressed in blue velvet and lace ruffles and caresses an elegant fawn greyhound. Shibby wears tough old peasant clothes, Lady Isabella exquisite silks; Shibby wields a sweeping brush, Lady Isabella gently holds a rose.

The uncanny likeness between the two women is the centre of the novel. Shibby's frantic attempts to reverse the chain of events and to pit herself against the inevitable *is* the expiation of Lady Isabella's sin of pride. At the same time she is as proud as Lady Isabella and every bit as determined. She inherits all her arrogance and single-mindedness; and her determination to put the family back into the Big House is as great as Lady Isabella's determination was to keep them there. The terrible reality for Shibby is that she herself is a part of the evil which she wants to obliterate; hence she refuses the doctor's offer of marriage to stop the sins from carrying on into another generation. She loves the doctor too, but she chooses a life of loneliness because of her illegitimacy, 'I wouldn't wrong you or your children.' Her one reason for living is to undo her ancestor's evil, to restore the Prendevilles to their rightful place.

She is a rock-like woman who can terrorise the whole village with a glance; to them she is the big woman with the bad eye, '*Droic h'uil!*' Like Charlotte Mullen and Julia Duffy she is the result of a mixed match, and like them she possesses strange powers which she does not understand, and sometimes cannot control. There is none of the spiritual refinement of Slaney or Christian in this simple woman. Her mind is elemental; she lacks self-knowledge and all analytical ability, but she has the depths of passion of Charlotte Mullen. Intense moods grab hold of her and, 'She lived them wordlessly. She was not conscious of uplift in spirit when things moved in accord with her manoeuvrings, or of gloom when they went, as she would have said, "agin her". She was happy or distressed; she was being successful, or being baffled; her plots were prospering, or failing—that was all there was about it. She did not discuss with herself her emotions, being entirely occupied with the facts that produced them.' She has the ordinary country woman's superstitions: she sits before a looking glass brushing her long white hair over her face, and then peering through the strands to see what the future holds; she reads teacups; she foretells which horse will win the race. On a still night the windows shake to tell her of her friend, Old John's death, 'I wouldn't say, but that it was himself was in it—coming to say good-bye to me, like.' Dreams and premonitions assail her; she possesses the power to make people do what she wants.

Her desire to separate Kit and 'Foxy Mag' who comes from the most degraded of the shebeens, with a mother in a lunatic asylum and a father who is drinking himself to death, brings her powers to the fore. She pursues the girl's destruction with all the force of her mind and soul (similar to the way in which the man in D.H. Lawrence's *The Fox* gets Banford). She struggles on an almost subconscious level, musing on the ways of death open to her—poison, or pushing her over the tower, or locking her up in the cellars of the Big House. They are more 'malign fancies' than plottings, half-waking dreams with none of Charlotte's conscious evil about them. It often seems that Shibby is as much the victim as the agent; that she has fallen into the grip of forces beyond her control. When possessed by these forces all she can do is grasp her rosary, and mutter prayers, 'whilst her great eyes, like those of some fierce, caged animal' stare at her victim. At any moment she can be thus taken,

> She felt as if it came from without, meeting and joining hands with what was in her soul. Something stronger than she, strong as she felt herself. Her fists were clenched, her head was bent forward. To one who had seen her then she would have looked like a snake ready to strike. Thus she stood, held by the power that had mastered her. She had gone outside Time.

Just as sexual jealousy reduces Charlotte to this dehumanised state, so it is hatred which grabs hold of Shibby. As events draw to a climax she suffers increasing visitations. The wind hurls a photograph of Kit to the floor, an ominous portent. 'A flood of hatred of Maggie Connor rose in her.' It is much more primitive than Charlotte's jealousy of Francie. Shibby is lying rigid like a dead woman, 'ill-wishing' the girl. Grey vapours rise in the bedroom and swirl around in changing shape; phosphorescent light is manifest on the walls, till Shibby loses consciousness, consumed by her malice. The storm assumes these evil vibrations and pounds the village and Shibby, till she finds herself at Maggie's door 'looking, with her blown white hair and long dark cloak, herself an embodiment of the storm'. When she finds the girl on the edge of the river she grabs her to stop her from committing suicide. The struggle is resolved when Maggie falls into the water. Shibby is left ignorant of whether she let go or the girl overcame her hold. Too many times has she willed the girl's death not to feel that she *must* have had a hand in it now it has happened. Did she let her go? Did she stop saving the girl from throwing herself into the raging river? Shibby, an ardent and regular mass-goer, falls to praying, but even now her pride is not staunched:

> 'Merciful God, Thou knowest . . . Thou knowest'—What did He know?
> The prayer was checked.
> She rose to her feet.
> 'I'll tell God no lies! Let the truth stand before Him. I'll take what's owing to me!'

She regains her composure standing alone on the rock: 'Through the wind there came again to her the note of the church bell; it came like a gentle hand that touched her, recalling her to a sense of the present, from the nightmare in which time was not.'

She acts as fairy godmother to Peggy and Kit; she wills them to love each other. She makes Peggy change her mind after she's lost her faith in Kit: 'she had, by sheer force of personality, and the unconscious hypnotic power that was hers, succeeded'. And yet she is not strong enough to turn the tide of events. The strength of Shibby makes the feeling of the inevitability of doom all the stronger: if she cannot alter fate nobody can.

It is an amazing portrait and an example of the writer's power that such a character can be made so entirely credible in her passionate hatred, and her adoration of Kit whom she spoils and pampers until at last she is forced to see his dissipation. When he asks what is to be done she has to tell him that nothing can be done now, too much has been done already. 'No more, my poor child, God help ye, no more than your father done before ye!— And no more than them that came before him—but too much— O God! Too much!' There is pathos in the scene. Shibby has our sympathy throughout, even when she is planning Kit's marriage with calculation and no thought of his wishes, even when she collects all the tatty junk. (She has not inherited her ancestor's taste, 'There isn't a stick in the room, now, but what's good . . . Lady Isabella herself wouldn't want better!') Shibby's efforts to restore a lost race, 'The King shall have his own again!', to resurrect and instil pride into a people that have fallen, are of tragic depth.

The Prendevilles seized what they wanted from the inhabitants of the island and built the tower to guard themselves from the wild Irish; then they built a ten-foot stone wall round five hundred acres of grass and woodland. Their superior attitude found its most fatal expression in the corrosive arrogance of the woman who disdained to meet even the other country people. When Shibby fights against the forces of decay she is as crazy as Cuchulain fighting the waves, and there is this feeling of doom, and the inevitability of fate throughout the novel. She is finally forced to recognise her failure when Kit sells the Big House.

> 'I'm done!' she said aloud, 'I'm beat. I done my best. There never was luck in it! There was too much pride and wickedness long ago, destroying the ones that came after— Pride and badness, all sorts. . . . God knows, I had the pride, but it's broke in me now.'

Lady Isabella's heart was broken by her children, Shibby's by Kit. The house, with its marriage stones, crests and coat of arms, belongs to the Prendevilles despite all their fecklessness; to Jas it was a 'd..d barracks' and to Kit merely worth its market price— without even John Weldon's sense to insure it. Only Shibby, striding about, 'the grey mass of her hair shining in the sun like a silver crown', sees the tragedy. But then she is 'the finest Prendeville o' the lot o' them, whatever way she was got!'

The epilogue is taken from the 1912 letter of Violet Martin which originally inspired the book:

I was driven off to a little desolate awful church, to which the Ardrahan clergyman drives out. I have *never* been at anything so wretched. The little church quite well built, but coated with mildew and damp, the decaying old prayer books stuck to the seats with fungus. The clergyman came out and dusted a pew for me before he allowed me to sit in it. I, a young man, and a policeman, were the congregation. The parson gave out a hymn, started it very well; I struck in, and he and I then sang a duet. When he found that I was well set, he sang an *excellent* bass in a low baritone. The youth and the policeman listened reverently to this unique performance.

In the afternoon Tilly R. and I drove over to Tyrone House—a bigger and much grander edition of Ross. A great square cut-stone house of three stories, with an area—perfectly empty—and such ceilings, architraves, teak doors, and chimney-pieces as one sees in old houses in Dublin. It is on a long promontory by the sea, and there rioted three or four generations of St. Georges—living with country-women, occasionally marrying them, all illegitimate four times over. Not so long ago *eight* of these awful half-peasant families roosted together in that lovely house, and fought, and barricaded and drank, till the police had to intervene. About 150 years ago a very grand Lady Harriet St. Lawrence married a St. George, and lived there, and was so corroded with pride that she would not allow her daughters to associate with the Galway people. She lived to see them marry two men in the yard.

Yesterday as we left, an old Miss St. George, daughter of the last owner, was at the door in a little donkey trap. She lives near in a bit of the castle, and since her people died she will not go into Tyrone House, or into the enormous yard, or into the beautiful old garden. She was a strange mixture of distinction and commonness, like her breeding, and it was very sad to see her at the door of that great house.

If we dared to write up that subject!

Beside the passage above should be this note of Edith Somerville's:

A few years after the publication of this book I projected a visit to the distant county in which X house stood. But the visit had to be abandoned, and X house must ever remain for me an effort of imagination, as during the Civil War that followed the Treaty of Peace, the fate that befell the Big House in our story was made actual.[3]

Perhaps Yeats should have the last word:

> What if the glory of escutcheoned doors,
> And buildings that a haughtier age designed,
> The pacing to and fro on polished floors
> Amid great chambers and long galleries, lined
> With famous portraits of our ancestors;
> What if those things the greatest of mankind
> Consider most to magnify, or to bless,
> But take our greatness with our bitterness?[4]

Somerville & Ross wrote two more novels: *French Leave* and *Sarah's Youth*. Both are primarily concerned with the position of a young woman in society, the one in 1884, the other in the 1920s. The possibilities open to the girls are not radically different. The two books are more lighthearted and superficial than any of the other novels, most remarkable in their zest and sense of fun after the solemnity of *Mount Music, An Enthusiast* and *The Big House of Inver*. The authors are delving into a subject which they can handle with complete confidence and this gives a poise and detachment to their writing. If nothing else, time (for Edith Somerville was sixty and seventy years old respectively when she wrote the tales) detaches them from the problems.

French Leave was begun in October 1926 and written with the usual amount of strain and stress, but more regularly than usual (two chapters a week on average) and the first draft was finished in a year. There was the usual list of distractions: a new bathroom, the decoration of the whole house, new curtains, cows bitten in the udders by flies, and an incessant stream of visitors and social engagements. Lady Violet Powell calls the novel an inferior *Mount Music*. There are similarities: the hero, James Anthony FitzAlleyne, Baron Coran, is, like Larry, a wealthy aristocratic young man, good looking, unintellectual, genuinely uncritical, liking most people and so very popular;

Lester, the rival, is like Barty in his social inferiority, his dog-like worship of the Ascendancy girl. His inability to speak to her in an ordinary voice is similar to Barty's adoption of his committee voice when he talks to Christian. Lester, after dancing superbly with Patsey, spoils it all by saying, 'Miss Kirwan, I wish I could express to you, how grateful I am for the—the privilege of dancing with you—'[5] and in dire straits he lapses into the style of the Church: 'I know I'm not worthy so much as to—' But it is really a quite different kind of novel from *Mount Music*, far less ambitious, and concentrating not on the Anglo-Irish as a social entity, nor on problems of religious prejudice, but simply on the life of a young girl in the eighteen-eighties.

It is Edith Somerville's last attempt at a historical novel and she is careful to get the details of clothes, furniture and travelling correct. Patsey, aged twenty, must wear what her mother dictates, no matter how much she personally dislikes the bustle, the elaborate bonnet of lace, roses and ribbons. She is expected to travel first class, preferably with a companion. There is a vivid picture of a journey from one county to another in Ireland. It involves a night on the road, four changes of train and a six-mile drive in a leaking and damp landau. This is upper-middle-class comfort. When Lady Kirwan arrives at Lord Coran's stately home:

> The bedroom, high and spacious, was gloomy and chill as the night, with massive mahogany furniture round its remote walls, and a catafalquian bed looming large in the darkness. Delia, on her knees on the hearth-rug, was engaged in tense conflict with a refractory fire, whose existence was only deducible from the smell of turf smoke. Mrs Moffat lighted two candles on the far-away dressing-table, that, like the fire, produced no appreciable effect. . . .
>
> For perhaps half an hour, Lady Kirwan lay shivering in the catafalque, coiled like a little dog round an unsympathetic stone footwarmer.

To Patsey the house, with its enormous stable-yard, six hundred acres of level grass, fir plantations, laurel coverts, four avenues—

the straightest of them half a mile long, tennis lawns and formal gardens, is like a mausoleum. The house is 'arid, inhuman, cheerless . . . the last resting place of mummified furniture from which all life had long since departed'. There is an equally graphic picture of Lester's lower-middle-class farm with its piano, horsehair sofa, black marble clock and semi-cured goatskin rugs. The meek little mother nervously stores up her egg money to buy her son the best broadcloth when he is ordained; and the autocratic, evangelical father believes he has God on his side when he goads his son into the Church. For him to merely *live* in Paris ensures eternal damnation. The full weight of class differences is realised in the relationship between Patsey and Lester; to the French and Americans they are a well-matched couple, both Irish, both Protestant, tall and handsome and passionately determined to be artists, but Coran expresses the Ascendancy Irish point of view. When he hears that Patsey has seen Lester in Paris he comments, 'Quite absurd to say he was a *friend* of Pat's—of course she *knows* him.' Patsey herself never forgets that despite Lester's looks and talents he is still Holy George's son.

The characters are all credibly of 1884 without losing any life. Sir Ingram Kirwan, Bart, M.F.H., D.L., J.P., ex High Sheriff of the County is less bothered about loss of political power and far more strong-minded and confident than Talbot-Lowry. He is said to have had his own way, all his life, in everything except the sex of his offspring. His five daughters are his burden and he is typically Victorian in his solution to the problem—marriage, 'unmarried daughters were superfluities, if not disgraces, to any right-thinking parent'. Education for girls was unnecessary, 'Much help this trash of Women's Colleges (just then coming into notoriety) would be if it were left to them to find husbands for the unfortunate girls whose parents were fool enough to send them to them! A five-and-twenty pound governess had taught all that was necessary for good-looking girls like his (with a share of their mother's fortune).' A girl's duty was to obey her father until she was married and then to obey her husband. He rules with a rod of iron and it has the inevitable result: 'affection for fathers of the school of Sir Ingram (a large and flourishing one during the first half of the nineteenth century) was a matter more of the Church Catechism and of theory than of practice (the practice being summarised in what may be called Lip-Service; in other words, a morning and evening peck on the male parent's jaw).' Patsey is not compliant; the clash between them is done with conviction—the scene, for example, where he loses his temper at discovering that she is responsible for the drag. He bellows and swears at her in front of the hunt, shouting that he would thrash her with his hunting crop if she were a boy and not 'an impudent young she-devil'. Patsey of course replies, 'Thrash away! I don't want any advantage!' His boorish treatment of his daughters is on a level with the rest of his sophistication; he shares Lester's father's prejudices about France. When Patsey goes to Paris he expostulates, 'What's she living on, I want to know? I want to know that! Frogs and dandelions, I suppose! She'll lose her looks and come back half-starved and no man'll look at her twice!. . . if she don't marry she'll starve! *I* can't leave her enough to live on.' Millie, Patsey's elder sister on the other hand, has been a credit to her father, marrying the affable, weak-minded widower, 'Fat old Dick', when she was in her mid-thirties and looked like becoming a problem. She was not only plain, but she 'had a touch of that High Church nonsense that she picked up in England,' but now Sir Ingram congratulates himself, for there she is, 'plenty of money, and every prospect of finding herself a rich widow some of these days!'

Millie's husband is silly enough to encourage Patsey to run away from home after her row with Sir Ingram, and to stay with them; and then he forgets to tell his wife about it. When Patsey arrives he is spineless enough to pretend not to notice all her luggage, and he merely invites her in for 'a bit of lunch'. Millie is only a minor character but she is well realised through the dialogue. She gets one in on her husband, as well as on Patsey for her thoughtless arrival, when she welcomes her with, 'We only got home the day before yesterday. We're rather upside down still! *Rather* a brief honeymoon, wasn't it? Only a scrap over a fortnight!' And she proceeds to politely let her young sister know just exactly how welcome she is, 'It *is* nice of you, Patsey dear, to come so soon to see us—though I must say you look very tired, and *I* think you ought to have rested and done nothing! Another day you must bring Papa over to lunch, and Jimmy Coran—I hear he's *so* nice—when Dick and I have shaken down a little more,' so that Patsey leaves her luggage outside and soon departs for Dublin.

The year, 1884, in which the book is set is of course two years before Edith Somerville met Violet Martin and the book is partly an attempt at reviewing those days. Patsey shares many characteristics and experiences with Edith Somerville, which doesn't make her less credible nor a less vigorous heroine nor less representative of young ladies of her time. Financially limited, with the smallest allowance and no money to spare for her to study she can only envy her younger brother. He has none of her gifts, and none of her seriousness, but money can be spent on his every whim while she can only be made use of as 'Dog-boy, and rough-rider, and under-groom', until she gives in and gets married. She envies Coran more than she does any-one else, 'She thought of his freedom, his strength, his money, his power to order his life as he chose'; and she tells him, 'When you want a thing most awfully you've only to stretch out your hand and take it. There's no-one to put handcuffs on you'.

The author's sympathies are naturally with the heroine but the novel never degenerates into sentimentality or preaching. The wedding which occupies the early chapters is done as lightly and as cynically and with as much detachment as any of their writing. Patsey is quick to see the pseudo-romantic; the cards which go out with the wedding-cake are, for her, pure humbug, 'The idea of old Millie transfixing Dick Villier's heart with an arrow!—it looks like a kidney on a skewer!' The 1662 marriage service, 'devoid as it then was of the comparative reticence of a later and less barbaric era, advanced, unflinching in its admonishments,' evoking only 'resentment and contempt' in Patsey. The difference between the promises made by the man and the woman infuriates her, 'The notion of obeying old Dick! They won't catch *me* "cherishing and obeying" . . . Easy to see that it was men wrote it,' and makes her even more determined never to get married.

Patsey's life in Paris as a poor art student is written with love and zest: the long days of sketching from eight a.m. to five p.m.,

the Anglican church on Sundays, the playing at house-keeping
on a strict budget.

> To sample of new crémeries, and there to receive six stewed
> prunes for the same price that *Le Père Fusco* charged for four,
> to buy a small gobbet of raw meat, and with it to wing her
> way home, like a hawk to its nest, and devour it, burnt to a
> cinder, for her dinner, completing the repast with what was
> known as a resurrection omelette, in which old forgotten
> things found their last home. . . .

This was fun for a young lady who was never allowed to boil an
egg at home, let alone do the shopping. The new friends, such as
the German Miss Henriette von Kappf, whose hair is cut short
and parted on one side, who wears collar and tie, Norfolk jacket
and a man's hat, 'If, as it seemed, her intention was to be taken
for an English schoolboy, only her petticoats frustrated it' are all
so exhilaratingly different from anything in Co. Cork. The very
streets of Paris are enchanting and Patsey's joy is communicated
to us, 'The sour vinous smells of the frequent *cabarets*, the whiffs
of rankly luscious cookery that issued from the open doors of
small restaurants, the mingled odours, all-pervading as the
ether of garlic and strange tobacco, were . . . airs of Paradise.'
So is the excitement of living for art and the judgment of one's
professor, so that one's whole world turns over at the words,
'*C'est pas mal! Pas mal du tout* . . .'. But despite all the professor's
praise Patsey must return home when her money runs out. All
she can do is write bitterly to her poor mother, 'Why didn't you
make me a boy, and give me a chance?'

The book ends with Patsey doing her duty and marrying Lord
Coran, a man whose greatest intellectual accomplishment is to
flick over the pages of a detective novel. The last words are given
in a letter of 11 June 1885, written by Patsey's mother to Coran's
mother—who has always presumed that the marriage will take
place.

> I wish I could persuade you to come and pay us a little visit.
> Jimmy is here, and we should all enjoy a sight of you so much.
> He is being *slaved* by Patsy to carry her painting-things about
> for her. They are out all day in this lovely weather. I think

they are both very happy. She says she will never give up what she calls her Career—and Jimmy says he hopes she won't—but you and I know more about matrimony than she does!

With politics and religion left far behind the novel is immensely good-humoured. At the same time it is sharper and crisper than the more ponderous *Mount Music*. There are snappy descriptions such as that of Sir Ingram, bored with his daughter's wedding-breakfast and wishing everyone would go away but necessarily polite to his guests as he moves amongst them, 'like a courteous thundercloud . . . pressing champagne on jaded matrons'. Despite the authors' disapproval of Sir Ingram there is no bitterness of tone; he is almost lovable, as when he reacts to Patsey's ordering the carriage for herself:

'I don't know what girls are coming to nowadays! I should like to have seen one of *my* sisters ordering a horse and trap and man out of the stables as if the place belonged to them! . . . Why, not even I myself would have done it—and I was the eldest son, mind you—not till he had a stroke and lost the power of speech!'

Jimmy Coran's limitations are more a matter of fun than anything else. When he went round his farm with the bailiff and the latter pointed at a group of bullock's saying they were Herefords, 'his Lordship had replied airily, "Oh, are they? I thought they were mine!"'

In 1929 Edith Somerville started going through all her old letters to Violet Martin, Violet's own letters and their diaries, hoping to find material for a new novel. She found none, and not until 1936 is there mention of the next novel. It is 'this difficult book that drags on'. In March that year Admiral Boyle Somerville was murdered, and Edith Somerville left aside her own work in order to finish the book he was engaged on. The next year Hildegarde, Lady Coghill, her sister, took over housekeeping so that Edith could have the mornings free in which to write. Her diaries show that on average she did no more than half an hour a day. On 30 November, 'Had a wonderful, undisturbed morning, from eleven o'clock to one thirty! The first for months (if not years), got ahead a bit in consequence.' She is 'desperately rheumatic and tired all the time' but by the end of May 1937 the book is finished.

Sarah's Youth is a remarkably youthful and spirited account of a young girl. Sarah is a twentieth-century Patsey but perhaps less interesting because less gifted, and quite lacking in introspection. Her half-sister, Kathleen, is the intelligent, fair and fey one, sensitive and psychic. She hears voices and communes with spirits, especially with Sarah's mother. The main interest in the book is the picture of Irish society—on Mrs Fitz-Symon's and the widow Delanty's level. The troubles are no bother to Sarah's father, Captain Tom Heritage, for he owns no more than his flower-garden, 'I've barely got grass would sod a lark!'[6] He and his wife are both gently comic characters. Mrs Hermitage may live in the Big House and be stepmother to the stately Sarah, but her language is her own. ' "I'm dead!" she began cheerfully. "I was just having a lie-down. I was sitting up all night, and I didn't get a wink with watching him like a cat and mouse. But he's good this evening, thank God!" '

Equally comic is Cousin Richard. He is an awful man. He has lost his nerve for riding but he insists on cutting a figure on the hunting field, merely taking out his resentment at being afraid on his servants when he gets home. He bullies them unmercifully in order to boost his morale. He is a gentleman farmer who has no more idea of farming than Jimmy Coran; when he reads in the *Irish Times* that the price of pigs has fallen, he gets terribly indignant, and then, 'he tried to remember how many pigs he had. Or had he any?' His father, a successful Dublin solicitor, has given Richard the fifty-acre farm to keep him out of trouble, but Richard is far too stupid to make anything of it. He feels obliged to ride about the farm but he is never sure which crop is being harvested. 'It didn't quite do to ask. It would look too much like ignorance—but one thing was so very like another— and then this sequence of crops—they were always changing things from field to field . . . ' He is made up of vanity, meanness and cowardice, and only the latter two save his skin where horses and women are concerned. He loves to be in love and he is as comic as Orsino in his deliberate self-indulgence in the emotion. He is in love with Sarah's stepmother at one stage, and then in

202 *Somerville & Ross*

love with Sarah. There is a fine scene when he has to reveal his love for Sarah to her stepmother: ' "Lucy," he said, with the impressiveness that he felt the subject demanded. "It came upon me like a clap of thunder! It was the last morning I was out with the hounds—before I got ill. I felt as if I was looking at her for the first time. It was ree'ly like St Paul having his eyes opened!" ' He is so moved by his own story that tears well up in his eyes as he talks, while Lucy just cannot control her laughter. Equally comic is his complete lack of sensitivity to Sarah when she has broken off the engagement which he has forced on her. He attempts to make things right by sending her each week the most expensive box of chocolates he can find. But there is always judgment in our laughter. He really thinks he can buy Sarah with a horse and the hundred pounds he lends her father. After these transactions, in his eyes, she belongs to him, and when she goes on a holiday without telling him he is furious, 'I call it all a damned swindle!'

The position of women in Anglo-Ireland in the nineteen-twenties was not so very different from what it was in Victorian times. Captain Tom Heritage, who is as quiet and mild a man as ever there was, is said to receive the news that his second child is also a girl with calm, when his first comment to the nurse 'had been to desire her to put it in a bucket of water'. But he makes the best of a bad job by reflecting, 'Girls don't want education . . . The two o' them together won't cost as much as a boy.' Higher up the social scale is Colonel Nick M.F.H., who is similarly afflicted with daughters, four of them. He is mockingly said to be such a conscientious sportsman that aware 'that a man couldn't serve God and Mammon' he neglects his daughters too, 'he'd be damned if he'd wrong the hounds for the sake of paying extortionate school-bills'. He too makes do with cheap govern-essess and when finishing schools are mentioned replies 'that the only finish he wanted for them was to get them off his hands, and girls were married for looks and not for brains.'

Captain Tom presumes that he can choose Sarah's husband and he is utterly shocked when she tells him she will make her own choice. Unlike Christian Talbot-Lowry, Sarah is not obedient, and even when her father has his heart attacks she refuses to give in and marry Cousin Richard. 'I'll only get married when I choose!' Captain Tom can never really bring himself to see that she means it; even on his death-bed he promises Richard that Sarah will marry him, 'Richard, me dear friend, I give Sarah to you!' Richard is ready to use every means within his power to bully her into marrying him, including quoting the Bible at her, 'Children obey your parents in all things; for 'tis well pleasing unto the Lord'.

The situation is the same as in the nineteenth and early twentieth centuries, when Talbot-Lowry blackmails his daughter into breaking off her engagement with a Catholic Nationalist; and Shibby and Old John plot and decide the terms of the marriage of Kit and Peggy, without a thought of what the young people think. In *An Enthusiast* Dan's and Eileen's parents plan their marriage with little attention to the feelings of the two involved. Car is wretchedly unhappy in her most unsuitable marriage which was made by her parents when she was still at school. Marriage is still the 'only gate into freedom' which most parents recognise for their daughters. Until they are married they can go on being unpaid maids, messengers, dog-walkers, horse exercisers, and entertain visitors. Peggy Weldon returns from her expensive education with nothing else to do until she marries.

All the young heroines, except for Katharine, do marry or are intending to marry by the end of the book, even Patsey. *Sarah's Youth* closes with the eighteen-year-old heroine deciding to be a whipper-in, 'I've decided that marriage is out of my line and I love hounds', but we are left in no doubt that in time she too will surrender and become the wife of the ideal Bobby Dryburgh. These last two books are not profound explorations of the inner thoughts and emotions; they are more simply concerned with the role of the young woman in her family and society. As such they are necessarily more superficial than *The Real Charlotte* or *The Big House of Inver*. They are novels of manners which do not go much further than a study of manners and conventions. But they are extremely readable, and they do put the far greater novels into perspective, and by doing so help us to see *them* more clearly.

The Real Charlotte and *The Big House of Inver* deserve to take their place beside *Mansfield Park* as well as beside Maria

Edgeworth's *Castle Rackrent* and Yeats's *Purgatory*. They are among the great novels of passion in English, necessarily Irish, but no more provincial than Dean Swift or Yeats. Somerville & Ross's achievement is to show their Irish lives as deeply and eternally significant.

Select Bibliography

BOOKS WRITTEN BY E. Œ SOMERVILLE & MARTIN ROSS

E.Œ. Somerville, *Mark Twain Birthday Book*, London: Remington 1884.

Geilles Herring and Martin Ross, *An Irish Cousin*, London: Bentley, 1889.

E.Œ. Somerville & Martin Ross, *An Irish Cousin* (revised edition) London: Longmans, Green & Co. 1903.

E.Œ. Somerville, *The Kerry Recruit*, London: Perry, 1889.

E.Œ. Somerville & Martin Ross, *Naboth's Vineyard*, London: Spencer Blackett, 1891.

Through Connemara in a Governess Cart, London: W.H. Allen, 1893 (previously serialised in *Lady's Pictorial*, 1891).

In the Vine Country, London: W.H. Allen, 1893 (previously serialised in *Lady's Pictorial*, 1892).

The Real Charlotte, London: Ward and Downey, 1894.

Beggars on Horseback, London/Edinburgh: Blackwood 1895 (previously serialised in *Black and White)*.

The Silver Fox, London: Lawrence and Bullen 1898 (previously serialised in *The Minute)*.

Some Experiences of an Irish R.M. London: Longmans, Green and Co., 1889 (previously serialised in the *Badminton Magazine)*.

Martin Ross & E.Œ. Somerville, *A Patrick's Day Hunt*, London: Constable 1902.

E.Œ. Somerville, M.F.H., *Slipper's ABC of Fox Hunting*, London: Longmans, Green & Co. 1903.

E.Œ. Somerville & Martin Ross, *All on the Irish Shore*, London: Longmans, Green & Co. 1903.

Some Irish Yesterdays, London: Longmans, Green & Co., 1906 (previously printed in various magazines).

Further Experiences of an Irish R.M., London: Longmans, Green & Co., 1908 (previously printed in various magazines).

Dan Russel the Fox, London: Methuen 1911.

E.Œ. Somerville, *The Story of the Discontented Little Elephant*, London:

Longmans, Green & Co. 1912.

E.Œ. Somerville & Martin Ross, *In Mr Knox's Country,* London: Longmans, Green & Co., 1915.

Irish Memories, London: Longmans Green & Co., 1917.

Mount Music, London: Longmans, Green & Co., 1919.

Stray-Aways, London: Longmans, Green & Co., 1920 (previously printed in various magazines).

E.Œ.Somerville, *An Enthusiast,* London: Longmans, Green & Co. 1921

E.Œ. Somerville & Martin Ross, *Wheel-Tracks,* London: Longmans, Green & Co. 1923

The Big House of Inver, London: Heinemann 1925.

French Leave, London: Heinemann 1928.

E.Œ. Somerville, *The States Through Irish Eyes,* Boston & New York: Houghton Mifflin Co. 1930/London: Heinemann 1931.

E.Œ. Somerville & Martin Ross, *An Incorruptible Irishman,* London: Ivor Nicholson & Watson 1932.

The Smile and the Tear, London: Methuen 1933.

The Sweet Cry of Hounds, London: Methuen 1936.

Sarah's Youth, London: Longmans, Green & Co. 1938.

E.Œ. Somerville & Boyle Townshend Somerville, *Records of the Somerville Family 1174-1940,* Cork: Gut & Co Ltd. 1940.

E.Œ. Somerville & Martin Ross, *Notions in Garrison,* London: Methuen 1941.

Happy Days, London: Longmans, Green & Co., London, 1946 (previously printed in various magazines).

Maria, & Some Other Dogs, London: Methuen 1949.

ARTICLES AND REVIEWS BY SOMERVILLE & ROSS

E.Œ. Somerville, 'Mrs Moloney's Amateur Theatricals', *Home Chimes* Vol.2 (2 May 1885), 408-12.

Martin Ross, 'A Night in the Suburbs', *Argosy* (September 1887), 66-75.

Martin Ross, 'Olympia to Connemara', *The World* (29 August 1888)
'A Delegate of the National League', *The World* (17 July 1889)
'Cheops in Connemara', *The World* (October 1889)

E.Œ. Somerville & Martin Ross, 'Slide No.42', *Lady's Pictorial* (Christmas 1890).

'The Primrose Path of Dalliance', *Black and White,* (26 November 1892), 609.

'Priests or Patriots?' *The World* (27 September 1893) 26-8.

'A Pool of Siloam', *Lady's Pictorial* (23 September 1899)

Martin Ross, 'A Speaking Contrast', *Irish Homestead* (December 1899)

E.Œ. Somerville, 'Ireland & West Carbery as A Sketching Ground. A Letter to a Member of "The Paris Club"', *International Art Notes* (May 1960) 82-5.

E.Œ. Somerville & Martin Ross, 'An Irish Problem', *National Review* Vol. 38 (November 1901) 407-19.

'The Desired of the People, by "A Looker on"', *National Review*, Vol. 42 (September 1903) 120-9.

'A Regrettable Incident', *Nash's Magazine* (November 1909)

'The Anglo-Irish Language', *Times Literary Supplement*, (5 May 1910)

E.Œ. Somerville, 'Old Wine and New', *Times Literary Supplement* (20 October 1910) 388.

Martin Ross, 'Two Views of Irish Politics', *Times Literary Supplement* (27 October 1910) 403.

E.Œ. Somerville, 'Masters of Horse', *Times Literary Supplement* (22 February 1912) 17.

E.Œ. Somerville & Martin Ross, 'With Thanks for The Kind Enquiries', Woman's Council of Conservative and Unionists Women's Franchise Association (May 1912)

Martin Ross, 'The Reaping of Ulster', *The Spectator* Vol. 108 (5 October 1912) 504-5.

E.Œ. Somerville & Martin Ross, 'At A Western Hotel', *Lady of the House* (November/December 1912) 15-20.

E.Œ. Somerville, 'Ireland, Then and Now', *Times Literary Supplement* (7 March 1918) 114.

'In the Kingdom of Kerry', *Times Literary Supplement* (4 April 1918) 161.

'The Intellectuals', *The Englishwoman* (May 1918) 85-88.

'Sonnet', *Literary Digest* Vol.59 (November 1918) 38.

'Misunderstood', *Irish Statesman* (6 September 1919)

'The Cult of the Peasant', *Times Literary Supplement* (20 November 1919) 667.

'Whyte-Melville and Others', *Times Literary Supplement* (16 June 1921) 377-8.

'Stage Irishmen and Others', *Times Literary Supplement* (30 August 1919)

'Extra Mundane Communications', *Country Gentleman* (November 1919)

'Matter of Opinion by a Retired Prophet', *Time and Tide* ('July 1921) 644-5.

'Court Ladies of Japan', *Time and Tide* (22 October 1921)

'Some More Irish Memories—I', *The London Mercury* Vol. 5 November 1921) 18-24.
'Some More Irish Memories—II', *The London Mercury* Vol. 5 (December 1921) 128-33.
'Snapshots in Sicily', *Time and Tide* (22 October-24 November 1922)
'Some Spanish Impressions', *Blackwood Magazine* (August 1926)
'Armistice Day in Southern Ireland', *Time and Tide* (30 November 1928)
'Certes, a Classic', *New Statesman* (15 March 1930)
'Ireland: the Re-Creators', *The Spectator* (23 January 1932) 103-4.
'For Richer For Poorer', *Cornhill* (September 1933) 343-51.
'Sic Itur ad Astra', *The Journal of the American Society for Psychic Research* (November 1935) 319-21.
'Twice Born', *Light* Vol.73 (July 1943) 229.
E.Œ. Somerville & Martin Ross, 'Two of a Trade', *Irish Writing* No.1. (1946) 82.

BOOKS ON SOMERVILLE & ROSS

Collis, Maurice, *Somerville & Ross, A Biography*, London: Faber & Faber 1968
Cronin, John, *Somerville and Ross*, Lewisburg: Bucknell University Press 1972
Cummins, Geraldine, *Dr. E.Œ. Somerville: A Biography*, London: Andrew Dakers 1952
Fehlmann, Guy, *Somerville & Ross, Témoins de l'Irlande d'hier*, Caen 1970
Hudson, Elizabeth, *A Bibliography of the First Editions of E.Œ. Somerville and Martin Ross*, with Notes by E.Œ. Somerville, New York 1942
Powell, Violet, *The Irish Cousins*, London: Heinemann 1970

UNPUBLISHED THESES ON SOMERVILLE & ROSS

Berrow, Hilary, 'Somerville & Ross', Ph.D. thesis, 1975, University College, Dublin.
Laurie, Hilary, 'The Correspondence of Edith Œ. Somerville and Violet Martin with their Literary Agent James B. Pinker, 1896-1922', M.A. Thesis, 1969, The Queen's University, Belfast.
Ormsby, Frank, ' "A Man of the People", an Unfinished Novel of Somerville and Ross', minor thesis, 1971, The Queen's University of Belfast.
Watson, Cresap, 'The Collaboration of Edith Somerville and Violet Martin' Ph.D. thesis, 1953, Trinity College Dublin.

ARTICLES AND REVIEWS ON SOMERVILLE & ROSS

Barlow, J.E.M. 'A Memory of Martin Ross', *Country Life* Vol. 39 (29 January 1916) 136.

Bowen, Elizabeth, *Tatler and the Bystander* (7 April 1948) 23.

Coghill, Sir Patrick, 'Opening Address' *Somerville and Ross: A Symposium*, (August 1968) The Queen's University of Belfast.

'Somerville and Ross', *Hermathena* No 79 (May 1952) 47-60.

Cronin, John, 'Dominant Themes in the Novels of Somerville and Ross', *Somerville and Ross: A Symposium*, (August 1968) The Queen's University of Belfast, 8-18.

Flanagan, Thomas, 'The Big House of Ross-Drishane', *Kenyon Review* Vol. 28, nol.1 (January 1966) 54-78.

Gibbes, E.B., 'The Case of "Bob F." Dr. E.Œ. Somerville's Testimony', *Light* (22 April 1937) 243.

Graves C.L., 'The Lighter Side of Irish Life', *Quarterly Review* Vol. 219, no. 436 (1913) 26-47.

Gwynn, Stephen, 'Lever's Successors', *Edinburgh Review* (October 1921) 346-57.

Kiely, Benedict, 'The Great Gazebo', *Eire-Ireland* Vol.2 (Winter 1967).

Lowell, Amy, 'To Two Unknown Ladies', *North American Review* (June 1919) 837-42

Lucas, E.V., 'The Two Ladies', *The Spectator* (1 January 1916) 9-10.

Lyons, F.S.L., 'The Twilight of the Big House', *Ariel* Vol.1 (July 1970).

MacCarthy, B.G., 'E.Œ. Somerville and Martin Ross', *Studies* Vol.34 (June 1945) 183-94.

McMahon, Sean, 'John Bull's Other Island: A Consideration of *The Real Charlotte* by Somerville & Ross', *Eire-Ireland* Vol.3 no.4. (Winter 1968) 119-35

McQuilland, Louis, 'A By Gone Ireland. The Humorous Story of Major Yeates and His Neighbours', *The Cork Examiner* (8 September 1936) 6.

Mitchell, Hilary, 'Somerville and Ross: Amateur to Professional', *Somerville and Ross: A Symposium* (August 1968) The Queen's University, Belfast. 20-37.

Moran, D.P., 'The Battle of Two Civilisations', *New Ireland Review* (17 August 1950) 323-36.

O'Connor, Frank 'Somerville and Ross', *Irish Times* (15 December 1945) 4.

O'Connor, T.P. 'A Book of the Week, The Shoneens', *Weekly Sun* Vol.5 (19 January 1895) 1-2.

O'Donnell, Donal 'The Novels and Stories of Somerville and Ross', *Irish Writing* No.30 (March 1955) 7-15.

O'Grady, Standish *All Ireland Review* Vol.2 (21 September 1901) 232.

'P & Q' *The World* (16 May 1894) 27.

Power, Ann 'The Big House of Somerville and Ross', *The Dubliner* Vol. 3 (Spring 1964) 43-53.

Tynan, Katherine 'Violet Martin (Martin Ross) and E.Œ. Somerville', *The Bookman* Vol. 50 (June 1916) 65-6.

'Mount Music', *Studies* (March 1920) 148-150.

'Vanishing Types in Ireland. Social Changes under the New Order', *The Observer* (16 April 1922)

Notes

Introduction (pp. 1-4)
1. Letter from 'Geraldine' to Violet Martin, 29 January 1915, (Q.U.B.)
2. Letter from J.R. Martin to Violet Martin, 14 January 1914, (Q.U.B.)
3. John Cronin, *Somerville and Ross*, Bucknell University Press, 1972, 100.

CHAPTER I (pp. 5-37)
1. *In the Vine Country*, 227.
2. Letter to Colonel J. Somerville, 1 February 1916.
3. Ibid., 26 July 1917.
4. Ibid., 1 March 1918.
5. Letter to Dame Ethel Smyth, 17 July 1922.
6. Ibid., 18 July 1922.
7. Lady Gregory, *Journals 1916-1930*, edited by Lennox Robinson, 1946, 14.
8. W.B. Yeats, *Collected Poems*, 348.
9. Letter to Dame Ethel Smyth, 13 September 1922.
10. Letter to Colonel J. Somerville, 4 August 1923.
11. Ibid., 14 April 1936.
12. Ibid., 9 August 1944
13. Ibid., 1 December 1945.
14. Letter to Count de Suzannet, 27 February 1935.
15. Letter to Geraldine Cummins, 20 March 1946, quoted by G. Cummins, *Dr. E. Œ. Somerville*, 1952, 174.
16. Ibid., p. 203.

CHAPTER II (pp. 38-56)
1. 'Two of a Trade' *Irish Writing*, 1, 1946, 85.
2. 'A Subterranean Cave at Cloonabinna', 1898, reprinted in *Stray-Aways* (1920), 81.

3. 'Cheops in Connemara' *The World*, October 1889, reprinted in *Stray-Aways*, 31.
4. 'Ireland, West Carbery, As a Sketching Ground, A Letter to a Member of "The Paris Club"' *International Art Notes*, May 1900, 82.
5. 'At the River's Edge' *The Englishwoman*, February 1914, reprinted in *Stray-Aways*, 9.
6. 'For Richer For Poorer', *Cornhill*, September 1933, 343.
7. MS T.C.D.
8. 'Two of a Trade', *Irish Writing* op.cit.
9. Ibid.
10. This and the following quotations are from commonplace books in Q.U.B.
11. 'The Anglo-Irish Language', a review of P.W. Joyce's *English As We Speak it in Ireland*, *Times Literary Supplement*, 5 May 1910.

CHAPTER III (pp. 57-84)

1. *Irish Memories*, 130.
2. This and the following quotations are from *An Irish Cousin* unless stated otherwise.
3. Letter to Colonel J. Somerville, 13 August 1943.
4. Ibid., 13 February 1936
5. This and the following quotations are from *Naboth's Vineyard* unless stated otherwise.
6. This and the following quotations are from *Through Connemara in a Governess Cart* unless stated otherwise.
7. This and the following quotations are from *In the Vine Country* unless otherwise stated.
8. This and the following quotations are from *Beggers on Horseback* unless stated otherwise.
9. This and the following quotations are from *In the State of Denmark*, reprinted in *Stray-Aways*, unless otherwise stated.
10. *Irish Memories*, 216.

CHAPTER IV (pp. 85-117)

1. *Irish Memories*, 231.
2. Ibid., p.21.
3. This and the following quotations from *The Real Charlotte* unless otherwise stated.

CHAPTER V (pp. 118-146)

1. This and the following quotations from *The Silver Fox* unless otherwise stated.
2. *Irish Memories* 252.
3. *The Weekly Sun* 19 January 1895, 1.
4. This and the following quotations from *Experiences of An Irish R.M.* unless otherwise stated.
5. This and the following quotations from *Dan Russel the Fox* unless otherwise stated.

CHAPTER VI (pp. 147-176)

1. Donal McCartney, 'From Parnell to Pearse', *The Course of Irish History*, ed. T.W. Moody and F.X. Martin, Cork 1967, 297.
2. This and the following quotations from *Mount Music* unless otherwise stated.
3. George Russell (Æ) 'An Unpublished Letter' in *Tribute to Thomas Davies*, Cork 1965, 211.
4. This and the following quotations from *An Enthusiast* unless otherwise stated.

CHAPTER VII (pp. 177-204)

1. This and the following quotations from *The Big House of Inver* unless otherwise stated.
2. W.B. Yeats, *Collected Poems*, 225.
3. Quoted in Elizabeth Hudson's *A Bibliography of the First Editions of the Works of E. Œ. Somerville and Martin Ross*, New York 1942, p.45.
4. W.B. Yeats, *Collected Poems*, 225.
5. This and the following quotations from *French Leave* unless otherwise stated.
6. This and the following quotations from *Sarah's Youth* unless otherwise stated.

Index

AE (George Russell), 153
Armistice Day, 32-3
Austen, Jane, 58, 67, 68, 100, 103, 105,
116, 203

Badminton Magazine, 47, 126
Beggars on Horseback, 74, 77-80, 83
Bernhardt, Sarah, 13
Big House of Inver, The, 46, 53-4, 149,
177-94, 203-4
Black and Tans, 23, 27, 51, 166
Black and White, 6, 77
Brontë, Charlotte, 37
Bushe, Charles Kendal, Lord Chief
Justice of Ireland, 1

Carleton, William, 55
Cassel's Magazine of Art, 13
Coghill, Hildegarde, (née Somerville,
sister of Edith Somerville), 18, 35, 36,
50, 178, 200
Collins, General Michael, 29
Cork County Eagle and Munster Advertiser,
170
Cronin, John, 4
Cummins, Geraldine, 36, 37

Dan Russel the Fox, 47, 139-46, 147
Darley, Bishop of Cavan, 9-11
De Suzannet, Count, 36, 76

Easter Rising, 1916, 20-23 passim
Edgeworth, Maria, 55, 152, 203-4
Eliot, George, 162
Elizabeth, Countess of Fingall, 1
Englishwoman, The, 21
Enthusiast, An, 42, 165-76, 178, 186,
194, 203

'Finger of Mrs Knox, The', 126-7
Forster, E.M., 149
French Leave, 194-200, 203
Further Experiences of an Irish R.M. see
Irish R.M. and his Experiences, The

Gaelic League, 148, 149
Graphic, The, 13
Gregory, Lady Augusta, 28, 29, 140
Gregory, Sir William, 62-3
Griffin, Gerald, 55

Happy Days!, 43, 44
Hardy, Thomas, 118
'Harrington', 133
Herbert, Emily, 88-89
'House of Fahy, The' 129
Hudson, Elizabeth, 175

Ibsen, Henrik, 83
In Mr Knox's Country see Irish R.M. and
his Experiences, The
In the State of Denmark, 74, 77, 80-83
In the Vine Country, 74, 75-7, 85, 87
Irish Academy of Letters, 35
Irish Cousin, An, 2-3, 19, 45-6, 57-69,
72, 84, 85, 150, 186
Irish Literary Revival, 49, 54, 127
Irish Memories, 4, 58
Irish R.M. and his Experiences, The, 32,
43, 125-39

Kipling, Rudyard, 55

Lady's Pictorial, The, 73, 75, 80
Lamb, Father, 26-7, 30
Lang, Andrew, 7
Lawrence, D.H., 190

Le Fanu, Sheridan, 58, 64
Lever, Charles, 75
'Lisheen Races, Second-Hand', 135
Llangollen, Ladies of, 80
Lucas, E.V., 47

Mahaffy, Rev. J.P., 153
Man of the People, A, 46, 47
'Man that Came to Buy Apples, The', 130
Martin, Anna Selina, (mother of Violet Martin), 15-16, 44, 63
Martin, Robert, (brother of Violet Martin), 7, 89
Martin, Violet,
  family of, 1, 2, 7
  friendship with Edith Somerville, 6, 19-20
  childhood, 7-11
  first meeting with Edith Somerville, 12
  visits Edith Somerville in Paris, 14
  the return to Ross, 15-17
  collaboration with Edith Somerville, 38-48
  love and knowledge of dialect, 49-56
  as tourist, 73-84
  toiling with *The Real Charlotte*, 85-7
  memories of Ross theatricals, 89
  dislike of *Dan Russel the Fox*, 140
  as model for Christian Talbot-Lowry, 159-60
  as originator of *The Big House of Inver*, 192-3
  see also Somerville, Edith
Mitchell, Susan, 21
Moore, George, 6
Mount Music, 42, 51-3, 147-65, 166, 175, 176, 178, 186, 189, 194-5, 202-3

Naboth's Vineyard, 69-72, 84, 85

O'Casey, Sean, 51
O'Connor, T.P., 118-19
O'Faolain, Sean, 181
'Oh Love! Oh Fire!', 125-6

Pearse, Patrick, 153
'Patrick's Day Hunt, A', 54
Pinker, J.B., 46, 47, 54, 139, 147, 152
Plunkett, Sir Horace, 31, 148

Powell, Lady Violet, 194
'Pug-Nosed Fox, The', 130-131

Real Charlotte, The, 8-9, 37, 46
  writing of, 85-7
  Somerville family's reaction, 87-8
  characters based on people, 88-90
  narrative technique and style, 90-98
  picture of society, 98-105
  Church of Ireland, 106-7
  Francie, 107-10
  Charlotte, 110-17
  Lambert, 113-15, 118-19, 144, 147, 152, 181, 186, 189-91, 203-4
Robinson, Lennox, 181
Ross House, 1-2, 7, 16-17, 18, 90, 180, 193
Ross, Martin, *see* Martin, Violet

St Leger, Warham, 6
Sarah's Youth, 194, 200-203
'Sharper Than A Ferret's Tooth', 134-5
Shaw, George Bernard, 158
Silver Fox, The, 46, 118-25, 159, 186, 189
Skibbereen, Battle of, 25-6
Slipper's A.B.C. of Fox Hunting, 18
Smyth, Dame Ethel, 19
Some Experiences of an Irish R.M. see *Irish R.M. and his Experiences, The*
Somerville, Adelaide, (mother of Edith Somerville), 13, 17, 87, 90
Somerville, Vice-Admiral Boyle, (brother of Edith Somerville), 1, 33-4, 200
Somerville, Colonel Cameron, (brother of Edith Somerville), 32, 88, 177
Somerville, Edith,
  family of, 1
  friendship with Violet Martin, 6, 19-20
  childhood, 13
  art student days, 13-14
  Drishane days, 12-13, 15, 17, 18
  political opinions, 21-32
  reaction to the Troubles, 21-32
  attitude to England, 24, 32-3
  love and knowledge of dialect, 49-56
  as tourist, 73-84
  toiling with *The Real Charlotte*, 85-7
  diffidence over *Mount Music*, 147, 152

the Troubles as fiction, 166-76
art student days as fiction, 198-9
see also Martin, Violet
Somerville, Hugh, (brother of Edith
  Somerville), 28
Somerville, Hildegarde, *see* Coghill,
  Hildegarde
Strand, The, 54
Suffragette movement, 17-18
Swift, Dean, 35, 204
Synge, J.M., 55

Thackeray, W.M., 55
Through Connemara in a Governess Cart,
  73-5, 77, 85, 86

'Trinket's Colt', 44-5, 133
Troubles, The, 20-31, 166-76
Tucker, James, 89-90

'Waters of Strife, The', 133, 137
Watson, Cresap, 38
Wheeltracks, 1
Wilde, Oscar, 129, 139
World, The, 7

Yeats, W.B., 29, 55, 175, 180, 188, 194,
  204